THE LAST STAR

A Study Of Marc Almond

◆

Jeremy Reed

CREATION BOOKS

London • San Francisco

credits

the last star
a study of marc almond
by:
jeremy reed
ISBN 1 871592 61 5
© jeremy reed 1995
first published 1995 by:
creation books
83, clerkenwell road, london ec1, uk
tel: 0171-430-9878
fax: 0171-242-5527
this edition © creation books 1995
design/layout/typesetting:
sailorboy pcp
design technician:
bradley davis
discography:
peter colebrook, michelle robek
photo credits:
as captioned or credit control
jeremy reed photographed by john robinson
cover shot:
penis in furs, copyright © brad branson 1995.

author's acknowledgements

for encouragement and support in the writing of this book I would like to thank james williamson and peter colebrook at creation books, michelle robek of vaudeville & burlesque the official marc almond fan club, holly elsdon for invaluable assistance, and john robinson for listening to sections of the book in progress.

—*J.R.*

*For
Immaculate*

CONTENTS

THE LAST STAR

"A long time had elapsed since the spider had opened her belly, from which two blue-robed adolescents had leapt, each holding a flaming sword, and taken their places on each side of the bed, as if to stand watch over sleep's sanctuary."

—Lautréamont

"The deepest experience of the creative artist is feminine, for it is an experience of conceiving and giving birth. The poet Obstfelder once wrote, speaking of the face of a stranger: 'When he began to speak, it was as though a woman had taken a seat within him.' It seems to me that every poet has had this experience in beginning to speak."

—Rilke

"And their names will inspire awe, as we are awed by the light from a star that has been dead a thousand years. Have I told all there was to tell of this adventure? If I take leave of this book, I take leave of what can be related. The rest is ineffable. I say no more and walk barefoot."

—Jean Genet

DIVA TENDENCIES

All afternoon the expectation mounts. In September the light's tigered gold, and the rain has organised the fallen leaves into a splashy batik pattern, a black and yellow print thrown across the streets. I've been concentrating on my writing all day, and listening to Marc Almond audios, the particularly good audience recordings of his two April 1987 International AIDS Day concerts, one at the Royalty Theatre and one at the Hackney Empire. Inspired, impassioned performances, in which his rendition of the anonymous folk poem 'When I Was A Young Man', a heartbreaking elegy invoking early death in an unrepentantly libertine youth, has stood out as the dramatic highlight in a set so texturally diverse that the singer has compounded French and Spanish influences with torch ballads, has had the creative temerity to sing us lyrics from Charles Baudelaire and Paul Verlaine, and has taken in songs by Jacques Brel as well as his own generously romantic and emotionally bruised compositions. The rich mosaic afforded by these concerts is unlike anything else in British music, for they combine Latin hedonism with French lyricism, and employ the intimate vocabulary of the forbidden being imparted to initiates.

Almond's decision to play the Royal Albert Hall, after a four year absence from touring in Britain, broken only by short acoustic sets at the Brixton Academy in 1990, and at the 5th Convention at Heaven in the same year, may or may not be a prudent one. The Royal Albert Hall is a suspect venue for tenor acoustics, and Almond is to showcase a retrospective of his career, an ambiguous gesture from a man whose live performances have grown progressively fewer since the dissolution of his backing musicians La Magia, in 1989, and the severance of his links with Annie Hogan, whose piano and keyboards had interpreted his vocals with intuitive sensitivity for the better part of a decade. But the assessment of twelve years of song informed by a passionate commitment to artistic truth, in which the singer has balanced commercial success with a reckless integrity aimed at immolating all past achievements, is long overdue, even if it offers no clue to Marc Almond's future direction. The chart success of *Memorabilia*, a compilation of Soft Cell and solo material, jump-started into popularity by the re-release of 'Tainted Love', the massive Soft Cell hit from 1981, has assured a raised profile for Marc Almond, whose variable and controversial solo career has attracted the devotional adoration of a cult and a corresponding hostility on the part of mainstream critics.

Three months earlier, in June 1992, Marc Almond had staged an unforgettable acoustic concert at the Liverpool Philharmonic, where backed by Martin Watkins on piano, his set had incorporated old Soft Cell songs like 'Torch', 'Youth', 'Where The Heart Is', 'Fun City', and 'Say Hello Wave Goodbye', as well as new songs like the plaintively elegiac 'Amnesia Nights' and the explicit gender dilemma voiced in the Charles Aznavour song 'What Makes A Man A Man'. An almost inexplicably one-off show, Almond's vocals had never been more resonant, and the permutations of his emotional range never more sympathetic. To the minimal stage props of red roses and a few red draperies, he had lived out the songs in his own inimitably gestural fashion, incorporating diva tendencies into a torch singer's agonised biography of emotive loss. For those who had heard tapes of the piano concerts Almond had performed in Japan the preceding year, the choice of material came as little surprise, excepting the handful of new songs incorporated into the repertoire. But what had arrived authoritatively was absolute reliance on the voice. Free of the computer sequences that had worked in such contradistinction to the sensitivity of the vocals on *Enchanted* and *Tenement Symphony*, Almond's strictly acoustic shows between 1990-1992 were a confirmation that the singer had arrived. And rather like Scott Walker before him, record company pressures had insisted that Almond prove himself commercially to counterbalance the losses incurred by his uncompromisingly individualistic material. And the noticeable absence of touring in support of both these albums had contributed on the one hand to a lack of confidence on EMI's part, and the failure to renew a contract which accounted for Almond being with Warners; and on the other, to the rumour that Marc Almond had not survived the defection of his familiar musicians, and would have difficulty regenerating the hubris to tour again.

But if neither of these rumours lacked credibility, then there was truth in the realisation that the diva was becoming progressively invisible to his public. 1985 had been the last year of really consolidated touring across Britain and Europe, and although the years up to the popular *The Stars We Are* album in 1988 had been characterised by sufficient live appearances to maintain a public profile, Almond seemed now to have exiled himself in Paris and New York, and to have adopted Maria Callas's aura of mystique, the torch singer's sequinned halo shining in the hermetic confinement of his apartment. And there were so many questions we still wanted to ask him, like what are the little rituals he adopts on the day of a concert, does he choose his own make-up with meticulous attention to details of skin toning, what book is he reading at present, does he write better songs in the autumn in accordance with seasonal dissolution, does he go out shopping for his own food, are the afternoons too long and the nights too short, and what fears jump at him like black snakes from Soho pavements? Does he read Jean Genet's novels for inspiration? *Our Lady Of The Flowers, Miracle Of The Rose, Querelle Of Brest, Funeral Rites,* and the controversially autobiographical *Journal Of A Thief.* Genet who marries a rose with a knife, a prison cell with a boat voyaging towards a new America, a foggy day with a thief escaping in a gondola across the black jewel of a Venetian canal, and who unites love with death in a single orgasmic scherzo, is the archetypal romantic realist behind Marc Almond's peculiarly Frenchified lyrics. And if Lindsay Kemp created a mime extravaganza from Genet's *Our Lady Of The Flowers,* so too a musical construct from the book should be created for Almond's voice, together with the sumptuously baroque props that underpin the novelist's lyricism.

Almond's live appearances in Britain had begun to decline in 1986. A histrionically elated performance at the London Palladium as part of the Soho Jazz Festival in October of that year had been followed by a consummate show at the same venue a month later, as the high point of a mini-tour. 1987 offered the Convention at Busby's in Charing Cross Road, the two International AIDS Day concerts, and then right at the end of the year two masterful vocal concerts at the Astoria, both of which were filmed by Japanese television and subsequently released as the video, *Marc Almond Live In Concert.* But British fans had to wait until the autumn of the following year for the brief tour that supported the release of *The Stars We Are,* with Europe and Japan likewise receiving only a brief quota of concerts. There had been the disastrous 1989 concerts in Europe when Almond, supporting The Cure, had received consistent opprobrium from audiences orientated to rock music, rather than the introspective dramatics of torch song. Something of an end was reached at the Pink Pop Festival at Laandgraaf in Holland in May of that year, when Almond, unsuited to performing in an outdoors festival, was received with remorseless disrespect by a coarser sensibility in the audience.

By 1989 all the signs were irrefutably pointing to the fact that Marc Almond's genre of music had transcended even tangential references to rock, and that his focus should be directed to the more sophisticated audience who had always formed the nucleus of his support. And for the intensely dynamic Brel concerts that Almond was to stage in Europe in April 1990, including a triumphant show at La Cigale, Paris, he was to appear in dark suits with formal white shirts, accompanied only by Martin Watkins on piano, and so the acoustic medium ideally suited to his voice range had now become the instrument through which he would interpret a generous selection of old and new material. There was also a defiant stance of anti-commercialism about this gesture which suggested a deepening of artistic integrity. Almond has subsequently criticised the production of *Enchanted* and *Tenement Symphony* as exploiting a sound antipathetic to the organic premises behind what are some of his best songs, and by failing to promote these albums with a keyboard orientated band, and instead choosing to play low-key acoustic concerts, he has accentuated the uncompromising isolation that surrounds a singer who backed by a large record label is nonetheless unwilling to subscribe to the protocol behind commercial success.

The problem is repeated for all artists who live on an edge, fuelled by individualistic conviction. Where does one go? The way to public consciousness is guarded by vapid censors, representatives of bourgeois standards who mainline compromised art into a mediocre representation of culture. Marc Almond no more fits the commercial criteria of the media than an imaginative poet does the tenets of social realism. And certainly his forays into commercial success as a solo artist seem to have had only limited success in adjusting the record buying public to the more durable qualities of his LPs. The massively successful duet with Gene Pitney, 'Something's Gotten Hold Of My Heart', a song that refuted popular belief that Almond was on a downward spiral into oblivion, was consolidated two years later by the facility with which his cover versions of Jacques Brel's 'Jacky', and David McWilliams's 'Days Of Pearly Spencer' coasted into high chart placings as evidence to his new record company that his commercial profile was undiminished. But it wasn't the whole story. When Almond was to release a song so sympathetic to his own sensibility that it could have been written for his voice, his inspired reading of Charles Aznavour's 'What Makes A Man A Man', the record was denied airplay on account of its references to gay culture, its sensitive depiction of a transvestite strip artist beleaguered by homophobia, and it dipped into obscurity with no PR support and no live promotion by the artist. Almond had once again scratched the veneer of public respectability, and found that public tolerance for gay ideals in Britain are as pointedly ersatz as they are prejudiced in favour of the majority. It was this song, when performed live at the Royal Albert Hall, which was to receive a standing ovation, and to seem so naturally to fit the singer's vocabulary that it appeared to be an extension of himself. And why should there be any sense of discredit in singing other people's songs? The art of writing good lyrics belongs to few, and yet most rock artists are prepared to record self-penned banality rather than work with lyricists. It's one of the reasons so many rock artists ossify round cliché, rather than develop lyrically to accommodate growing older. Marc Almond's own songs stand with the best in European writers in his genre, people like Jacques Brel and Charles Aznavour, and his willingness to assimilate and record the best material written by others has deepened his artistic sensibility, contributing greatly to the expansion of his own repertoire. And I can think of no-one other than the French singer Léo Ferré, who has been prepared to sing us poetry in the way that Marc Almond has embraced lyrics by Charles Baudelaire, Arthur Rimbaud, and the Spanish poet Federico Garcia Lorca. The seriousness of this undertaking aside, there has to exist between the artist and his audience a particularly sensitive rapport in order to achieve the realisation of poetry becoming song. Almond is unique in that he has attracted to his music the undeviating loyalty of a literate audience wholly sympathetic to the incorporation of decadent poetry into a programme dictated by song.

What is it like to be a torch singer? Is it so very different from being a poet? It's a role usually adopted by a woman with diva propensities, we tend to place in this category Marlene Dietrich, Billie Holiday, Dinah Washington, Edith Piaf, Juliette Greco, Shirley Bassey, Dusty Springfield, and the various chanteuses who take up with crimson dresses, black gloves, and a smouldering lipstick bruise for lips. It's a particular genre inspired by extremes of passion, and one which makes dramatic the joys and devastating pains of love as they are observed in a solitary spotlight. The protagonist of the song is invariably rejected, but celebrates the agony involved in being loyal to memories. It's a mode of singing which has been adopted by gay culture, as well as the solitary in love, and those who just favour camp histrionics, for the better part of a century. Almond would insist quite rightly that the interpretation of torch songs should be heartfelt, and that there should be no separation between singer and song. It is a belief that he has often taken up in interviews, and in his concerts he has exemplified his conviction that all true singing is experience relived. And this commitment to truth in part accounts for the compulsive adulation which infuses his admirers. There's no being a part-time Marc Almond fan, it's more that his music is assimilated into your emotional life, and is there as consolation for the indomitably blue hours that pervade your life. There's no subtle area of pain that his words don't evoke, and for the listener there's a sense of shared compassion, a realisation that someone else has been in that place, and has walked back home under the desolate night rain without any hope for tomorrow. And in turn the song becomes a star worn in the heart, a constellation that visits suffering.

Male torch singers have been few. It's more a French genre, characterized by the likes of Charles Aznavour, Léo Ferré, and Serge Gainsbourg, although these singers belong to a masculine sense of identity, and fail to share with Almond diva and androgynous propensities. Even Scott Walker whose aching baritone ballads are the closest precedents to a field Almond has made exclusively his own, seemed uncomfortable about defending an area of the emotions better given to a female sensibility. Walker's ambiguous sexuality, and his sensitivity to the sort of poetic lyrics that Marc Almond was to adopt and also write, had him progress just so far, but to a level way beyond his contemporaries, before he retired at the height of his fame into a closed and inexorable solitude. Walker was the first English singer to fully embrace Jacques Brel's lyrics, and to record a number of the songs that Almond was to take into live concerts and the recording studios in the eighties. It was Scott Walker whose visibly palpable sensitivity to tragic lyrics had his hands shake on stage, who gave us the likes of 'Jacky', 'My Death', 'Mathilde', 'If You Go Away', 'Next', 'Funeral Tango', 'The Girls From The Street', and 'Sons Of', as well as his own complex and romantically flavoured compositions in which loneliness or unrequited love formed the nucleus of the song. And it was Walker who early on encountered the opposition that record labels give to serious and therefore potentially uncommercial material, and who, like Marc Almond later, had to navigate a perilous course between recording more mainstream material for release as singles, and keeping his true interests afloat through album material. In his brief but highly prolific years with Virgin, Almond seems to have been given the creative latitude to go entirely with his instincts, and during that period to have recorded a diversity of uncompromising material that was expressive of his true musical interests at the time. How else would we have got his marvellous renditions of Brecht's 'Pirate Jenny' and 'Surabaya Johnny', and the extraordinary cover versions that comprise *A Woman's Story*? The latter set of songs are amongst the most consummate of his vocal successes and are graced with an enthusiasm and intensity that he seems to have maintained throughout the sessions. There's a total commitment to those songs with their full blown balladeering traumas put across to us with the singer refusing to switch gender in the interests of the song, and instead singing from the viewpoint of a woman. Few singers have ever adopted the female persona with such harrowing authenticity as Almond's passionate declaration in 'A Woman's Story' that he lives 'As a woman who was passed around'; his empathy with women who suffer the infidelity of their partners perfectly fulfilling the tenets of torch extremism. There's a huge risk and vulnerability advanced by singing songs from the understanding of a woman when you're a man. The singer's professed love of drag bars and transvestites, some of his songs like 'L'Esqualita' and 'Madame De La Luna' being named after gay cabaret bars, has left him uninhibitedly open about recreated gender and androgyny. And don't we all look towards the generation of a third sex, a new species in which gender differentiation is dissolved, and in which the marriage of anima and animus are fused into perfect union? Songs like 'L'Esqualita', 'Her Imagination', 'Torch', 'Exotica Rose', and 'Madame De La Luna', portray the profound suffering that comes of living out the duality on a human level. When a man makes up he is open to street violence. What is permissible on stage undergoes a hard journey as it's translated to street level. Years of making up have given me a peculiar insight into human prejudice. Men express manifest hostility or ridicule when they encounter one of their own sex in makeup, for it challenges the repressed feminine within them, a fact aggravated by the favourable response given to androgyny by women. The conventionally straight man finds himself thrown off balance by the immediate sympathy that exists between feminine men, and women. The song 'What makes A Man A Man' portrays through Almond's heartbreaking timbre the victimization that comes to a drag stripper. 'Exotica Rose' narrates the life of a transvestite who is married and whose drag act supports a wife and children. Rose lives out a conscious bifurcation of identity, and in 'Her Imagination' a transsexual who has become the focus of neighbourhood gossip is referred to as having been 'such a happy boy'. The psychological compulsion to identify with the opposite sex is recorded from the earliest decadent histories of the Roman and Byzantine emperors, right through to the sacred rights of the shaman who adopts a woman's appearance in order to receive inspiration. Men sensitize anima in order to heighten creative potential. When I work on poetry and fiction making up is a ritual I do in order to heighten concentration and maximize creative energies. Singers, dancers, and performance artists wear makeup so as to differentiate and establish the space of their being set apart from the audience, and because creativity is about the celebration of androgyny.

It was Scott Walker's 'Big Louise', a song which Marc Almond was to cover on his first solo venture *Untitled* which allowed the subject of transvestism to openly take a place in song lyrics. In 'Big Louise' the loneliness of the protagonist is evoked through the realisation that 'the sad young man's gone away', leaving in his place the vulnerable Louise who is beleaguered by loneliness and gossip. We are told of Louise that 'tears smudge her lipstick'. She is alienated, transspeciated, and cut off from conventional society by reason of her adopted sexuality. Louise is in many ways the prototype for Marc Almond's authentic evocation of TVs and transsexuals, a lyric concern that not only occupies most of his recording career, but also the thematic obsessions which dominate in his collection of poems, *The Angel Of Death In The Adonis Lounge*.

Right from *The Transvestite Memoirs Of The Abbé De Choisy*, an authentic account of transvestism in late seventeenth-century French society at the court of Louis XIV, a growing literature on cross dressing has preoccupied a sympathetic sector of the public. Oscar Wilde's criminal trial involved evidence of young men dressing as women, Jean Genet's novels embraced the subject, and rock music popularized the image with Mick Jagger wearing a Mr. Fish white dress, and Lou Reed eulogizing the likes of Jackie Curtis and Holly Woodlawn, both members of Andy Warhol's TV entourage. Finally it took David Bowie to embody the whole thing, and through Ziggy Stardust to present the image of a genderless android. Strutting on the stage in high stilettos, fishnet tights and a leotard, Bowie's essentially homoerotic magnetism appealed to the youthful Marc Almond, who has recorded how as a member of the Bowie fan club, he watched his hero fix his eyes at a Ziggy Stardust concert, and proceed to use them as the emotional focus for his stage projection. Although essentially a traditional singer, whose songs are concerned with love and death, Marc Almond was brought up as a descendant of the glam rock of the seventies, and an adolescent of the punk movement. In terms of immediate influences he found himself drawn towards the music explored by the New York Dolls, Johnny Thunders, and Suicide, as well as early on establishing an interest in Johnny Ray, and Dusty Springfield, as two proponents of torch ballads. And although the electro-music created by Soft Cell repudiated guitar-orientated rock, Almond has never quite disowned his origins. In covering songs like Suicide's 'Ghost Rider', and Johnny Thunders' 'Born To Lose', even if they belong to the more ephemeral end of his discography, he has in a sense paid homage to the prototypes behind his first interests in music.

But in a career informed by variable and eclectic tastes, it is Almond's durable contributions to torch music which best exemplify his particular genius. "We are all in the gutter, but some of us are looking at the stars" Oscar Wilde tells us in *The Picture Of Dorian Gray*, a maxim that seems central to the spirit of Marc Almond's music. It is in the smoky blue, passionately tremulous dramas of his redemptive ballads that Almond best finds a measure on suffering. The creative expression exalts pain, and by giving voice to it transforms the experience into an act of compassionate sharing. Almond has always insisted on singing from the heart, and attributes his love of Spanish music to that cathartic quality. 'With Spanish singing there's always been a rough edge, the voices are often very broken through smoking cigarettes or drinking. The voices are never technically perfect, but they always have something that's stirring and passionate and goes to your soul. It's something that even if you don't understand the language, you know what the songs are about. I've tried to put that into my own singing. I don't think I'm technically a good singer at all, I'm very unbridled and uncontrolled, but that's what singing's about. Telling a story and conveying something, making someone believe you're singing. Nothing attracts you to words that don't stand out from a song.'

And to sing with the sort of passionate conviction that Almond demands, requires the integration of voice and lyrics. Poetry has a wound open into a red rose, and lyrics from good songwriters should convey a similar quality. Inspiration should be like catching a star in the hands and transferring it to the page. And Almond's own lyrics have explored a subject matter which is instantly recognisable as his own. What began as an excavation of lowlife and sleaze, and the general public has never quite forgotten the notion of 'Tainted Love' as being attributable to the singer who so successfully espoused its virtues, has deepened with Almond's maturity into a lyric concern for all outsiders, the gay people, transvestites, transsexuals, and underworld figures who populate his imagination. He has done for songwriting what Jean Genet achieved for the novel, and that is to embrace the taboo and convert it into art. Most rock lyrics comprise condescending cliché, but Almond, whose successive record companies have insisted he contend for popularity in the charts, has avoided any involvement with platitude. Even the commercially orientated Soft Cell hits like 'Bedsitter', 'Say Hello Wave Goodbye', and 'Torch', created an authentically sad and angular world for youth.

And the lyrics have proved sufficiently durable for the singer to resurrect and rework the material into acoustic concerts throughout the early years of the nineties. Almond's tour of Japan in August 1991 saw him lift the poignant elegy 'Youth' from his recorded archives, and re-interpret it through the sensitivity of piano accompaniment, as well as the more poppish 'Where The Heart Is'. And with the inclusion of 'Torch', 'L'Esqualita', and 'Say Hello Wave Goodbye', the singer appeared not only to be promoting *Memorabilia,* but to be refinding material which enhanced by his greatly improved voice has stood the test of being incorporated into his working oeuvre.

What a performer brings to the stage isn't what the audience sees, the two hours in the spotlight, but a lifetime's experience which has contributed to the person being there. An artist's mystique is compounded of what the audience conjectures about his or her life. And how did he get there across the city? Was he driven in a closed car by friends, did he come by taxi, and what did he see in that journey? Was there a girl in a red dress crying outside a telephone booth, did he hope the lights would stay red a little longer so the journey would be protracted, and the intensified moment prolonged? The little instant in time that would never come again, the reflection on his past and the people he would have wished were there to see the concert. But the lights were rapidly changing, and two gay clones were standing outside a bar kissing, and a greengrocer was running up his striped awning, and all the time the adrenalin was rising and his heart racing at an impossible speed.

We are always impatient for more of Almond's voice. The product is always too small and the concerts too few. The diva retains his inviolable mystique so as to offer hubristic excess on stage. Described early on in his career as 'a small, skinny poof in a black dress', Marc Almond has gone on to adopt various stage personae, but integral to all his changes is the notion of the diva as self-dramatized victim personifying a wound that is essentially unhealable. The voice in performance is cathartic only in the sense that it confides and universalizes a subjective spectrum of emotions, it does little to assuage the singer's pain. When he exits from the stage his personal problems remain as a reality, and performance serves only to create the illusion that within the dramatic components of song something has changed. And so much of what a singer does has to be committed to audial memory. We live with the voice in our head, an intimate form of possession which is far more pronounced than the process of reading, in which our dialogue with the text is a silent one.

In *The Queen's Throat*, Wayne Koestenbaum's extraordinarily illuminating study of the operatic singing and codes of diva conduct, he writes of the singer's pretence to be divine, and of how the invented persona adopted on stage comes to be identified with the singer himself; a belief that becomes obsessive on the part of fans, and accounts for the sort of devotional cult who follow Marc Almond. Koestenbaum writes: "Diva conduct, whether enacted by men or women, whether, indeed, we feel that diva conduct differentiates between men and women, has enormous power to dramatize the problematics of self-expression. One finds or invents an identity only by staging it, making fun of it, entertaining it, throwing it – as the ventriloquist throws the voice, wisecracks projected into a mannequin's mouth... No single gesture, gown, or haughty glissando of self-promotion will change one's actual social position: one is fixed in a class, a race, a gender. But against such absolutes there arises a fervent belief in retaliatory self-invention; gay culture has perfected the art of mimicking a diva – of pretending, inside, to be divine – to help the stigmatized self imagine it is received, believed, and adored."

I came to take a serious interest in Marc Almond's music at the time of the release of his controversial *Torment And Toreros* LP. The latter was savaged by the sort of insensible critics who common to both the music and literary worlds, disparage whatever threatens their personal limitations. So often critics simply define their own vanishing point, and fail altogether to connect with the space that goes beyond it. Almond's suite of songs, held together by a bruised death-wish, and charged by anger at the commercial pressures surrounding his career with Soft Cell, were lyrical and visionary, spiky with romantic realism, and entered into one's hearing like a panther carrying a rose in its teeth. An album of fine balances, the scalding invective aimed at the music industry in 'Catch A Fallen Star' is offset by songs of deep emotional intensity, like the resonantly haunting 'In My Room', and the dramatically sensitive medley comprising 'Narcissus', 'Gloomy Sunday', and 'Vision'. Everything about the album attracted attention, right down to Almond's thanking his sympathetic doctor in the credits, and to the chaotically improvised concerts staged at the Duke Of York's Theatre in St. Martin's Lane. Almond who was still nominally affiliated to the commercially orientated Soft Cell was creating a schizoid rift in the band's future, by accentuating a music which employed violin, cello, flute, and piano, as well as guitar, bass, keyboards and drums. In doing so Almond appeared to be insisting that his voice was the dominant instrument, and that his future lay in the interpretative finesse of his vocals. In more ways than one the diva was being born.

And in 1983 as in in 1994, what separated Marc Almond from his contemporaries was both his concern with a European tradition of song, as well as an art of recognizably retrieving lyric from the death it has suffered in the hands of anti-literate rock composers. And there was the initial voice. Untutored, impassioned, resonant with hurt, often singing flat, but already on the way to becoming the incomparably fine instrument it is today. Anyone disquieted by Scott Walker's untimely withdrawal into silence was compensated by the realisation that Almond had not only arrived, but would go on to supersede Walker's vocal prowess. By the time of recording 'You Have', Almond's brilliant but insufficiently praised single from 1984, the singer had placed himself at the forefront of British vocalists, developing an uncategorizable style which blended torch singing and cabaret with the more intelligent fringes of rock. And the expansive improvement in the singer's voice capacities during the period of 1984/85 suggested just how hard he was working at technique.

From Baudelaire onwards, by which I mean the beginnings of the modern sensibility, the committed artist has worked at an angle to society. Poets have a particularly hard time due to lack of any support system, and the negligible performing facilities made available to them. Almond, while belonging to a far richer profession nonetheless inherits the outsider's role. Uncomfortable with any distinct tradition, unwilling to be assimilated into mainstream music, Almond remains an artist who occupies the margins and is dangerous by reason of his individuality. Success is invariably the enemy of spontaneous creativity, and by inhabiting a role just sufficiently viable to attract commercial support, but at the same time uncompromisingly artistic, Marc Almond has been able to up-end preconceived notions of popular success and to present serious lyrics to a cult who have kept him alive. In this way his achievements have grown to be eminently durable, and have passed into the vocabulary of song.

And Almond would rightly argue that if you sing notes, you need a purposeful lyric content. His suitability to a cappella renditions of song, as well as to sensitive piano accompaniment, means that he lives by the resonance of words. His breath informs our emotions of the conflicting joys and pains of love, and as such he is the most subtle interpreter of pain, cruelty, jealousy, awareness of advancing age, death; in other words the whole emotional spectrum which is otherwise the business of poetry. Almond's voice explores the inner fissures, it breaks into us in the manner of segmenting an orange, and asks that the song becomes a source of reintegration. And when he takes violence for a subject it's with tempestuous empathy for unequal relationships, as in 'The Animal In You', or 'Love Amongst The Ruined', where the damaged lover is *"Waiting at the station/For my train to ruination."*

But it's predominantly as an elegist that Almond excels, and by elegy I mean that poetic form which commemorates, celebrates, and evaluates passion peculiar to loss or death. 'St. Judy' elaborates a fictional life of Judy Garland, one of the many torch singers Almond has integrated psychologically. The lyrics eulogize the self-destructive death cult of the artist whose style extends to the astonishing confession, *"And if I die before I wake up/I pray the Lord don't smudge my makeup."* The singer's own death-wish is evident in his revelling in the idea of *"high heels and a pool of gore"*, as he evokes a portrait of Judy dead on a hotel floor. Almond's elegies are many, and are perhaps nowhere more pronounced than in the funereal suite of songs which go to make up *Violent Silence*, arguably the most eloquent set of S&M lyrics ever to be recorded, combining as they do salient perversion with reflective tenderness. Almond's role as a contemporary elegist finds suitable expression in the song 'Champagne', which is minimalistic, stark, and portrays the life of a New York dancer degraded into strip at a 'low rent nude review', The Show Palace Theatre on 8th Avenue. Champagne's drug habit and suicide are recounted non-judgementally, Almond's sympathies implying that the majority invariably force minorities into untenable situations.

We're still waiting for the Royal Albert Hall concert. The excitement has been mounting for weeks, and the earlier show at Nottingham on 20th September 1992 has been a foretaste of the spectacular dramatics to come. London seems different on the days when Marc Almond is due in concert. Aren't the carnations redder in their street display, and the coffee darker and bitterer to the palate, isn't there a particular perfume on the air – I recognize it now as *1000* by Jean Patou – and isn't the impulse there to go out and buy red carnations or red roses? There's a delicious sense of ritualisation involved in the hours of waiting for the only voice to come on stage.

If in terms of subject matter Almond has made the ethos of transvestism and transsexuality his own, then in terms of performance he is acutely conscious of singing from a woman's point of view. And commenting on his ability to adopt a woman's point of view rather than a gay man's, and particularly in respect of the song 'A Woman's Story' he tells us: '"A Woman's Story" is still one of my favourite singles, and again it was something for me to play with, singing a song from a woman's point of view. I've often liked to mix genders around, play with them in songs, and sometimes sing them from a woman's point of view, not from a gay man's point of view, but a woman's. I think the best songs are written for women, you see, and a lot of singers I like are women. I couldn't do it as 'A Man's Story', because it isn't a man's story. I just sang it as it was, and didn't turn the genders around. Of course, the record company then started getting a little confused...'

Virgin were deeply troubled, and with the non-commercial slant of *Violent Silence*, the suite of songs Almond had recorded for the Georges Bataille Festival at the Bloomsbury Theatre in 1984, being released to a subdued response, followed by a string of uncompromising singles including 'Ruby Red', 'A Woman's Story', and 'Melancholy Rose', there seemed little manoeuvring point, particularly as Almond's next album was to be the acoustic *Mother Fist And Her Five Daughters*, a record of dark obsessions that disappeared without proper recognition or commercial fulfilment.

British audiences are shocked by diva tendencies. In 'St. Judy' Almond takes up the refrain *"I've wanted to do it for years"*, the *"it"* being that sense of total realisation, a man rushing out into the rainy street in a sequinned gown, arms lifted to the sky, a woman pushing her animus to an edge whereby she imitates the behaviour of a male drag artist, these are moments of breaking out when gender is not so much transcended as transferred. And camp is often about transference. The adoption of simulated gender is an act, in the same way as singing demands the adoption of a role sometimes foreign to the artist. In a *Gay Times* interview with Paul Burston, Almond spoke of his diva tendencies in terms of creating an image for himself independent of his looks and physique. 'It probably has a lot to do with being a small person. You're surrounded by people who threaten to swamp you, so you want to make bigger gestures than anyone else. I'm very aware that I can be a bit of a tragedy queen. If there's not a tragedy there, I'll go ahead and create one. I can turn something very small and inconsequential like a bad write-up in *The Pink Paper* into something huge and important complete with threats of violence and plenty of drama... I think there are elements of Saint Judy in all of us. But I also think I'm the first person to send myself up. The only way I've got through twelve years of tears and traumas and diva routines is to make a game of it all.'

And the illusion is maintained with perfection. The audience identify the singer with his songs, and the voice, particularly in Almond's case, passionately supports that belief. Divas live in a state of metamorphosis, and the stage is the ideal setting for such conduct. Pain and the emotions of loss can be recounted from behind a screen. *"Well let's all put on our sequinned dresses/and end it all in tears/Let's all holler, and beat our breasts/ending it all in tears/Christ I've wanted to do this for years."* —'St. Judy'

Readers of Neil Bartlett's *Ready To Catch Him Should He Fall* will remember the unforgettable bar scenes in the book, or rather diva scenes, in which Madame sings her one song each night, and so perfectly is she identified with the lyrics that a whole private mythology is born from this nightly gesture. And what Madame wants is all of it. The impossible gesture, the one that reverses age and misfortune, the one that promises love, gain and continuity as opposed to solitude, pain and fragmentation.

Very few poets have covered a field that Marc Almond has made distinctly his own, the ethos of transvestism and transsexuality. The closest to Almond's preoccupation with the subject as a source of lyric inspiration is the poetry of John Wieners, whose broken lyricism and identification with female suffering has placed him as something of a cult outsider in poetry. Born in Boston in 1934, Wieners has become a cult icon to the gay underworld, and the purity and genuine sadness of his work has reflected his own drug-ravaged and predominantly solitary existence. Wieners adopts the diva role in the course of writing, and chooses to take on a woman's identity through his poetry. In the poem 'To H' he writes: "I like Sunday evenings after you're here./I use your perfume to pretend you're near/in the night. My eyes are bright, why/can't I have a man of my own./Your wife's necklace's around my neck/and even though I do shave I pretend/I'm a woman for you/you make love to me like a man." Arguably Almond could sing a lot of Wieners' lyrics, and it's significant that Wieners is obsessed by Billie Holiday's plaintively elegiac love songs, and throughout his poetry identifies with glamorous femme fatales – Lana Turner, Marlene Dietrich, Judy Garland, the late Jacqueline Onassis. Empathetic adoption of the female persona allows the artist to aspire to adopted gender, and so release himself from the inhibitions of an inherited role. The passionate theatricals of Almond's performance, and one might also say the presence of duende, allow him to over-reach and transfer to a state of dynamized androgyny.

It's taken Marc Almond a long time to outgrow the image of sleaze with which he was associated by the music press. Encouraged by his floridly decadent paeans to lowlife like 'Sex Dwarf', 'Seedy Films',

'Gutterhearts', 'Disease And Desire', 'Ruby Red', and the infamously onanistic 'Mother Fist', Almond was perceived as a purveyor of songs which corrupted, a distinctly unEuropean way of responding to material which is aesthetically decadent. Branded by the image of leather, studs, and heavy makeup, British journalists narrowed Almond's field to one in which the general public might have imagined the singer hanging out in a Soho alley, brandishing a bullwhip and a torch dipped in infected blood. Rock journalism is ill-qualified to appraise torch singers, and what in Almond was a lyric identification with the underworld, in the way that Baudelaire chose to write about Parisian vice, or Jean Genet the deflowering of machismo, was accentuated and treated with censorial judgement by the mainstream press. Almond partly revelled in the debased image accorded his act, but was privately and deeply aware that notoriety was detracting from the serious poetics of his songs. 'I had a Spanish interview that I'd done, and the headline for it was "The Judy Garland Of The Garbage Heap." It was my favourite description of me, the themes of glitter and dirt, the tarnished glamour. I've always liked playing parts, playing around with images, in the way that David Bowie, T Rex and Roxy Music used to do, and I've always thought I've done that with humour, kind of sending myself up as well.'

But inwardly he would be the first to admit that the despair and frustration that came from having superlative songs denied air play, and audiences continuously interrupting his performances by the need to engage him in salacious camp repartee, were in the long run counterproductive. In Europe that problem doesn't exist in quite the same way. Audiences are better attuned to the seriousness of a singer's intentions, and the fact that great concentration is required in the act of singing. And it's not that Almond has compromised by appearing less often on stage, or has modified the lyric concerns of his material, it's more that he has made a shift in demanding a more mature reception to his work.

Diva tendencies, according to Wayne Koestenbaum, involve a love of queens. "The diva loves queens because pretending to be a queen is an occasion to divorce the body from the soul, to assume lofty and hieratic alienation; pretending to be a queen also helps the diva imitate figures in her past who might have ignored or abused her. Imitation is a form of mourning-through-identification: you imitate what you wish you could explain." And in 'L'Esqualita', arguably Almond's most discerning portrait of a diva, he sings of the drag queen's histrionic arias as a consummately adopted role, and one for which the audience suspend belief in favour of the singer's declamatory agony. *"OK so it's ham/But she means every word/In a ten minute ballad of despair and blood/With one hand to the bosom/Paid for by the ballad/And somewhere in there is a deep love for love."* It's all familiar territory to Marc Almond, an invented sexuality seeking consolation by way of dramatically agonized performance. Aren't we all bored with hieratic gender distinctions? The latter denominations uphold the sort of plutocratic machinery behind warfare and capitalist tyranny. Wouldn't it be healthier to think the politician is wearing lingerie under his bland suit, and has learnt to feminise his psyche? All trans-creatures, that is to say those who choose to make of their sex a fluent identity, constrained neither by inherited genetics nor sociological conditioning, are creatures of the coming Aquarian age in which the androgyne will find easy accommodation. For the present, invented or adopted sexual identity is proscribed by the proletariat, ridiculed and disparaged on the street, and vilified by the tabloids as contributing to the disease and moral attenuation under which we live. It's an uncomfortable ethos, and Marc Almond's songs have done much to combat convention, and not by the misdirected political anger of which he rightly disapproves, but through the creative expression of song, which together with poetry and art achieve revolution on an inner plane, and contribute much more durably to the dynamics of change. And 'L'Esqualita' not only celebrates drag, but it points to the claustrophobic isolation of the act – it is segregated in clubs, in this instance a Spanish Puerto Rican drag club on 8th Avenue New York, and as such is the focus of a particular audience. *"Conchita Piquer/She will take on the whole floor/This Carmen in cling film/Will bathe in your applause."* It's a world in which every detail is magnified, and in which desperation is offset by outrageous humour and camp send up. After the act the drag queen reverts to a solitary misidentified victim of society. In the song Almond sings, *"She'll live a few years/But she'll have some adventures/Then sing of her sequins/With tears and with traumas."* And in 'St. Judy', he catches the supreme gesture, *"I love it when they throw up their arms."*

A sympathy to diva qualities is necessary to any understanding of Marc Almond's life and work. Throughout a career that now runs to fifteen distinguished years, he has openly celebrated and elegized the diva in every aspect of performance. And the Royal Albert Hall? It's time to be getting there for the spectacular extravaganza. There's little that Marc Almond can't do with the increasing warmth and range of his voice. And it's odd for him to be carrying that special gift. People can't see it in the street, or know that it's there. It's like poetry, it's like any gift, it's there as an invisible strength, but it's suggested by the person's aura on close contact. A luminous sensitivity implies the inner process, and artists are set apart by a mystique attached to creativity. It's got to do with a particular neurological charge, and a vulnerability that points to intense inner preoccupation. And creativity is an ongoing process, it's a way of life and not an occasional demand. Catch a glimpse of Marc Almond in Wardour Street, or Brewer Street, and of course he's inwardly preoccupied. There's the work to be done, ideas for new songs, the seriousness of keeping an aura vibrant, and there's the practical necessity of avoiding people who would intrude upon mystique. Perhaps he's singing 'When I Was A Young Man' in his head. There are the crowds outside Madame JoJo's and the Raymond Revue Bar, the propositioning cries of marketeers in Berwick Street, the whole colourful insurgence of Soho as it filters through the London afternoon. There's the occasional transvestite out on the street in makeup: the afternoon's a sort of suspended mirage before the night arrives. What do torch singers and divas do in the afternoon? There's a famous shot of Maria Callas opening or closing the curtains to a spacious apartment window, and the photographer has captured a moment of solitary mystique, Callas confronting a world from which she is hiding, the unsharable agonized recognition of being apart is visible in her features before she disappears from sight. For the creative sensibility there's always a division between inner and outer realities. The world is either too close or too far. When you meet a torch singer by chance, hand him or her the bouquet of red roses you imagine yourself to be holding.

It's the show tonight. The sky's sprinkled with clusters of coruscating stars. We're waiting for the only voice. Dear lovers of the only voice.

IN DE SADE'S SHADOW

When Soft Cell arrived on the scene in 1980 as a quirky phenomenon employing the histrionic cabaret vocals of a diva, and the computerized notations of an offbeat keyboard player, their oddity couldn't have been more pronounced. The guitar orientated glam-rock icons of the previous decade were either extinct or burnt out. Marc Bolan had died in 1977, David Bowie had effectively cremated his inspirational zeitgeist in 1980 with the recapitulative 'Ashes To Ashes', Lou Reed was at the time nosing into oblivion and semi-retirement, and the saliently dissonant thrust of punk had mutated to a second wave of goths. At the turn of any decade there's a faltering, old modes of expression hang in tentative suspense, while the new have still not properly arrived. Cabaret disco, as one might conceive of Almond's initial creative expression, was an unexplored genre, and potential competition like Depeche Mode and Spandau Ballet altogether lacked the vocal expertise that was Almond's.

The meeting of Marc Almond and David Ball at Leeds Polytechnic in 1976, and Ball's recent purchase of a synthesizer for £450, with money inherited from his dead father, was to lead to Ball's composing electronic soundtracks to Almond's improvised cabaret performances, in which the singer, dressed in masks and outré androgynous costumes, recited his lyrics before coming to develop a singing technique. 'The music I was playing – Frank Sinatra meets The Cramps; Throbbing Gristle meets Ella Fitzgerald – wasn't commercially acceptable to most of the Leeds scene at the time.' And because of hostility and evident isolation in terms of breaking through to the London scene, in order to finance his music, Almond had to take jobs behind the bar at the Leeds Playhouse, and as a cloakroom assistant at the Warehouse, the city's most avant garde attempt at a disco. And already we sense in Marc Almond the beginnings of an indomitable inner conviction that he had the potential to be a star. Wearing the blacker than black eyeliner and mascara which were to be distinguishing characteristics of his gender difference when Soft Cell surfaced to international acclaim, we're also aware of the warm humour and strength underlying Almond's apparent vulnerability, qualities which were to sustain him throughout a career alternately assassinated by critical hostility, and sustained by cult fanaticism. As an unknown, whose student performances had suggested S&M tendencies, and whose exhibitionism had caused him to strip on stage and smear his body with catfood, Marc Almond for all of his overt nervousness and palpable sensitivity was inwardly determined to succeed. And certainly success wasn't to be achieved through the couple's self-financed journey into the studio to record the *Mutant Moments* EP in a limited pressing of two thousand copies in 1980. The four songs featured on the EP 'Metro MR X', 'L.O.V.E. Feelings', 'Potential', and 'Frustration' were examples of minimal electronic pop, and none of them allow for Almond, who is predominantly singing flat, to realise the inimitable vocal genius he was to acquire over the next five years. But despite the obscurity surrounding the record's release on Big Frock Records, the EP came to the notice of Stevo, an eccentric young entrepreneur who at the time was running in the Sounds music paper, the 'Futurist Chart', which focused on the potential of new or obscure bands. Despite his impoverished education, alleged semi-literacy, and pronounced difficulty with speech, Stephen Pearce had given up hod-carrying to become a DJ, and in time the founder of Some Bizzare, the successful record label which manages Marc Almond to this day. 'I liked Soft Cell because there was a lot of feeling and emotion in them. I liked the sleaze and trash. They were heavy and commercial on different sides.'

It was Stevo who, in compiling a Some Bizzare album of new representative talent, had Soft Cell record the extraordinary 'Girl With The Patent Leather Face', a song in which Almond's preoccupation with the grotesque is countered by a corresponding compassion for a girl whose face confines her to an anomalous solitude. This girl who studies fashion glossies longing to have the attributes of a model, is also possessed of the malevolence to avenge herself on the model types she would emulate. Almond has spoken of his admiration for J.G. Ballard's *Crash*, a mid-seventies futuristic novel of astonishing imaginative genius in which an apocalyptic autogeddon occurs on the Hammersmith fly-over, and in which Vaughan the white-suited protagonist develops a perverse voyeurism as a photographer obsessed with taking shots of crash victims in all the complex geometry of their wound lesions and geometrically dislocated bodies. There's a resonance of *Crash* in Almond's lines, *"The girl with the patent leather face/Hangs around the mutant*

bars/She tampers with machinery/So other beauties crash their cars."
The lyric is crafted and imaginative in a way superior to all of his
British songwriting contemporaries, and it suggested to the discerning
that the individual vocal talent who had arrived was also a literate
composer of unorthodox lyrics. And with Soft Cell signing to Some
Bizzare, who would in turn license them to Phonogram for a
thousand pounds advance, the way was set for them to go into the
studio and record 'Memorabilia'. The latter is another example of a
densely written lyric which succeeds by injecting cyclical cut-up into
the writing. In this song Almond extols the insignificant things which
constitute the memory of having been in a place. And with a
dance-beat lifted from a Donna Summer record, the song became a
club hit, elevating Soft Cell to cult status, and sufficiently appeasing
Phonogram's need for the band to have a commercial hit to allow
them to go on and record 'Tainted Love', the offbeat Northern soul
number to which Almond was to apply the emotively bruised vocals
which were to take the song to the top of the charts. A club song
previously sung by Gloria Jones, 'Tainted Love' ideally suited the
persona Almond chose to occupy at the time. The song hints at gay
sleaze, it's almost Wilde's "the love that dares not speak its name",
despite the comparatively innocuous lyrics. Almond's appearance on
Top Of The Pops was calculated to accentuate the songs implications,
and dressed in black leather fetish wear, together with a percussive
array of bangles, his eyes articulated by mascara and eyeliner,
audiences assumed that Almond and Ball were a couple, and that the
song elegized prejudices against gay love. But no matter the
erroneous assumptions, 'Tainted Love' proved to be a commercially
infectious international hit, its minimal electronics and impassioned
vocals preparing the way for Almond's audacious formula for cabaret
disco. And while Almond's sexual orientation seemed self-evident, he
remained ambiguous about his gay propensities, preferring like a true
diva to luxuriate in mystery.

Often victimized for his appearance, and threatened in clubs by
displays of homophobic machismo, there was a generative feeling of
revenge in Almond's person in the way he carried 'Tainted Love' to
immediate success. In a *Sounds* interview later in the year, Almond
spoke of the undefined gender which often characterizes the people
in his songs. 'So when I write lyrics I'm never thinking about anybody
as having a defined sexual gender. It's not being faceless either. Nor
even being conscientious or worthy on my part. It's just taking away
the labels, that's all... Our music's really non-sexual despite talking
about sex so much. I know what you mean when you say it's
celibate. It doesn't point out a him or a her.' Despite the efforts of the

gutter tabloids to vilify Almond's name, and label him as a purveyor of perverse sex rites, this deeply sensitive individual has guarded his privacy as a necessary and sane prerogative to surviving in a music world dominated equally by sensational and disposable values. Who is Marc Almond? The person he elects to be at this moment. And to those who have paid discerning attention to his lyrics over the years, there has been little doubt as to his gay orientation. The ambiguity he maintained early on in his career with Soft Cell, suggesting an ambidexterous, ambivalent approach to sexual interests has been altogether dropped with the growth of his solo career, and the realisation that his voice is the determining instrument of his success. Almond has never adopted socio-political grievances over being gay, or attempted to propagate a pink banner; his method has been one of contributing to a body of song in which gay relations have been a primary focus. In 1981, he couldn't risk the endorsement of homosexuality as a lifestyle, rather he avoided gender affiliation and identified with the mixed up emotions that preoccupy youth. But in a 1993 *Gay Times* interview Almond was more specific about his distaste for collective ideologies, and his belief in the individual affecting changes by way of the creative act. 'I go out on the gay scene and I see a lot of very diverse people. Just because they're gay it doesn't mean to say they have much in common with one another. There are people who have HIV and people who don't have HIV. I've known so many people with HIV who've been written off by their gay so-called "friends". I've witnessed the appalling attitudes some gay people have towards drag queens and transvestites – that whole "let's keep the trannies at the back" attitude. That's part of the reason I hate Gay Pride. I'm just not convinced that half those people drinking themselves silly in the park even like each other.'

These are the considered reflections of a man in his late thirties who has proved himself to be an amazing vocal talent. But for the first eighteen months of their commercially successful career, which spanned the *Non-Stop Erotic Cabaret* and *Non-Stop Ecstatic Dancing* LPs, together with six endemically infectious dance hit singles, Soft Cell were reviewed by mainstream journalists as a depraved idiosyncratic scene who would prove to be one of the more ephemeral phenomena of the eighties' music trends. Disparagement and critical hostility tempered by jealousy directed at Almond's versatility as a recording artist have surrounded much of his career. Recapitulating on that career in a *Melody Maker* interview in 1990, and subsequent to his massively successful duet with Gene Pitney, 'Something's Gotten Hold Of My Heart', it was not without irony that Almond commented on the price of commercial success. 'In the early days of success with Soft Cell, there'd be a lot of animosity thrown in my direction from people I'd meet in the street, people shouting insults at me or threatening me in pubs. Since last year's success, I never get anyone picking on me. Because it was a duet with Gene, I think it was sort of my key into acceptance by the mainstream, which was great fun. It was very strange being accepted and quite a challenge.'

The paranoid legacy that Marc Almond has inherited from public opprobrium accounts for the manifest vulnerability he displays in the London streets. His slight, nervous figure hurries through the Soho alleys as though a wolf might be on his trail. But it's also to do with protecting his inner gift, and the need to keep that inviolably separate from the curious. The artist is distinguished by a particular inner resonance, a highly attuned nervous sensibility which distinguishes him from others. The dynamics of that energy have to be preserved. Parents are usually the first to misunderstand its direction, education would seek to uniformize it, and the collective to ridicule or annihilate it. Almond has told of his drunken father's brutal inimicality to his 'Tainted Love' appearance on *Top Of The Pops*. 'For my own father, the Soft Cell *TOTP* experience couldn't have been more devastating had Christ himself appeared in our living room and ejaculated into my mother's handbag. "They're freaks, y'know," he raged, tying me to the bed for the night, "I was in Bahrain with the RAF and I know a puffy weirdo when I see one." Years later, I remembered Dad's old habit of crying softly, whilst pissed, to his *The Complete Gene* boxed-set compilation and wondered how he'd taken the Almond/Pitney collaboration.'

'Fun City', which he introduces in his 1991 acoustic concerts as the first song he ever wrote, was originally released not by Soft Cell, but as a single exclusive to the Marc And The Mambas Fan Club. The song points to Almond's considerable despair and confusion as a young man; a sexual identity crisis has the protagonist leave home and live as a rent boy in London. A decade later Almond was to pitch the theme with greater eloquence in 'A Love Outgrown', a moodily plaintive ballad about having to leave his hometown Southport, for fear that his despondent isolation in a claustrophobic seaside resort would result in him being locked up in an institution. Abortive teenage suicide attempts were a part of his emotionally confused upbringing. 'What I didn't realise was that it's illegal. I was arrested and sent to a mental institution – THE PEOPLE IN THERE! You wouldn't believe it. It certainly made me think twice about attracting that sort of attention again.'

Almond has always nurtured a healthy contempt for superficial success, and the sort of gestural vapidity that often accompanies plutocracy. His rise from humble beginnings at the Leeds Warehouse to international stardom in the course of a year, brought out in him an innate revulsion for the whole parasitical echelons attached to the music industry. Three minutes of 'Tainted Love' had completely changed his life. The sleaze invoked by songs like 'Secret Life', 'Seedy Films', 'Entertain Me', and 'Sex Dwarf', from the *Non-Stop Erotic Cabaret* album had afforded him the reputation of being a perverted latter day de Sade, an S&M deviant disciple of the Divine Marquis, a nefarious purveyor of vice intent on corrupting the nation's youth. Almond who had moved to a flat in Brewer Street in Soho, only minutes away from the notorious Raymond Revue Bar, and the transvestite mecca Madame JoJo's, was presumed to be an initiate to Sadean practises. That he felt a natural gravitation to lowlife is expressed both in his lyrics and his personal comments on the subject. 'If my Mum was walking through Piccadilly Circus, she wouldn't see the rent boys, the young male prostitutes standing up on the meatrack. She would just see a lad leaning up against a railing. I know he's leaning on a railing because he's on the meatrack and he's looking for business. I can tell by the eyes. But I've always found glamour in the squalor. There's always something really glamorous and sparkling in the filth and the seediness. That's what I find curious. I have a fetish about those places.'

It was with the blander, more instantly saleable 'Bedsitter', that Soft Cell continued with success as a singles band, and the video portrayed Almond looking angelically camp in gold eyeliner, acting out the solitary predicament of a young person alone in the city, whose only cathartic release is that of going out to clubs for kicks. This song together with the poignantly moving 'Say Hello Wave Goodbye' confirmed Soft Cell's profile as one ideally suited to feeding youthful angst with a sensitive and empathetic evocation of perennial traumas: love, betrayal, loneliness, and emotive turbulence. It's the deeply sensitive 'Say Hello Wave Goodbye', arguably one of the best written lyrics of the eighties', which suggested something of the direction Almond would take when he came to pursue a solo career. As a lyric writer he is the finest of his generation, and yet little critical attention has been devoted to the rich decadence of his imagination, and the way that imaginal sensibility is transferred to the social ethos in which he lives – the Latin hedonist directing his sympathies towards the sexual pariahs – the transvestites, transsexuals, whores, people who live as socio-ideological and genetic outsiders to the uniform mob. There's a distinctive flavour of compassion for these people in every Almond composition from 'Fun City' to his most recent work. There's hardly a sadder introduction to any song than *"Standing in the door of the Pink Flamingo/Crying in the rain/It was a kind of so so love/And I'm gonna make sure it never happens again."* Whatever one's love and sexual preferences the theme rings true by reason of its universality. *"How I love any kind of love"* Almond sings in 'There Is A Bed', and it's impossible not to listen to his elegies without a realisation of tolerance. Gay and straight love celebrate the same passionate aspirations and the same impossibly traumatic rejections. When Almond re-did the vocals for 'Say Hello Wave Goodbye' in 1991, the accompanying video portrayed gender ambidexterity, overtly gay young men and beautiful girls walking through the blinding rain, while the singer sits at a cafe table upon which blue irises have been placed. Speaking of its five minute length, Almond commented, 'It was impossible to cut the lyrics. It was dreamy and romantic. It told the story of a prostitute. It was really great hearing it on the radio and people saying "Oh, what a lovely song."' The song's original chart placing was No.2, and the success of this densely textured ballad was a prophetic indicator that Marc Almond was only just beginning a career that would graduate towards his prestigious distinction as an internationally renowned torch singer.

But there were internecine pressures that threatened the band with dissolution from the outset, and despite the commercial success of their initial album, and first three singles, Almond was angularly opposed to the pressures that Phonogram attempted to impose on Some Bizzare's artistic license. Stevo has always pursued a policy of licensing Almond to a contractual recording company, and Phonogram who had taken Soft Cell on for a parsimonious £1,000, were anxious that they should continue with the commercial appeal instated by 'Tainted Love'. Almond who was anxious to depart from electronic music, and to perform live on a level with the audience, without any intermediary barrier of a raised stage, found himself increasingly estranged from the corporate's intentions to have him transmogrified into a celluloid pop star. By the time Soft Cell came to record their fourth consecutive hit 'Torch', with the video featuring Cindy Ecstacy, it seemed obvious that Almond's romantic realism as a lyricist was in time going to take him out on an individualistic trajectory which had little in common with chart music. In fact there's nothing like 'Torch' in early eighties' music, and nothing as good as it since.

The song is typically about a transvestite torch singer in a club. 'The song was actually inspired by a Billie Holiday-type singer with a white gardenia in her hair and a blue sparkly dress, a very sad blues singer in a club. And a person who sees his life in her song.' There should be a newly created state for trans-people: a Transsexual Empire in which transvestites and transsexuals delight in their difference, instead of living as outsiders who are ridiculed for their appearance even within the gay community. The notion of monadic, heterosexual dominance has so often proved radically counter-productive to human advancement, with its preoccupation with warfare and machismo avarice in business, that it's time for a new trans-ideology to replace its outmoded conventions. Almond within the context of song has accommodated a persecuted sector of society. His compassion and sympathetic understanding for sexual outsiders, while it has brought him the suspicion of the media, has nonetheless proved a durable expression within the parameters of song. Almond has lent dignity to drag and transvestism. His beautifully sensitive reading of the Charles Aznavour song 'What Makes A Man A Man', remains the ultimate singer's rendition of a drag theme involving homophobia and human marginalisation. 'Torch', while lacking the explicitness of the Aznavour song, carries with it a subtle distillation of pain. *'I'm leaning on this bar/Listening to you sing,/And your sad song rings in my ears/And I start to cry,/He's searching,/She's showing,/See him held in a deep, deep, spell,/He knows she's glowing."* The interchange of gender implied by the lines is perfectly in accordance with Almond's preoccupations, and there was an air of desperate romance to the song which had it create a blue mood with an intense luminosity in the centre. 'Torch' charted at No.2, just narrowly missing the premiere position granted 'Tainted Love', despite its being much the finer song. Almond was unrepentant. 'Soft Cell have always had these ambisexual overtones. It's another side of the subversiveness. The sexual mystery going in and out of the songs. I don't often direct songs at a particular gender. It's more ambisexual. It's what delights quite a lot of people about Soft Cell. And disturbs quite a few.'

'What', the band's next single, had instantaneous commercial appeal; a catchy pop number not written by Almond, and scanning with predictably rhythmical naivety, it is a song which nowhere specifies gender – we assume a man is addressing a woman, but it may be otherwise. Despite its success, contentions between Almond, Ball, and Phonogram were at breaking point. It appeared manifest in the video cut to promote the single that Almond had exhausted his sympathies with commercially orientated music. The song just wasn't him, but it repeated a contagious formula that Soft Cell had developed in the studio. What seemed to be transparently apparent was that the voice was frustratedly superior to the songs being recorded. And almost as an undercover refuge to sanity, Almond was beginning to record the more serious suite of compositions he was to put out later in 1982 as *Untitled* from Marc And The Mambas, the group of musicians who were to serve as the creative catalyst to his becoming a solo artist. As an album of obsessional influences combined with virtuoso lyricism, *Untitled* was to prove the blueprint to next year's controversial work of genius, *Torment And Toreros*. And given that Soft Cell had re-mixed and repackaged six of their most identifiable songs as the mini LP *Non-Stop Ecstatic Dancing*, and by doing so had established the precedent for a whole decade of issued re-mixes, this salient marketing stab could also be read as an ironic statement by Almond that, like Rimbaud's assassins, he was preparing to strike. Dave Hill reviewing the Soft Cell album for the *NME*, exposed what he though was a formulaic pattern to Almond's success. "It's all too obvious. Marc has very capably internalised the complete back-catalogue of camp artistry, merging that perennial Cabaret mythology with a few Earls Court leather bar cyphers, and a bit more twittering theatricality, to create a fluffy, fluttery pink vision of decadence which leaps luridly at you from every modern media device." Almond was becoming categorized as a purveyor of vice, someone who embodied a nefarious satanism, who was refused the rights to buy an apartment in New York because he was considered undesirable, and yet he clearly captivated a disaffected youth into buying his records. There was a suggestion of mass empathy on the part of his public. The tainted one had established an image of camp androgyny every bit as pronounceable as the newly discovered, but revamped, Quentin Crisp. Only Almond was eminently more shocking than the reticent Crisp. And it had become *de rigueur* that the press should attempt to devaluate Almond by accenting what they considered to be a spurious camp. In reviewing 'What' *Sounds* commented, "The weirder Almond attempts to be, the more sordid the contexts he creates, the more fetishistic the outfits in which he drapes his pale runtish form... the more utterly, sweetly, safely ordinary he appears to be."

Reactionary animadversion to creative difference is common to all the arts. Critical censors in music, poetry and art exist to reinforce the notion of an immutable status quo. There's the erroneous idea that genius needs only to be devaluated to conform. Almond had no such intentions. His energies were stretched over recording two new albums, the acclaimed Soft Cell LP *The Art Of Falling Apart*, produced by Mike Thorne and recorded in New York in the autumn of 1982, and his own *Untitled* suite of songs released at the end of the same year. To insiders, and the more sensitive sector of his fans, the release of *Untitled* pointed towards the restive dissatisfaction that Almond was showing towards Phonogram and the pressures to create hit singles. Soft Cell had always fought shy of extended touring, choosing to engage in a few select appearances, and then go underground for months; a policy Almond has maintained throughout his solo career, preferring to accentuate mystique rather than translate his music into common acceptance. And besides, performance is about giving, it entails an emotional generosity which is distinct from the practise of going through the motions every night with routinal inauthenticity. A Marc Almond concert is about marrying life and death through the extremes of passion.

On the edge of disintegration as a band, Almond and Ball worked with Mike Thorne in his 54th Street studio on the more texturally layered and lyrically darker *The Art Of Falling Apart*. Almond's themes on this album are the obsessive Baudelairean ones: revenge, love, death, disease, age, and betrayal, an amalgam of decadent concerns that have remained constant in his cumulative opus. In a *Sounds* interview in 1988 Almond drew attention to how a decadent sleaze image associated with his work had prevented attention being given to its lighter aspects. 'People only scratch the surface of what I'm about and take too much of it for granted. They fail to see that there's more there. Often I'm told, you write about the seedy side of life or the sleazy side of life which I hate, hate, hate. I think it's other people's fascination with that that's responsible. I have written about the darker emotions or the outsider, but it's outweighed by the other material I write. I very much write about love, about simple emotional things, about life and travel and social comment, which is what a lot of these so called seedy songs are all about. It's other people's fascination for it, a very British attitude that homes in on anything sexual in your work and blows it out of all proportion.'

There's considerable truth in this. No-one reads a poem of Baudelaire's without entertaining the biographical preconception that the author had syphilis, and was prosecuted for obscenity and blasphemy. No-one comes to a Marc Almond song without some awareness of the singer's reputation for decadence. And often the desire to invoke evil has as a source its polarised opposite: innocence. Creativity often confuses the issue because the artist comes to be associated with his work. Public image implies the affiliation of one to the other. And the songs on *The Art Of Falling Apart* do explore a seam as dark as a tunnel in the underworld. They are premonitory of themes Almond was to pronounce more resolutely in his solo career. In songs like 'Heat', Almond focuses on the theme of numbers, a topic that was to prove the subject of a later banned single from the same album. *"Do you use our bodies like cigarettes/Do you need them for ego/Do you need them for sex."* Betrayal and anonymous sex is a recurring theme in Almond's work. The figure of the sexual outlaw down in the park featured in 'I've Never Seen Your Face', and 'Night And No Morning', both maturer expressions of sexual excess voiced by his solo career, owes his thematic origins to Almond's early writing with Soft Cell. The desperation in these early songs, which was to culminate in the apocalyptic cry of despair in 'Soul Inside', suggests the drug-fuelled writer's personal immersion in the New York scene, and his discovery of clubs like L'Esqualita, The Baby Doll Lounge, The Grapevine, and the Hellfire Club in which Puerto Rican transvestite torch singers eulogized a bondage subculture.

There's a real sense of psychophysical disintegration in Almond's forays into the New York scene. His songs of that period relish a masochistic self-loathing, as well as a deviant celebration of his encounters. But out of the sexual turmoil came the resolution to survive, and even if Soft Cell wavered with shifting foundations on the edge of the abyss, there was still a powerful sense that Almond would survive, and do so because he subjectively values his creativity. *The Art Of Falling Apart* vibrates with paranoia, depression, disillusionment and hysteria. Soft Cell were living and moving too fast: their mercurial success and corresponding rejection of commercialism had all happened within eighteen months. Perhaps there were too many singles, and with Phonogram monitoring a formula for chart appeal, Almond and Ball saw themselves as manipulated simulacra caught up in a momentum established by record company accountants.

Almond was typically explicit about his discoveries at New York's Hellfire Club. 'It was so uninhibited, there was everything there- whipping, bondage, people into urinating and whatever, but very out in the open, and encouraging voyeurs as well – and I found it was a real relaxation. Standing at the bar drinking, you don't feel shocked, you feel you can be any sort of person – your true self – 'cos nobody really cares, they're all too busy being their real, true, basic inner self.' And certainly the scorching themes of 'Heat', and 'Numbers', and the album's title track demand a concession to self-debasement. Almond's beginnings were too humble, and the contestancies to his early fame too antagonistically contumacious, for him to nurture any illusions about the glamour attached to pop icons. There's a sense that almost

---

everything Soft Cell achieved was against the grain, and got by subversive energies directed against their record company.

In Stevo, his Some Bizzare manager, Almond found a willing conspirator. Some of Almond's aggression towards a manipulative record corporate was voiced in a *Melody Maker* retrospective in 1986. 'We were always annoyed that Phonogram never believed in us. They were proved wrong, but we always felt let down. They never had any enthusiasm for what we wanted. There was a continual battle with them just to get things released. I just find most of the people in record companies totally sick-making.' For anyone intent on individually liberated creative expression, Almond had chosen a constrictive medium, and some of the sexual shock in his lyrics is clearly aimed at countering his frustration at media prohibitions. 'Numbers' was the first really uninhibited song about casual gay sex, and one which laments being consigned to an endless cycle of impersonal contacts. It was also the first clear indication to Phonogram that Almond was quite prepared to sacrifice a single's commercial potential for his belief in artistic integrity. None of the singles released from the highly successful *The Art Of Falling Apart* carried much chart prestige, 'Where The Heart Is', 'Loving Me Hating You', and 'Numbers' indicated that Almond's attempts to address psychological issues through electronic music were exposing a radical contradiction between his work's serious intentions and its trivialization by the media.

There was clearly no way in which Almond would be able to put out a song like 'Martin', which was included on the 12-inch single packaged with the album, in its own right. One of Almond's virtuoso explorations of deviant rites, the lyrics recount the story of a youth obsessed with the desire to kill, a psychopath who stays in bed and hallucinates; a theme inspired by a George A. Romero film in which a vampirical teenager drinks the blood of the women he murders. Once again Almond was seen at his best empathizing with the disaffected, and those separated from reality by extreme fetishes. Martin sees a face at the window, a hound under the bed, and the insurgent clamour to kill rises in his blood. It was a courageous topic to entertain at a time when the bland lyrics of music's new romanticism were focused towards the mundane girl meets boy imagery.

Almond's forays into the shadow areas of his psyche, and the dark confessions of his romantic sensibility as they were realised through *Untitled*, and *Torment And Toreros*, the two albums he released with the Mambas simultaneous with his career with Soft Cell, will be the subject of a seperate chapter; for they also represent the beginnings of his concern with song, and the adaption of personal favourites written by others to his voice. It was a tangent necessary to the singer's artistic survival, a sign that he wished to differentiate his work from a pop formula, and concentrate on a mode of expression that would prove creatively durable.

Soft Cell were to outlive the crises surrounding them at the time of recording *The Art Of Falling Apart*, and were to return to live performance in the spring of 1983. But Almond was clearly under severe nervous pressure, fuelled by a cocktail of liquor and drugs to mollify the hard edges of experience. There were reports in *Sounds* of Almond and Stevo marching into Phonogram's offices, after learning that 'Numbers' had been released with a sticker offering a free copy of 'Tainted Love', and wrecking the A&R department's fourth floor office, Almond clearing gold discs off the wall, and Stevo smashing a glass door with a fire extinguisher. Almond's frustration at what he conceived to be exploitation and obtusity on the part of his record company, fired a policy of uncompromising recrimination that was to last until he finally left Phonogram for Virgin in 1984.

Soft Cell performed at the Hammersmith Palais on March 7th 1983, supported by the Venomettes as backing singers and with Gary Barnacle on sax. They played two nights to rapturous applause, Almond proving to be re-energised by renewed contact with a live audience. Writing the concert up for *Sounds*, David Dorrell remarked how 'Almond embodies each figure perfectly, contorting and eventually squeezing the cruelty – the life blood – from each strangled persona, each agonised lyric.' And twisted or agonised very much describes the emotional spectrum of Almond's singing at this period. From the tortured ballad 'Loving Me Hating You', to the sexual iconoclasm of 'Numbers', through to the deeply sensitive elegies 'Youth', and 'Say Hello Wave Goodbye', Almond's performance at the Hammersmith Palais suggested a man who, in his late twenties, had compressed every form of emotive experience into his turbulent life to date. The voice sounded like a bruise opening out into a black rose. The electronic cabaret provided a stage upon which the singer's real life dissolution was incarnated through art. And the inner cataclysms that Almond projected through his live act in triumphant performances repeated at Liverpool, Derby, Brussels, and then on tour in Spain, were to find impassioned release through his work with the Mambas on *Torment And Toreros*, the album which was to prove a controversially turbulent distillation of his creative energies. Right on the edge, Almond was heading towards breakdown and hospitalisation as a consequence of alcoholism. Dangerous times: the self-immolative persona of the artist on stage was becoming a mirror reflection in life. Almond was using copious amounts of vodka and tequila to withstand the pressures of having to prove himself a commercial artist. Although Soft Cell had taken to the stage again, and were to engage in a bizarrely successful tour of Spain that summer, all hints of creative fulfilment on Almond's part seemed to have disappeared. Above all a singer, Almond was denied by the limitations of dance music, and Soft Cell's orientation, the eclectic versatility of material that he was able to adopt with the Mambas. One has only to hear Almond perform 'Youth', and 'Say Hello Wave Goodbye' acoustically, songs that he has included in piano sets with Martin Watkins, to assess how much improved his vocals are since a time in which his voice strove for distinction against the electronic components of sound.

If Soft Cell's demise occurred at the time of the furore surrounding Almond's announcement of his retirement from recording in August 1983, then their commercially polarised, blown-away-in-a-storm single, 'Soul Inside', was a tempestuous recrimination against Phonogram. An up-tempo, personal register of agony, Almond's unforgettable plea *"And I just want to scream to the sky"* rips across consciousness, the fine vocals imposing controlled restraint on the desperate theme. And even though Soft Cell were contracted to record a last album before their farewell concerts at the Hammersmith Palais in February 1984, the video accompanying the single, a wind tunnel in which Almond smashes Soft Cell ephemera, together with gold discs mounted on the wall, suggested an explosive valediction to record company manipulation. 'Soul Inside', proved to be a commercial hit, and suggested that Soft Cell could successfully mutate to cabaret rock instead of cabaret disco, but there was to be no going back on Almond's decision to quit, and to pursue a solo career independent of Soft Cell and the Mambas. And even if the turbulently autobiographical *Torment And Toreros*, the double package Almond was to release with the Mambas in that same summer, was received with vicious critical animosity, the album's achievements couldn't be overlooked, forming the innovative template for his future recordings.

It was in early August that Almond, enraged by the critical invective directed at *Torment And Toreros*, and tabloid sensationalism suggesting that he had been stomach pumped because of the quantity of sperm in his intestines, issued a confused statement to the press which announced the demise of the Mambas, and the implied jeopardy surrounding the recording of the Soft Cell album, *This Last Night In Sodom*. 'If there are any future recordings they will be extremely few (if any), which will come as a great relief to those who find my singing a pain in the ears.' Almond referred to himself as 'Increasingly confused and unhappy within the music business', and went on to say 'I no longer wish to continue on the recording side of the music scene, whatever that may be and whoever I may be.'

Almond's threat to retire from singing seems in part to have been provoked by Jim Reid's review of *Torment And Toreros* in *Record Mirror*, in which Reid called the album "Four sides of ill-disciplined doodling, it deals with familiar Almond obsessions, i.e. the generally scabrous side of life. I'm afraid I find Marc's murky travelogues neither outrageous nor daring but simply tedious." Hearing too that HMV had banned the record for alleged obscenity, Almond in a nervously distraught state arrived at Jim Reid's desk in the *Record Mirror* offices in Long Acre, brandishing a bullwhip. Almond's sensitivity to criticism, something shared by all creative artists who subjectively identify with their work, was to lead to his writing heated letters to the music press following the uncomfortably ambivalent reception given to his *The Stars We Are* album in 1988.

Clearly, Almond was undergoing a breakdown: he had worked desperately hard on the *Torment And Toreros* album, saturating the songs with deep emotional input, but the heady Latin sound investing the music was too passionately overreaching for the British market. Something of the destructiveness that Almond was feeling at the time filtered through to the final Soft Cell album *This Last Night In Sodom*. 'I think that both of us felt that Soft Cell was very limiting. And we were very rebellious with the last album, we wanted to make it as hard and uncommercial as possible. We deliberately recorded a lot of it in mono, going back to punk in a way and, I suppose, reflecting a lot of drugs we were taking then – it was very speedy.'

This Last Night In Sodom is the closest that Soft Cell came to authentic sound, and the songs portray Almond's vulnerability and inner questioning as much as they do on his solo material of the time. The two singles chosen from *Sodom*, 'Soul Inside', and 'Down In The Subway', are pure desperation. *"There was no one to phone/I just chewed at the time/I was waving goodbye/To control of my mind"* he sings on the agonisingly painful 'Soul Inside'. 'Down In The Subway' envisages suicide on the tracks, and a corresponding loss of mental control that will embrace death rather than compromise with a life of indifference. Is there no-one who has ridden the subway without contemplating the fantasy of throwing themselves in front of a train? The underground encourages a compulsive gravitation towards danger. The risk of being down there is huge. When you're in mental tatters as Almond was at the time of recording the song, the fantasy of death provides a refuge from the intractable horrors of life.

Most of the songs on *This Last Night In Sodom* depict intrinsic disintegration. 'Where Was Your Heart', and 'Surrender', are confessional songs about loneliness, being used by sexual partners, and hanging on for dear life in a state of terminal disillusionment. Almond is both attracted and repelled by gay promiscuity. The feminine within him looks for the security of monogamous love, whilst the masculine within him rejects it and seeks out the constant renewing of experience. Anima and animus are in perpetual contention, and nowhere more than in the work Almond recorded during this conflagratory period.

On their way out, Soft Cell could afford to take risks, and it's in the anthemic torch melodramatics of 'L'Esqualita' that Almond most emphasises his sexual proclivities. Arguably the best song that Soft Cell ever recorded, it's one that begs re-recording in conformity with Almond's much improved voice today. 'L'Esqualita' synthesises a Puerto Rican drag show in which the diva *"tugs at the reins/Of a hundred chihuahuas"*, wears cheap aftershave, and spends the money intended for rent on a new dress. This depiction of the drag ethos, a world Almond has made his own within the purlieus of songwriting, oscillates on a knife-edge between ostentation and parody, glamour and self-loathing. The conversation offstage is typically affected. *"Chi Chi at the bar/Dressed à L'Esqualita/Talks of Johns and Joans/And tomorrow's rhinestones."* Within that space nothing else is important. He is a she and she a he. No-one better understands that dichotomy than Almond. And overlaying all the posturings of adopted gender is something as profound as truth: *"And somewhere inside is a deep love of love"*, a realisation that asks for universal redemption. Pain so often breeds love, and the song reads like it was written in blood. 'L'Esqualita' is worth everything Soft Cell ever recorded, and the song pointed the way forward for Almond to live out corresponding dramatics as a solo artist.

Soft Cell's valediction to the world came in two shows played at the Hammersmith Palais in January 1984, one of the two nights being captured for the excellent bootleg double album *The Art Of Tearing Apart*, the cover depicting a girl in black stockings and a spotted face-net semi-squatting above a toilet.

In an interview given to Don Watson backstage at the Palais, Almond prognosticated a typically debauched future. 'I'm going to write some more songs, keep a low profile for a while for a change, go to a few places, Puerto Rico, Tijuana – then I'm going on my dysentery tour of the world, round the most scummy and diseased places like Bombay and Tangiers. Then in June and July I'm going to do something else, not the Mambas but something quite similar. I'm going to do something which I've never done before and just play everywhere in Britain that I possibly can.'

But beneath the desire to maintain a Sadean profile for sexual rites was the serious artist. Marc Almond had no intention of abandoning singing, and in a refutation to his own press statement about retirement, he had warned 'I'm going to sing ten times more and ten times louder to annoy all those who criticize me. I'm not finished and Dave's not finished either.' A reputation and a fanatical cult had been established. Almond's Brewer Street flat had become a shrine of decadence to his Cellmate, and Gutterhearts fans, the myth was only just beginning to establish its controversial momentum. Marc Almond would undergo chameleonic metamorphoses, but in disbanding Soft Cell he had buried the notion of commercialism *per se*, and was now set on establishing an artistic career through the resonant instrument of his voice.

photo: Peter Ashworth

photo: Peter Ashworth

TRAUMAS, TEQUILA AND A BLACK HEART

Contemporaneous with his career with Soft Cell, and in pursuit of the serious creative tangent that his voice demanded, Marc Almond's tempestuous prolegomena to becoming a solo artist in 1984, was the two studio albums *Untitled* and *Torment And Toreros* which he recorded with the Mambas, and the series of concerts he performed with the latter in late 1982, and in April and December 1983. The singer also regarded the Mambas as a collaborative experiment with influences he was anxious to integrate into his still formative solo career. 'The great thing about Marc and the Mambas was playing a whole load of low-key concerts' he remembers in retrospect. 'I enjoyed the loose framework of working with other musicians, and it was also a way of performing other people's songs I had always wanted to do. The loose framework offered me the chance to work with Matt Johnson and Jim Foetus and other people, whose company and input I thoroughly enjoyed.'

The Mambas' sound pivoted round the classically trained Annie Hogan's piano, and for the next seven years, that is right up until Almond disbanded La Magia in 1989, Hogan's audience popularity and intuitive sensitivity to Almond's voice provided the nucleus to his sound. Small, blond, and self-effacing, her keyboard and piano finesse is an integral part of Almond's recorded and live repertoire. She alone of the talented musicians who passed from the Mambas to the Willing Sinners and finally La Magia, players who included Billy McGee, and Martin McCarrick, received the respect of the audience as an individual distinct from Marc Almond's identity. The versatile Mambas escalated to a telescoped orchestra with the inclusion of Lee Jenkinson on bass and guitar, Steve Sherlock on sax, and the Venomettes, a classically trained string section. It was the ideal unit with which Almond would deconstruct the public conception of him as still another transient supernova whose fame was based on a disposable commercialism. *Untitled*, cheaply and starkly recorded, was the first clear indication of Marc Almond's musical preferences, and as such served as a template for the lugubrious torch songs which were to become the dominant characteristic of his art by the mid-eighties. In this, his first venture into acoustic cover versions, Almond empathised fully with the emotional charge needed to deliver a slowed down version of Scott Walker's 'Big Louise', a masochistically bruised cover of Lou Reed's 'Caroline Says', and a tentative reading of Jacques Brel's 'If You Go Away', in which the tremor in his voice predicts tears on a rainy London night. What emerged from *Untitled* was not only the singer's complex sexual psychology, but a deep sense of the mysterious inner biography he had been cultivating since his teens. For all of its apparent intimacy of dark confession, *Untitled* was a reminder to Almond's fans of his essential secrecy. The songs suggested that his real preoccupations had little in common with the Soft Cell persona who had been written up as a resilient icon of sleaze. *Untitled*, as an assemblage of songs, seemed much truer to the serious and overwrought romantic sensibility Almond was intent on shielding from an intrusively antagonistic world. 'I just looked at it as a notebook for things that might develop in the future. I wanted to prove that I wasn't just a brainless pop star, stuck with a name, and couldn't do anything outside that name.'

The title song was in itself a real triumph of lyric expression, an evocation of loneliness and self-doubt, with the song's protagonist anxious for the future. Melodic enough to have done well as a single, the song awaits retrieval from Almond's archives. There's something authentically haunting about the refrain that isolates the outcast in a night walk across the rain-doused city. *"It's such a shame when I'm out in the rain/All the curtains are closed/It's a sad scene I know/I try not to care/That I'm going nowhere/See it slide down the drain/Washed away with the rain."* These lines often recur to me at times of deep despondency, out walking in Soho, or reflecting on the difficulties entailed by keeping a creative gift alive in a technocratic society. There are three outstanding Almond compositions on this early exploration of the dark psyche: 'Untitled', 'Angels', and 'Empty Eyes', all songs written with a lyrical density and interiorisation, and all concerned with the desperate conflict between inner and outer worlds which the private person forced to go public encounters. And still living alternately in Leeds and in a flat at Earls Court, notorious for its junkie inhabitants, Almond's nervous crises and emotional turmoil were graphically reflected in songs like 'Angels', Almond's account of a breakdown he experienced in LA as a consequence of brutal exploitation. Recalcitrant since childhood, and uncompromisingly individual, Marc Almond has always resisted logos, causes and record company domination. 'Angels' speaks of life on the West side of the world, *"Where the wind hisses through the meat hooks"* and the mega-rich crawl through the city in limos en route to tyrannical emporiums in the black heat. The singer realises that if he once lets go of the last vestiges of his inner reality, then he'll flip into madness, chaos, and beyond that death. This powerfully memorable evocation of a city on a plain inhabited by disposable stars carries with it connotations of the retributive holocaust that enveloped Sodom and Gomorrah. There's no help anywhere, the gulf yawns with psychotic fire, and the protagonist finds that even the lover he had believed in out there goes silent on the telephone, and is dead cold. When things break down inside, when the nerve communications are broken or misdirected, there's nowhere to go. And to be on the edge of the blue Pacific, the curve of the universe stretching beyond, is to invite ultimate isolation. In his Soft Cell years, Almond found it impossible to cope with America. During the recording of *The Art Of Falling Apart*, Cindy Ecstacy discovered the singer in tears in the street, just wanting to go home. And Almond himself has spoken of being driven across America in the back of a Rolls Royce, high on acid and making no sense. Almond remembers Soft Cell's one disastrous tour of America in 1983, as having been partly ruined by toxic excess. 'Dave and I were basically very untogether people, and to keep us in line all through a tour is practically impossible. That's why we hardly ever toured. There had always been a demand for us to tour the States but we never got it together. The American fans were incredibly over-enthusiastic. We played three nights in LA and I couldn't get through a single song without people climbing up on stage and grappling me to the floor. One bloke threw his arms around me and I fell to the floor and was concussed for about ten minutes.'

In *Untitled* Almond was free to explore and make sense of the emotional turbulence that was threatening to engulf him. In a way his two double albums with the Mambas were a lifeline back to sanity, and by writing and singing about extremes of behaviour, he was able to reconnect with an inner truth independent of fame and the demands to make commercial records. Almond courted stardom, but rather like the suicide who wants to fake death, he was unwilling to invalidate the principles in which he believed in order to adopt the spurious tenets of fame. Most of the anger distilled in his work with the Mambas pivots on this unresolved conflict. *Untitled* is considerably more subdued than its successor, but the music charts the collision of a self-immolative personality with a hostile reality. It is a perfect S&M marriage.

In a highly perceptive evaluation of what Almond was doing with the Mambas, Steve Sutherland writing for *Melody Maker* conjured up some of the artist's fraught dilemmas. He considered Almond 'A romantic, celebrating his agonies, burning himself out for the sake of his songs, pushing himself further, wantonly over-stimulating his senses into dullness and on into deeper perilous cravings.' Certainly the contents of his solo material, and that written for the last Soft Cell sessions, including a ravaged celebration of sexually transmitted disease in 'Disease And Desire', suggest that the singer had unleashed a black tornado in his unconscious. But there's a necessary reservation here in that confessional autobiography is invariably in part fiction. Almond has often commented on how unlike his songs he appears to people who are meeting him after having been immersed in his work. The separation between the artist and his work rests on a sensitive balance, and to conflate the two, most often leads to disillusionment amongst the fans. We write about experiences in which the participation is imaginative as well as those derived from life. The best writing usually embodies a combination of both states.

Untitled might be described as a process of black alchemy, the gold is rarely sublimated except by way of the voice. The compassionate intimacy of the narrating line demands immediate sympathy on the part of the listener. And what thrills about the songs is their density, they form the textural richness of poetry written for the singing voice. Almond's songs make everyone else's seem anaemic by qualitative comparison. More in the tradition of French *chanson*, he has given poetry to British song.

Marc and the Mambas were to perform most of the *Untitled* LP at the Drury Lane Theatre on 5th December 1982, an event that prepared the way for the series of concerts at the Duke of York's Theatre in April of the following year. Apart from showcasing solo material, the extravagantly experimental concerts were a platform for Almond's inimitable repartee, the question and answer system imparting a warmth and love to performance which is an inseparable characteristic of his early live shows, in the same way as he had insisted that early Soft Cell concerts were performed without a stage, and on a direct level with the audience. The Mambas concerts were as much about audience participation as they were a means to Almond discovering his increasing vocal potential. In his own words 'The Mambas was a real opening up of myself. Suddenly all the things I thought I couldn't do because it didn't fit into the framework of Soft Cell were given a release. I was learning lots of lessons about myself, like the fact that I wasn't going to take shit anymore.' There was little support from Phonogram for the Mambas project, the corporate viewing it as non-commercial and a disquieting pointer to the inevitable split that would occur within Soft Cell.

Amongst its unpredictables, *Untitled* included a highly melodic version of Syd Barrett's 'Terrapin', as a look back to Almond's art student days when Barrett had been a formative influence, as well as the protracted cruise into the sexual underworld, 'Twilights And Lowlifes'. The latter is one of the most searching of Almond's songs about sexual outlaws, and explores the world of a closed circle who pass pieces of paper containing sexual fantasies to each other beneath public toilet doors. The song offers no redemption for the participants, it just records the danger and immediacy of the risk. There's a desolation and pervasive sense of ruin attached to the lyrics. *"Kick down the door afraid of what you'll see"* describes the move towards attempted self-realisation that the narrator seeks.

Almond has quite rightly never made public proclamations about being gay, instead he has allowed his lyrics and his sympathetic support of gay causes, like his two concerts in April 1987 for International AIDS Day, and appearances at International Gay Happening at Krefeld in July 1993, and on New Year's Eve 1993 for Jeremy Joseph's G.A.Y. at Astoria 2, to stand as confirmation of his sexual and not ideological propensities. It takes a long time to assimilate and interiorise sexual difference, and Almond had no intention of demystifying his sexual ambivalence at this early stage of his career. His concerns like those of any true artist have been to place his creative work first, and to allow public speculation about his sexuality to accentuate the mystery surrounding his person.

Untitled made no great chart impact, although it did get into the latter regions of the Top Fifty. In retrospect it can be seen to have served as a necessary precursor to the more dramatically and idio-syncratically extreme *Torment And Toreros* which was to follow in the summer of 1983. An autobiographical demand to be taken seriously as an artist, as well as an album of Spanish and French influences, *Torment And Toreros* was fuelled with a vindictive passion on Almond's part to be considered as a singer and songwriter. The diversity of material he was prepared to take on, ranging from his own passionate compositions, to Jacques Brel's 'The Bulls', Peter Hammill's 'Vision', and to songs made popular by Scott Walker and Billie Holiday, 'In My Room', and 'Gloomy Sunday', was a sensitive delight, and a lesson to his contemporaries in the knowledge of song.

There's never been anything especially British about Marc Almond's music, his influences tend to be hedonistically Latin, French and sometimes Eastern. It's this amalgam of textural sources worked into a mosaic peculiarly his own, which gives the music distinctly universal qualities. In his interview published in *Tape Delay*, Almond spoke of his sense of estrangement from the British public, a sentiment endorsed by every British artist who finds himself in conflict with the narrow parameters of xenophobic provincialism. 'I collect a lot of music by Eastern singers from places like Egypt, Morocco, and the Middle East. I really wanted to go to those places because I loved the music so much and I needed to actually taste the culture. I always think that there's nothing really English or British about me whatsoever... I like things that have a very exotic flavour- Spanish and Middle Eastern stuff. It is something that has developed from listening to music, listening to records and visiting places.'

Torment And Toreros was Almond's first liberal injection of the exotic into the staid formula of British music. This brutally romantic suite of songs, sometimes sung too hurriedly, and lacking in places the intonation he would learn with a maturing vocal technique, is nonetheless one of his most flagrantly uncompromising offerings. In his new material he could be heard staking out areas of passion, poetry, and sexual defiance such as had not been heard in this country before. There was rage, duende, flamenco, chaos, and above all the impassioned will to be heard as a singer disaffiliated from rock music. All of Almond's problems at the time, drugs, liquor, the enervating pressures of being a star, fans ringing on his doorbell all day, the police keeping a video camera trained on his Brewer Street apartment, all of his desperation and inner sense of disintegration were focused into the making of *Torment And Toreros*.

Recorded at the expense of health and pocket, *Torment And Toreros* is a fiery evocation of romantic realism in contention with an ethos that had sold out to Thatcher's despotic materialism. The acerbically venomous 'Catch A Fallen Star' was Almond's whiplash polemic aimed at the cheap values of the music industry, and the imagery in this song contrived to have the LP banned by chain stores. In imagery that would have delighted Paul Verlaine, Almond describes a superannuated star brought to near extinction by the machinations of the world with which he has to deal. *"And this town is a potpourri of disease/Can you smell the herpes from the scum-/Sucking fucks who hang round/The same suckers each midnight."* There was to be no compromise in a song aimed at projecting vitriolic rage at an industry that demanded insincere image. *"What you earn heaven knows/It goes straight up your nose"*, Almond comments by way of bitter self-confession. The tempestuous vituperation contained in 'Catch A Fallen Star' is extended to the personal realm of love in the song that follows on from it, the distraught, overwrought 'The Animal In You', a seething recrimination against a smashed love affair, an unrequited matching of balances that proves to be a twisted love involving physical violence, and the breaking up of a room.

The whole album flexes with Latin passion, and the honesty of committed emotion allows the elegiac to contrast with the uplifting and vivacious. 'I love raw Spanish flamenco gypsy music', Almond said at the time. 'It's just like another type of soul music. It's very sad sounding, very emotional. A lot of these influences have rubbed off on the album, but it's not obvious. Don't expect an album full of maracas. "The Bulls" uses castanets, but it's done in a very tongue-in-cheek way. I love the imagery. There's a lot of cruelty in it – the treatment of the Spanish gypsies, which is why the music is so sad. The imagery is fiery.'

But mostly the mood of the LP excels by way of its slow desperate torch songs, which allow full range to Almond's dramatics, and the sense of inveterate suffering that his voice portrays. The loss of innocence and love rendered in 'My Former Self', themes repeated in 'First Time', and 'Your Love Is A Lesion', are poignantly autobiographical recreations of the bitterness involved in the experience of losing love. Memory can be rather like a spider slowly dismembering a fly, and in 'Black Heart' one of the two singles released from the album, a tormented narrative of being consumed by harrowing memories, there's little redemption offered by imposing a past love on the present. There's only a black heart at the core of the apple. Love with all of its bittersweet resonance is the constant leitmotif of *Torment And Toreros*. A thematic preoccupation usually associated with female singers, Almond reversed the roles by using anima to incorporate the concerns of deep hurt and tenderness into a male repertoire.

Attempted consolation and recurrent disquiet alternate as the modalities of this music. The cover versions of Scott Walker's 'In My Room', a song of aching blue loneliness, and of Billie Holiday's 'Gloomy Sunday', and Peter Hammill's 'A Vision', a song Almond has revived in the nineties for live performance, all lament a love that has gone, but which still remains in its power to hurt. You can come home five years after someone has left you, and resume the same unresolved recriminations in your head. Female singers like Sarah Vaughan, Bessie Smith, Nina Simone, Shirley Bassey and Dusty Springfield have all pursued the theme of unrequited love, but never quite with the vengeance that Almond imparts to the volatility of songs like 'Torment', and 'The Animal In You', in which the desire for revenge is tempered by a corresponding masochistic longing to be hurt.

Torment And Toreros was a testing and demanding package, and one that asked of the listener a peculiar degree of empathy. At times the material risks being pathological as in 'Boss Cat', and 'A Million Manias A Day', the latter song being a direct transcription of Almond undergoing a nervous breakdown. Reviewers criticised the concept for its over-emphasis on subjective traumas, and felt that the excessive interiorisation of neuroses was a substitute for musical direction. And to Almond who was still living out the furious dilemmas he had channelled into his music, any sort of pejorative criticism was construed as a personal affront. 'It was about this time' he tells us, 'I became very frustrated and even angst-ridden. I've always got angry about things, but during these months it would spill over into rage. I was living on a nervous, neurotic knife-edge. A lot of people said the album was too intense and contained too much pain – it's not easy to listen to, but I think as time goes by, people will recognise it's greatness.'

The album's greatness lies in its inconsistencies, and in the blood-wedding it establishes between love and death, exalted aspiration and the desire to belong to an arena of failure. When you over-reach on an inner trajectory there's always the need to compensate by creating a death fantasy. You can't climb the gold ladder to the stars, so you elect a ritual descent into death. The album's poetic equivalent is Robert Lowell's *Life Studies*, the personal book he published in 1959; one in which his autobiographical line *"My mind's not right"* was to usher in a whole mode of confessional writing, as well as liberating the poet from a past in which his work had been praised for its academic overtones. *Torment And Toreros* is Almond's *Life Studies*, the suite of songs in which he projected his blood-profile into the public arena. The image of him raising a bullwhip to one of the album's intransigent reviewers seems an appropriate metaphor for the occasion. Doubtless picked up from one of the sex shops which cluster around the Raymond Revue Bar, the instrument of violence only reinforced the notion that Almond lived in the shadow of the Divine Marquis.

Torment And Toreros is fired by the manic energies that Almond professes to bring to a hedonistic lifestyle. Underlying all his work is the desperate attempt to isolate and retrieve the moment. He speaks of having put four lifetimes into his own, and of having a passion to extract ultimate realisation from each day. Writing poetry, song lyrics, making sketches, feeding fragments of melody into the tape recorder he keeps with him for that purpose, travelling, seeing friends, engaging in the scene, are all expressions of the omnivorous passion Almond nurtures for life. And recalling his life in Soho at the time of his nervous disintegration Almond remembers, 'When I lived there, there were nightly police raids, and opposite the flat where I lived there was a sandwich shop on the corner of Brewer Street, and that was the ultimate in divey places. I used to watch the goings on every night from my flat window – it was always a haunt for transsexuals, most of whom were very good friends of mine. It was real voyeurism. I must have plastic bags full of Super 8 film containing close encounters and pick-ups.'

Torment And Toreros established the polarities of critical reception by which Almond's work has continued to be assessed. Inspiring either passionate devotion or acrimonious rejection Almond has suffered the price of all those whose art tests the limits. Wouldn't anyone with integrity prefer adverse criticism to polite acceptance by unimaginative reviewers?

It's wrong to construe *Torment And Toreros* as just a set of histrionic self-confessions, it's far more than a funereal summation of the morbidly exacting pressures surrounding the singer's life and work at the time. 'I started working on it in an extremely low period, when my depressions were becoming really bad, and I thought the only way to deal with them was to use them positively. Side Two is the very low side, but as the album goes on, it gets more up, almost as if reaching for the light at the end of a tunnel, and that's why I ended with Rodgers and Hammerstein's "Beat Out That Rhythm On A Drum", just to sort of let it all out.' But if the album was critically conceived to be a black book, a grimoire of baroque and exhibitionistic neuroses in which the metaphor of the bull being slain in the corrida found its extension in Almond's tormented psyche, then the music was also an act of creative generosity. It's easy to convert pain into negative passivity, but to channel displaced energies into a positive focus is the nature of art. Almond had to pay the price of receiving the largely pejorative criticism of reviewers attempting to miscategorize his work. Disorientated by the lack of a Soft Cell formula to the music, and the inclusion of strings rather than electronics, Almond's intentions were seriously misassessed. The singer was able to point out the healthy direction of his new work in comparison to the more accessible songs he prepared for Soft Cell. 'I wanted the listener to feel exhausted by the end of it because a lot of the songs are about me, and extremely personal. When I write for Soft Cell, I tend to write in a more observing way, looking, documenting. Here I've been freer and I've prepared the music and just done the vocals straight off over the music, working the melody line as I go along, feeling my way forward.'

The Mambas made live appearances at the Duke Of York's Theatre in St. Martin's Lane on the 27th, 28th and 29th April 1983, and again on the 18th and 19th December of the same year; their unrehearsed spontaneous shows allowing Almond intimate rapport with his audience, and the chance to stage songs which have never been included on any of his official recordings. Songs like Judy Garland's 'Blue Prelude', the distraught 'Switchblade Operator', and 'Muleskinner', and a piano accompanied 'Jacky', the Brel song that Almond was to convert into a hit almost a decade later, were interspersed with songs from *Untitled* and *Torment And Toreros*. The Gutter Hearts fan club released album *Bite Black And Blues* affords versions of otherwise unreleased songs taken from the 18th December show, a concert in which Almond was also to perform 'Fun City', and 'Sleaze', two of his earliest recorded songs with the Mambas. The back of the album sleeve depicts a bottle of Cusano Rojo mescal, the drink which he was using to assuage his nerves at the time.

The deceptive casualness of these shows in an intimate Victorian theatre, with the audience's ribaldly camp frivolity entering direct into the concert as a live current, only served to accentuate Almond's vulnerability in delivering a poetry that jumped like black rubies for the throat. Already the immeasurably sad voice was pointing to how the gravity of his work would deepen as the decade advanced. The concerts were as much a testing of audience reception as they were an indication of the singer's diverse musical repertoire. By the time of the December concerts at the Duke Of York's, Soft Cell had officially split, but during his April appearances with the Mambas Almond was able to assess the possibilities of his taking a sector of consolidated support towards a revised future. With his hair long, and dressed all in black with a scatter of jewellery, Almond developed the witty immediate repartee with his audience which was to persist as an indelible characteristic of his shows for the next four years. Catching him on the first night at the Duke Of York's, Mark Cooper reported: "Marc's audience is almost the finest thing about the

Mambas. While Marc camps it up like a Hollywood actress and plays the star, his faithful female followers keep him down to earth. His audience love him and laugh at him. The mix couldn't be healthier." Almond's concerts have always been staged on the knife-edge tension that exists between the unmitigating seriousness of his material and the audience's desire to find intermittent relief by attempting to send up the artist's vulnerability. At the Duke Of York's the safety margin allowing for the right balance between artist and audience was sometimes violated. But what was generated was a familial warmth, a feeling that the bonding between singer and his devoted admirers was one that would endure. And it was courageous indeed to perform the poetically sensitive medley: 'Narcissus'/'Gloomy Sunday'/'Vision' to an audience conditioned to the dance-accessability of Soft Cell's music. The Spanish influence in the concerts was represented by Almond's voice, at the time his favourite singers were a Spanish couple called Lola and Emmanuel, rather than the Mambas' music. 'The influence is more in the singing, because I love the way the Spanish sing, they just shout it out straight from inside them.' Most of the material performed in the April concerts was previously unknown to the audience, and in December Almond was to incorporate surprises like a sympathetically expressionistic version of Lou Reed's 'Walk On The Wild Side' into shows that already professed a voice greatly improved in technique from the April sound, and promising the maturer range that he was to develop over the next three years. One of the highlights of the 18th December show was an inspired saxy version of 'Sleaze', delivered as an encore. Its reference to 'Hanging round these backstreets in the Soho after hours', was a theme to be taken up in the celebratory requiem 'You Have', in which *"the cavernous alleys"* are undoubtedly the complex of courtyards and narrow alleys which make up the arterial maze of Soho. They are evocatively numerous: St. Anne's Court, Meard Street, Bourchier Street, Rupert Court, places where the sexual outlaw steps out of the shadows at a received signal.

1983 was also to see Almond engaged in diverse collaborative work. He was to sing on Psychic TV's 'Guiltless', and to appear on the TV show *The Switch* performing Suicide's 'Ghostrider' with Jim Foetus, an incongruous grouping that was to lead to the release of 'Flesh Volcano', the material that Almond and Foetus were to record together in 1984 and 1986. Later in the year Almond was to perform at the New York Danceteria under the grouping the Immaculate Consumptives, a conglomerate which featured Almond, Nick Cave, Lydia Lunch and Jim Foetus, a diversely chaotic experiment that was still another step towards Almond's refining an image and sound necessary to his future as a solo artist.

Apart from Soft Cell's valedictory concerts at the Hammersmith Palais in January 1984, Almond was to keep a low profile until May of the same year when a solo single 'The Boy Who Came Back' suggested a rejuvenation of his artistic integrity. And due to meticulous voice coaching, his substantially increased vocal range promised to continue the serious and uncompromising way forward that his work with the Mambas had indicated. A new deeper, resonant timbre was instantly recognisable in his voice, and the song presented a renascent image, the man who had defied temporary retirement and the redoubtable setbacks of critical disparagement to come back with formidable conviction and an inimitably re-attuned voice. 'The Boy Who Came Back' is Rimbaudian in its theme of the conflict between innocence and experience. The poet Rimbaud, a visionary genius, who had in his formative years created an imaginative body of work which was to serve as a blueprint to surrealism, and the poetic experimentation of the twentieth century, had a childhood marked by successive attempts to run away to Paris. Rimbaud's poems like 'Au Cabaret-Vert' celebrate life on the road, his boots ripped up by the desire for journey, he tells us that for a whole week he had been in the open countryside, walking away from bourgeois conventions towards a future informed by poetic vision. Almond's protagonist in 'The Boy Who Came Back' is likewise an explorer, *"Joy held his heart as he took to the road/Cast all his sorrow to the breeze"* and in the process he encounters age in the succession of seasons, and loss in love, but is sufficiently young to assume time is still on his side to make reparations. It was the perfectly chosen song for the moment, a transitional lyric that found the singer in his late twenties facing the end of one youthful decade, and understandably apprehensive about the future with its black doors opening out on age and death. The *puer aeternus*, or the dream of perennial youth is the companion of all artists. The imagination outruns age, and assumes a transcendental domain independent of the body. Almond's songs record this struggle, and are very much about the attempt to burn within the immediate and go beyond it. Oscar Wilde once attended a birthday celebration party dressed in a black mourning suit to express his grief at growing a year older. A torch singer's lyrics embody the same sentiment, the voice trying desperately to retrieve youth and to celebrate moments isolated in time by their emotive intensity. The day you walked into a bar direct into the eyes of the perfect stranger. The night a thunderstorm lit up the heavy garden roses and you ran out with someone into that blinding, sparkling downpour. The time you realised you really were alive and the individual moments tasted sharply good like an orange. Almond's voice conveys the evocative timbre on which the big experiences, life, love, and death hang. And in performance all of those colliding emotional planets arrive in the eyes, the throat, the heart, and on the tongue. His personification of these states accounts for the intensity he imparts to live delivery.

Seven months were to elapse before Almond returned to live performance with a new accompanying band The Willing Sinners. During this time he had been working with Mike Hedges as a producer on the material that was to surface in October on the *Vermin In Ermine* LP. September was to see Almond play a prestige concert at the Royal Festival Hall, appearing there on Saturday 8th after having played a low-key preparatory date at Chippenham Goldiggers on September 4th. A period of public inactivity had been rich in creative rewards. At the Royal Festival Hall he was to showcase entirely new material, his focus being concentrated on most of the *Vermin In Ermine* material, as well as on surprise songs like 'Stories Of Johnny' which was to go on the later album of that title, and the disarmingly sadistic 'Healthy As Hate' which he was to perform later in the month in the Georges Bataille Festival at the Bloomsbury Theatre. The latter song was to form part of the funereal suite *Violent Silence*, arguably his greatest and most underrated achievement of this period.

On stage at the Royal Festival Hall in a scintillating pink sequinned jacket, which he tells us he bought in Morocco, his hair short, and his eyes black with mascara and eyeliner, Almond manifested a formidable confidence in comparison to the hesitant and unrehearsed formula he had established with the Mambas in the previous year. Beginning with the renascent theme 'The Boy Who Came Back', he was quick to tell the audience that he would like to have established the event at 'Leicester Square public conveniences', now closed to the public, where most of his friends were regularly in evidence, before giving a first airing to the plaintively sensitive 'Stories Of Johnny'. Completely disowning his past repertoire, Almond introduced material which was a blueprint of his personal obsessions, the songs invariably idolizing hustlers, rent boys, thieves, addicts, losers and drag artists. There was to be no remission in the celebration of life's degenerate spectrum. A rousing version of Scott Walker's 'The Plague' set the way for a pathology of damaged relationships explored in songs like 'Ugly Head', 'Crime Sublime', 'Love Amongst The Ruined', and 'Healthy As Hate'. Prostitution, with the emphasis on rent boys, was eulogized in both Cole Porter's 'Love For Sale', with Almond telling the audience that Porter had written the song to praise a twelve year old boy, and in his own compositions 'Pink Shack Blues', and 'Solo Adultos' which similarly emphasised what he called a love of 'young flesh.' Histrionically glamorizing lowlife is the quintessence of a decadent sensibility, and Almond's concert material explored every facet of the underworld.

Writing this evening up for *Soundcheck*, Hasi Howells noted how "Marc, complete with shimmering Liberace jacket, did everything in his power to make the show as informal and seemingly unrehearsed as possible to fight off the inevitable crisis – the convulsions of fame. The evening turned out to be a privileged peep into Marc's surprisingly fresh re-vamped cabaret. Despite his slight change of direction he is still the strumpet of misery, filth, crime, grime, loneliness and love and this is just yet another angle to his divine A.B.C. of immortality."

Vermin in Ermine was the singer's first album with the Willing Sinners, and his last for Phonogram, the label with which he had been in heated contention ever since Soft Cell had elected to release artistically integral material at the expense of commercial viability. While *Vermin In Ermine* shares thematic interests with *This Last Night In Sodom*, it employs a richer and more sophisticated vocal technique, something that Almond attributes to working with Mike Hedges as a producer. 'Mike was perfect for me to work with because he loved experimentation and all the strange ways of recording things, but at the same time he brought all the odd ideas together into something that was coherent, and started to bring out a really good sound in my voice as well, giving me more confidence. In the early days of Soft Cell, I used to go in and do the vocals in one take. People had always said I was an out-of-tune singer, and there was something uncontrollable about my voice. But Mike brought a lot out of me. He was very instrumental in contributing to the sound of those first three solo LPs.'

Vermin In Ermine extols the shadowy side of life, in a way that invests the dark with a romantic glamour, and finds Almond aligning with his Gutterhearts aficionados; but it's also a collection of songs that allows for the lyrical tenderness of the torch singer. The three singles taken from the LP are all ballads, 'The Boy Who Came Back', 'Tenderness Is A Weakness', and the masterfully evocative 'You Have', a song he tells us he wrote for a friend who jumped off the cliffs at Dover. These three songs set the tone for the opulent agonized love ballads that Almond has come to make his own. The emotional mood of his songs swings between a rose and a snake.

Love and revenge. Sweetness and venom. His voice pleads and rejects, cajoles and stabs. One minute he carries a rose in his teeth, the next a knife. And there is no other singer who marries life and death in such an impassioned symbiotic relationship. 'I'm the sort of person who likes to have the keys to the city. Maybe it's childish naivety in me or plain stupidity. I write about death a lot because I love life so much as well. Like anybody with a Leo trait, I try to cram as much into my life as I possibly can. And to be aware of life you have to be aware of death as well. It's always there as a threat or even a promise, some sort of dark exotic lake that you can dangle your toes into occasionally.'

And bearing in mind the writers for whom Almond has expressed admiration, J.K. Huysmans whose synaesthetically exotic *A Rebours* proved to be the testament of decadence, Jean Genet whose romantic prose poems exonerate theft, homosexuality and death, and J.G. Ballard whose extraordinary futuristic novels re-anatomize the concept of death, it's little wonder that Almond's own writing consistently takes up these themes. 'Tenderness Is A Weakness' is a song of devastating solitude, and one which evokes that condition through a study of both sexes, her predicament and his, both are locked into forms of solitary derangement. Her claustrophobic tension and his, mirror Almond's own phobic state of distress in crowds, a condition for which he was prescribed Valium for many years. 'Tenderness Is A Weakness' with its video directed by Derek Jarman is an enervatingly beautiful portrait of pathological behaviour bordering on madness. *"Blow her away/Like ash in the ashtray"* Almond sings, his heart embodying the pain of his actions, the rejection he expresses of a possible love for both characters turns in on himself, the singer becoming the imagined victim of the song's exploration of unrequited love. *"Love has no part in my destiny"* he sings by way of an ingrained biographical truth, Almond's nature being one that quickly and easily falls in love and as soon grows disenamoured and hungry to search out the next amorous experience.

Reviewing the album for *Disc*, Betty Page commented, "Marc's voice has ripened to unparalleled levels of strength and expressiveness, and he uses it here to full effect, acting his heart out. And he's still a brilliant storyteller in the great tradition of 'jewel in the gutter' shockers." None of the three singles, which are arguably the most accessible songs on *Vermin In Ermine*, received any high profile, although 'You Have' found Almond in superb voice, the vocals indicating a more controlled tenor's range and a richly compassionate tone that was to be consistently applied to the many elegies he has recorded in the past decade.

The material on the album also reflects Almond's preoccupations at the time with entertaining risk and challenging danger. There's a spirit of temerity in him which likes to confront potential hostility on both psychological and physical planes. Around this time he was almost murdered in Marrakesh, he was mugged by two members of the Moroccan Air Force, who after having robbed and stripped him, stood there discussing whether to just beat up their victim or to kill him. Chased through Soho by football hooligans, threatened by the Mafia in Spain, and constantly challenged at street level by the public, Almond found danger a stimulus to creativity. In addition, there were the perennially beleaguering Gutterhearts either assembled in the street outside the Some Bizzare offices, or congregating near Almond's home in a mansion block in Brewer Street. No fanclub had ever shown quite such fanatical devotion, and there were constant run-ins with the Soho police who suspected Almond's devotees of taking drugs. Talking to *Sounds* about the Gutterhearts phenomenon at the time, Almond expressed a concern for their general safety. 'Sometimes, they come all the way from Margate. It's incredible. I like standing and talking to them. If I'm busy, they don't mind, they understand, anyway they come down to meet each other as well. While we were on tour a group of them were travelling around to every concert, and they were staying out all night on the streets which made us feel responsible. It's also been a concern that the Gutterhearts have been picked on by the police in Soho. One girl had her school books tipped out onto the pavement and was called a lesbian, another was punched in the face by a policewoman who then said "I want an excuse to get you." But all that doesn't deter them...'

Almond's reputation, enhanced by the release of *Vermin In Ermine* had established him as an icon of the sexually and politically disaffected. He had come to represent a cult of the shadows, and his name was mentioned in connection with a synthesis of decadent components centred around gay and perverse sex. He was considered to be a black ritualist and someone who vilified innocence. Moral evaluations of his work were expressed by BBC censors, the gutter tabloids, most notably *The Sun* and *The News Of The World* were quick to accentuate any item of sleaze they could connect with Almond. But he continued under distraughtly ravaging pressures to do what he had always done: outdistance his contemporaries by the seriousness of his work and voice. While the

---

vitriolic contumacy flew, Almond was deeply concentrated on his work, and two weeks after his Royal Festival Hall concert he was to appear at the Bloomsbury Theatre in a suitably controversial celebration of Georges Bataille's work, Bataille being the French writer who had devoted his life to a profound psychological investigation, in fiction and theory, of erotic extremism. Bataille's totally uninhibited portrayal of every form of sex in his collection of stories *The Story Of The Eye*, and his seminal texts about the erotic, *Literature And Evil* and *Eroticism*, had afforded him a strong cult following, and a pervasive underground influence on all sexually controversial writing. Almond elected to play *Violent Silence* supported only by backing tapes and presenting an integral suite of songs largely written for the occasion. Many of his admirers would claim that this particular concept remains his finest project to date. Arguably Almond's most integrated and extended elegy, the work is a seamless whole. *Violent Silence* with its Bataille associations allowed him complete freedom of sexual expression. The funereal connotations, the gothic S&M overtones, the black glyptic poetry which sparkles in the dark, and the agonized phrasing in which the lyrics are delivered constitute one of the most memorable pieces of modern music to come out of the eighties. It's impossible to hear these intimate confessions about ruined and desperate relationships without being deeply moved.

It was late in the evening of Wednesday 26th September that Almond dressed in black stepped on stage to the piano overture 'Blood Tide'. An astonishingly concise virtuoso performance, the songs that comprise his 'Love And Murder' offering are unparalleled in their minatory references to *"maim and murder."* Almond's lyricism was as close to Jean Genet as it was fitting to a Georges Bataille Festival. Anyone who has read Genet's poem 'Le Condamné A Mort', with its lines which Almond has quoted as amongst his favourite in poetry, "Let's dream together, love, of a hoodlum/big as the universe, body splashed with tattoos/He'll strip us, lock us into bondage cells,/And show us how between his golden thighs..." will recognise in the *Violent Silence* lyrics a direct empathy with Genet's transcendental marriage of love and death. Almond is the Genet of song, and the voice he imparts to these particular lyrics opens doors into strongholds in the psyche. We advance down corridors in which smoky torches blow and a mad child rubs petroleum over its legs and offers us the match. These songs live under the black cloak of genius.

Right from the first song 'Healthy As Hate', we're introduced to a world of bruised emotions, and masochistic impulses. *"Sometimes when it rains/I have the urge to break a window/Put my wrist out to the air/And watch the red blood flow."* So intense is the singer's desire to have a bad love ejected from his system, that he would even contemplate murder to be rid of the offending person. Lyrically superior, and informed with truer emotion than Lou Reed's suicidal sequence *Berlin*, Almond's baroque S&M sequence remains the most extreme set of love lyrics ever committed to record. There was great courage involved in offering these sentiments to an audience, and in releasing them two years later as the LP *Violent Silence*. The progress of the songs goes from outright hate to reflection on that source, back to hate again. The lyric turns on the possibility of murder or suicide. To kill love or to kill oneself. But Almond reminds us with suitable irony that these emotions are cathartic, they are as healthy as hate. 'My songs', Almond was later to tell us 'stink of back rooms, bar rooms, sweat, semen, sawdust, absinthe from Madrid, mescal, roses, gunpowder and dew-drenched oakwood.' The songs on *Violent Silence* smell of dank river water, blood, leather, sweat distilled by pathological anger, rainy cemeteries, dogs stepped in from the storm. They are a merciless celebration of evil committed in the name of love. The material comes out of the unconscious desires that Almond nurtured as a child to explore the dead and rotting bodies of animals. 'I was obsessed with dead hamsters' he tells us, 'I used to bury them in baked bean cans, in the back garden, leave them a few weeks, then dig them up to see how they smelt. I was fascinated with death and decay. I'd find dead birds and cut them open with a stone to see the maggots that would inevitably crawl out. All I used to think about was the innards of dead animals, day in and day out. Obsessed with things rotting away.'

Violent Silence is organised around the notion of decomposition. It's so supremely individual in its unsparing evocation of vicious emotions and extreme sexual fantasies, that the songs never fall short of the masters to whom they pay homage: Georges Bataille and Jean Genet. *Violent Silence* is for connoisseurs of the forbidden. It sits in a record collection like a rare piece of erotica in a personal library. One listens to it at particular times, a day when one needs to be shut off from the world, or is entertaining a mode of thought that intersects with its gothic libido. The minimal music accompaniment also affords Almond's voice the gravely compassionate tone that the lyrics demand. In this respect *Violent Silence* is more closely affiliated to *Jacques*, and *Absinthe*, than any other of his albums, all three carrying a conceptual unity that impresses by the consistency of its poetry.

What we need is a video to accompany *Violent Silence*. A closed château in autumn, a leopard sitting on top of an ebony piano, a child in a leather face-mask running down one of the interminable corridors carrying big yellow chrysanthemums. And the scene changes to a building by the river, a smoky grey day with the river swallowing its own tail, and a young man dressed in black decamping from a funeral car and finding a young boy *"Lying half in half out of the water."* The savagery of imagery in 'Things You Loved Me For' is a venomous distillation of Sadean impulses. *"I broke a large bottle on the edge of your cranium/You stared up smiling to eyes of oblivion/I sent you down to dirt and delirium/When you began screaming I spat in your mouth..."* As a complement to Bataille's exploration of sexuality and evil the songs capture just the right tone, as well as being prompters to the singer's unconscious preoccupations.

Love, desire, sin, fire, glory, destruction are the key notes to *Violent Silence*, the fraught mosaic marrying the absolutes good and evil in a bloody shroud. These songs are the equivalent of Baudelaire's 'Litanies To Satan', the poem carrying the refrain "Satan have pity on my suffering." They are hymns to kitchen knives and *"running petroleum all over your legs."* They exist right on the edge of psychopathology and draw the listener into a twistedly subjective ethos: *"I was dragging your face around the floor/Somebody's boot heel in your mouth."* And it's the sensitivity with which Almond relates extremes that gives the songs their awesome tension. In the hands of a lesser artist the material would be sensational instead of controlled and emotively resonant.

The sequence ends on the valedictory note *"I will never love again"*, the singer exiting on that dramatically resigned gesture. *Violent Silence* was remixed for release in 1986, but disciples of the work also cherish the bleaker atmospherics of the audience tape of the concert that has been in circulation amongst fans since 1984.

Almond finished the year by undertaking a full tour of Britain to consolidate his new career and the release of *Vermin In Ermine*. It had been a year of exhaustive changes and creative fertility. His versatility of singing styles had centred round torch and cabaret, and with a change of record label in 1985, he was in his two years with Virgin to record a diversity of material that gave him unchallenged supremacy as the most individually gifted singer of his generation.

RUBIES AND A JACKAL'S HEAD ON THE WALL

In 1985 Marc Almond left Phonogram, and in the summer of the same year was licensed by Some Bizzare to Virgin in a lucrative deal that promised the singer considerably more creative freedom than he had experienced with his former label. Almond's mystique and notoriety were riding high at this point of his career, and photographs of the interior of his flat, taken the previous year showed him surrounded by masks, bullwhips, chains, his two pythons Sodom and Gomorrah, and an assemblage of human skulls, while the stuffed heads of a jackal and hyena stared from the wall. The diva was cultivating the sort of domestic interior sanctioned by Huysmans in his novel *A Rebours*. Notably Almond's favourite book, Huysmans has the valetudinarian protagonist of his novel Des Esseintes cultivate exclusive aesthetic tastes in his retirement from the world. As an obsessive serendipity endowed with great wealth, Des Esseintes sets out to gratify his every sensory anomaly. He makes a collection of tropical plants, he studies the bacilli of sexual diseases, he distils perfumes and associates them with musical harmonies, he has a relationship with a young boy after a chance encounter in the street, he has a tortoise with a gold shell encrusted with jewels parade in front of him on the carpet. He surrounds himself with the books and paintings best suited to his morbidly refined sensibility, and withdraws from the world to the silence of his house at Fontenay. Oscar Wilde drew greatly on this book when writing *The Picture Of Dorian Gray*, and incorporated it into his text, Dorian referring to it as "the strangest book he had ever read." *A Rebours*, or *Against Nature*, as it is translated into English has continued to exercise an inexorable fascination on successive decades of degenerates. The book celebrates the perverse and the decadent, and is a mystic liturgy to corruption. Wilde called it "A poisonous book. The heavy odour of incense seemed to cling about its pages and to trouble the brain." *A Rebours* is an experimental journey in which Huysmans evaluates surfeit of the senses against possible spiritual asceticism. The book is a quintessential product of *fin de siècle* purple prose, and an exhaustive inventory of bizarre tastes. Together with Rachilde's *Monsieur Venus*, and Wilde's *Dorian Gray*, *A Rebours* has remained a seminal and influential text to writers as diverse as Proust, Genet, and William Burroughs. It has also entered direct into the expressions of counterculture; and the gothic fashions arising in the post-punk years of the early eighties are in part an extension of Huysmans' *A Rebours*. Almost all decadents end up reading this book.

Almond, who in 1985 was to sport a platinum streak, something he claims to have done to match the stuffed hornbill he had acquired for his collection, seemed in every trait of his life to be a representative of Huysmans' infamous novel. His body was becoming the surface for a visible mosaic of tattoos. The skulls, hearts pierced by daggers and flickering serpents which have steadily increased over the years were beginning to be recognised as a perverse fetish, so too were the rings that he wore on each finger, the most pronounced being the image of a skull. With his drinking-straw thin body, gold, cross-shaped earrings, and constant makeup, he stood out as belonging to no sector of fashion other than his own. He had become his own creation, and had attracted to him a cult whose loyalty was unshakeable. He was not only the diva of Soho, but a voice winning international respect for its inimitable emotional qualities.

Almond was to begin the year by playing dates at Manchester Hacienda on January 29th, Canterbury Marlowe Theatre on 30th, and London Hammersmith Palais on 31st. And in addition there was news of him lining up five nights of 'special events' at Soho's Raymond Revue Bar from March 12th to 16th, concerts which sadly never materialized. In the same year there were also plans for Almond to take up a week's residency at Ronnie Scott's club, but likewise the intended project never got off the ground.

Almond's repertoire at his January Hammersmith Palais concert opened with the heartbreakingly evocative Tim Rose ballad, 'Morning Dew', a song and elegiac theme ideally suited to his voice; and incorporated material that was to be included on the *Stories Of Johnny* album, like 'Always', and 'Love And Little White Lies'. The Tim Rose song, and 'Love Amongst The Ruined', an Almond composition that was later to be included on a compilation tape *If You Can't Please Yourself, You Can't Please Your Soul*, were welcome additions to the diverse material carried over from his rich 1984 concerts, the singer interspersing his own songs with generous cover versions of 'The Plague', 'Love For Sale', and 'Black Mountain Blues'.

Alive to every possibility of camp histrionics and inductive sleaze, Almond was free to organise performance around the rapidly developing instrument of his voice. His work was stamped with an authoritative individualism given to none of his contemporaries, and this together with his uncompromising belief in poetic lyrics were, as the year progressed, to steadily alienate him from the mainstream ethos.

British fans had to wait until June before Almond returned to live performance with two nights on the 13th and 14th at the new London Fridge on Brixton Hill, and a month later he was to sign to Virgin in anticipation of the respective 'Stories Of Johnny' single and album release in August and September of the same year.

A surprise chart resurrection was Almond's decision to duet with Jimmy Somerville of Bronski Beat on the old Donna Summer dance hit 'I Feel Love'. Largely conceived as a protest against Summer's antipathy to the gay movement, and the devastating progress of AIDS which had triggered her remarks, the medley 'I Feel Love/Love To Love You Baby/Johnny Remember Me' raced to the top three, a dispiriting realisation for Almond that success was available through infectious dance rhythms, rather than through the uncompromising torch songs that were by nature his innate creative expression. As transient as the song proved, it nevertheless raised his public profile, and was an indicator to his prospective label Virgin that he retained the potential for a commercial career.

Almond made a dramatic and acclaimed return to the stage in June with his two nights of showcasing new material at the London Fridge. Dressed simply in a white cotton shirt and jeans, his hair streaked with platinum, he ran on stage like a diva, his hands behind his head, his bottom prominently angled to a rapturous audience. Feeding on the dynamized intimacy of the venue, and utilizing an improved vocal technique, Almond's two performances were inspired by a Grand Guignol of emotive passion. One would have thought the devil was in attendance, dressed as a scarlet-haired goth and staring up at the stage with mesmerised gold eyes. Almond offered a barbed bouquet of new songs, the melodic ballads which were to find find their way on to *Stories Of Johnny* were variegated with the empathetic brooding romanticism of 'When I Was A Young Man', and a superb a cappella version of Judy Garland's 'Blue Prelude'. Writing the concert up for *Melody Maker*, Ziyad Georgis commented: "Utilizing his outrageous style, he has an uncanny knack of seducing people into his private world, creating a symbiotic relationship between himself and his fanatical fans. despite possessing a tongue filthy enough to rival Joan Rivers', the over-riding impression is that Marc is treated as a cuddly toy by his audience – albeit one that they may wish to engage in extravagant sexual fantasies."

What had become apparent by 1985 was the strength of Almond's individuation, and despite having his blood vampirically siphoned off by the music press, he had little or nothing in common with the genres of music they were promoting. It was his rumoured lifestyle, his confessional temerity, his stance as a controversial maverick, and his willingness to jettison commercial props which attracted a conformist press to his liberties. Almond has pursued a career, popularized by a press whose allegiance is to the formulated modes of music he has consistently deconstructed. He is the only male torch singer to have won his sequinned laurels through music press advocacy, and at the same time to have maintained his ideals.

'Stories of Johnny', a song that has remained a consistent favourite of the singer for live performance, became his first proper hit single as a solo artist. A plaintive Almond composition about a boy loser, a social misfit who is angular to all conventions, the song had a crepuscular feel to it, as well as a suggested innocence in contention with experience that smacked of the autobiographical. It was a theme to which Almond would return with the lyric 'Waifs And Strays' from the *Enchanted* LP.

Almond saw the song as 'A dedication in a way to all the famous record and literary and film Johnnies. Anyone from Johnny Rio to Johnny Guitar to Johnny B Goode, the list is endless. He is a romantic hero. He's a loser, wastrel and vagabond, but a prince at the same time. He's so fictional he's almost faceless.' Johnny could be anyone, he has the characteristics of the rent boys who used to hang out at Piccadilly Circus in the eighties, and is better conceived as the archetypal vagrant, the rebel who like Rimbaud decides at the earliest of ages to take to the road and circumvent social responsibilities. He is the perennial youth who will never come in from the rain. There's one on every street corner and death receives them before age.

Stories Of Johnny manifests eclectic influences, and was a much more commercially accessible album than its predecessor, or either of Almond's two releases with the Mambas. Torch, jazz and dance music are integrated into material that is essentially romantic and contentiously autobiographical. 'Traumas' sets the tone for the ruined but celebratory lover who narrates the disillusionment of being in and out of love, but never stable or happy. Memory is the faculty that a torch singer most values. The past is re-lived as a criterion which the future will never fulfil. There's a consolation in internalizing a damaged or unrequited love, and Almond excels as an exponent of this medium, as do so many of his influences like Johnny Ray, Peggy Lee, Scott Walker and Charles Aznavour. *Stories Of Johnny* is essentially torch singing to dance instrumentation. Take away the accompaniment and the songs are slow and deeply expressive of pain. And speaking of the title track in retrospect Almond was to say, 'The song was about a young guy I knew who smoked heroin and who later died – hence the line, "My smoky lover will take me away for ever." Most people I know find their way into my songs.'

Despite the greater tranquillity evident in his new collection of songs, the singer's life continued to be fraught with alcohol and personal problems. He turned up to one interview after having been thrown out of a Soho newsagent's, the man brandishing a knife at him, and then had to fight his way through the ever vigilant Gutterhearts keeping sempiternal watch outside the Some Bizzare offices. Much in the style of a Huysmans' devotee, he proceeded to relate the fetishes included in his house. 'I collect stuffed animals, and masks, and any exotic ephemera. In the hall there's two stuffed baby tigers, and a chihuahua under a glass dome. I had a male and female chastity belt on display too, but they intimidated people. Upstairs it's a bit like the Congo with lots of rotting vegetation – mini palms and bamboo curtains and a warthog head on the wall.' But a cultivated eccentricity and inveterate love of decadence were absent from *Stories Of Johnny*, which has proved to be the least controversial of his LPs. Perhaps in favour of his new record company, or as an admission that some commercial profile was necessary if he was to undermine the system, Almond delivered the successful product that was to lift him off the ground with Virgin.

Stories Of Johnny was favourably received by a music press who had lacerated the duende of *Torment And Toreros* and the aggrandisement of sleaze on *Vermin In Ermine*. The jazz swing and the opulent vocals on the Mel Torme number 'The House Is Haunted' were particularly singled out for praise, and reviewers commended what they saw as a mutation from confessional neuroses to genuine sorrow. Almond was extolled for exercising restraint and control on both his vocals and material. Reviewing the LP for *Melody Maker* Colin Irwin praised the consistency of "suberbly constructed songs of durable strength which rise effortlessly above the mire of most pop music. And while 'I Who Never' is a majestic ballad with certain qualities that might even appeal to Miss Shirley Bassey, for once in his life Marc retains control and resists the temptation to go totally over the top." The reviewer also noted the new optimism infusing the work, and considered that Almond had transcended his earlier preoccupations, and by no longer using his songs as weapons of despair, they had come to "acquire a defiant, even optimistic edge."

Stories Of Johnny has a cushioned Mike Hedges sound, and it would be interesting to hear Almond do acoustic versions of some of the real songwriting successes like 'Traumas', 'I Who Never', 'My Candle Burns', and 'Always'. The real content of the songs, that is their evocatively emotive lyricism, is often obscured by the arrangements. The overall mood of the lyrics is tenebrous and melancholy, whereas the arrangements are technically positive. But *Stories Of Johnny* came as a welcome assurance to Almond's fans that he could slip effortlessly in and out of commercial postures without compromising his integrity; a strategy that he has maintained to this day.

If Virgin were deluded into the belief that they were to market a mellower and more tractable artist, then the foundations for this belief were to prove short lived. Under their progressively dissatisfied aegis Almond was to release a stream of controversial singles, two uncommercial mini-LPs, and the notorious *Mother Fist And Her Five Daughters*. It was a typical turn around on the artist's part and a revelation of the contempt he felt for any sort of compromise.

The commercial successes of 'I Feel Love', and 'Stories Of Johnny', suggested that Almond was still eminently saleable, and that if separated from what was erroneously construed as the confessional neuroses of his first three solo projects, there was every chance that he would prove a successful competitor for chart titles. But the singer's interests lay elsewhere, and over the next year he was to record cover versions and original compositions that had little in common with contemporary trends in music. This would hardly come as a surprise to the aficionados who knew of his preferences through live performances, nor to those who realised that the popular viability of *Stories Of Johnny* lay in the arrangements and not the lyricism and tenor of the songs.

Almond was to pursue his most sustained tour of Britain in the autumn of 1985, but in September of the same year he was rushed into hospital for an emergency operation to remove his appendix. He was also diagnosed as suffering from liver deterioration caused by indiscriminate drinking. 'I was rushed into hospital that night with peritonitis and hepatitis. God, was I suffering, a ruined liver and appendicitis at the same time... I've stopped drinking since the hospital. I used to drink bottles of tequila or vodka. Now I just drink tea.'

A few weeks later, he was back on stage in marvellous vocal form, pursuing two hour concerts with a live-or-die torch singer's fanatically stylised heart. Almond projects a passion that no other British singer has ever realised, his voice having direct access to his heart. The symbiotic catharsis for the audience is one that opens out doors of self-realisation and the inexhaustable possibilities of love. Leave a Marc Almond concert and you want to swallow a red rose.

Almond's autumn concerts embraced a diverse spectrum of material. Opening either with Tim Rose's 'Morning Dew' or the gay vicissitudes inherent in 'Blond Boy', a song that deserved to be more than a B-side to 'Stories Of Johnny', he was consistently brilliant in revising his repertoire to include old and new songs. Amongst the latter were 'The Room Below', and 'Melancholy Rose', both of which were to be included on the *Mother Fist And Her Five Daughters* LP, as well as the torch ecstasy of 'When I Was A Young Man', and an almost baritone a cappella version of 'House Of The Rising Sun'. Smouldering ballads like 'Big Louise', and 'You Have', were juxtaposed against the more accessible 'Love Letter' and 'Love And Little White Lies'. 'Torment' was revived to reflect the torch singer's constant mood, 'A Woman's Story' was given a first live airing, 'Pink Shack Blues', and 'Joey Demento' were pointers to male lubriciousness, and 'I Who Never' was resonant with a desperately unrequited love. The concerts were tear-drenched and perversely decadent. Almond was more than ever mastering a style which married Charles Baudelaire to Judy Garland. And for the first time in British song, poetry had found representation through a voice with a popular following. What the French had always achieved through the union of lyrics and voice was being won by Almond at a considerable price. Two superlative London concerts at the Hammersmith Palais and the Dominion Theatre on the 4th and 5th of November respectively, were the highlights of an escalating momentum which was to carry the singer on over-reach into the following year. Arms waving, and body somatizing his pain, perilously thin and dynamized with duende, Almond was like a flamenco dervish singing blues ballads. The cultural cross references bled to isolation in his voice.

Roger Hill was there at the Royal Court Theatre, Liverpool, to capture

---

Almond on stage. He noted how "You're left balancing the pleasures of that apricot middle register against the shrill shock of the melodramatic high notes and the vulnerable unaccompanied tenor. If the general affect is amusing, downright burlesque at times, particularly between numbers, there's still space in 'The Flesh Is Willing' for authentic agony to break through. Tonight was short on tragedy, but only just." Where Almond tends to be disparaged by the unsympathetic, it's usually due to the combination of his nervous idiosyncrasies being in conflict with his inherent seriousness. There are people who are embarrassed by dramatic emotion, and who disparage the somatics of performance, and it is this desensitised sector of critical opinion which attacks poetry or song when it is delivered with authentic heart conviction. "A voice is like a dress; playing a record is sonic drag" Wayne Koestenbaum tells us in *The Queen's Throat*, and there's very real truth in that, for in the act of performance, and nowhere more so than in torch singing, the singer is androgynized, and it's the sense of ambivalent sexuality which communicates to the audience, or in the case of a record to the listener. In concert, Almond was sublimating his own abjection, and instating a diva iconography in which the victim is winner by virtue of celebrating his loss. Torch singing presents the irrefutable paradox of triumph through ruin. And the vocabulary of transcending loss is a physical one, arms thrown in the air, head tilted back, eyes closed on the romantic agony of squeezing the bitter pain sweet.

Although the songs weren't to be released until the spring of 1986, Almond recorded most of *A Woman's Story*, his suite of romantic cover versions, in September 1985. His phrasing had never appeared better than on songs demanding a stylised emotional exorcism. Reviving the Phil Spector song 'A Woman's Story', and singing it from a woman's point of view without any concession to gender, Almond rounded the song to symphonic passion. The diva's stage embodiment of the lyrics was an act repeated in the studio. With stunning orchestral arrangements managed by Mike Hedges, Almond grew to a vocal maturity that surprised even his closest admirers. The title song which portrays the life of a drugged, promiscuous and used woman, someone ruined by the wrong habits, found a corresponding association with numbers in gay sex, the partners not even knowing each other's names. In a more concealed way it was Almond's most overt sexual proclamation since the controversial storm surrounding 'Numbers'. With epic production, he immortalised Phil Spector's song of a libertine loser, and then proceeded to cover Eartha Kitt's 'The Heel', Procul Harem's 'Salty Dog', Scott Walker's 'The Plague', Johnny Ray's 'The Little White Cloud That Cried', Peter Hammill's 'Just Good

Friends', and Lee Hazelwood's 'For One Moment'. It was a diverse range of material to entertain, and Almond's version of Eartha Kitt's spiky narrative of revenge 'The Heel', also saw him adopt a woman's role to convey the song's classic tale of jealousy and betrayal. The exercise in gender transference had never sounded so authentic. Almond was heard committing hedonistic regicide in order to adopt a diva's tragic identification. "Disturb gender, and you disturb temporality; accept the androgyne, and you accept the abyss", Wayne Koestenbaum tells us in *The Queen's Throat*.

The two songs which adopt masculine primacy, 'A Salty Dog' and 'The Plague', are both outsiders' stories of journeying through apocalyptic landscapes composed of psychological and physical components. The more controlled desperation inherent in Scott Walker's version of 'The Plague' is re-translated by Almond into an up-beat antagonism. With the press having labelled the endemic virus AIDS, the plague, the song took on immediate, sinister connotations with Almond's adoption of Walker's paranoid, alienated confessions. Almond is naturally closer to Scott Walker than he is any other British singer. Both artists share an awareness of European influences, and both have attempted to work with poetic lyrics in a climate that has little sympathy with articulate song. Almond like Walker before him, has trod a precarious line between commercial success and cult adoration. Walker's celebrated reclusion and inviolable mystique are qualities increasingly inherited by Marc Almond, whose public appearances have grown fewer over the years, with a corresponding growth of mystique. Almond's version of 'The Plague' is a deeply assimilated one, and is delivered with a vitality that loses none of the song's original terror. And who else could cover Scott Walker to no loss? Almond's repertoire has also included Walker's 'Big Louise', and he has reinterpreted a number of the Brel songs that Walker made a part of his own identity: 'My Death', 'If You Go Away', 'Next', and 'Jacky', the latter becoming a hit single for both singers.

'A Salty Dog' was retrieved for Almond by a friend in New York, and the marine imagery and the homoerotic world implied by sailors is at once consonant with his sensibility. Almond, born in Southport, was brought up by the sea, and at an early age taken for long walks across the shore by his grandfather. It's little wonder that the sea is the natural element which recurs in his songs, with 'The Sea Says', and 'The Sea Still Sings', and 'A Love Outgrown' being amongst the best of his songs which recall that childhood preoccupation. There's a sense of the ocean running through his imagery, the sea represents spiritual freedom, it's the element that is untamed by man, and appears closest to original creation. From Baudelaire onwards, *"le voyage"* has represented the quest for a blue infinity. 'A Salty Dog' ideally fits Almond's vocal range, and adds the image of sailors to the implied sexual ambivalence that permeates this unusual set of songs.

Almond has always nurtured a love of Johnny Ray, a singer who underwent a prison sentence for homosexual offences in less tolerant times, and one who like Almond attempted to find some level of compromise between commercial and integrated song. Almond's version of 'The Little White Cloud That Cried' is suitably melodic, and while the song touches on the sentimental, it is nonetheless redeemed by the obvious homosexual metaphors of the cloud as outsider, condemned to suffer for its difference. The song is an act of personal homage on Almond's part to a talented, but largely forgotten singer. Almond's natural sense of empathy allows him to take up Johnny Ray's quiet despair, and without protest re-establish the song as a sexual outsider's tale of exclusion. In an interview 'The Sinner And The Saint' given in 1986, Almond spoke of his dislike of prejudiced people, and of his admiration of the obsessive and the extreme. 'I hate those who don't give others a chance – prejudiced people. I like obsessive people, those who take things to extremes. I have a real dislike for the human race in general, but a real sympathy for its suffering. I tend to feel sympathy for the individual, the loner. I hate the mob in society, that destructive element to creativity.'

One could argue that all true creativity is the result of the individual in contention with society, and where art conforms to social dictates it is a dead expression. Inspired art is generated by individual subversion, and revolution happens on that inner plane. And song contributes directly to bringing about changes in our sexual and social lives. Chanson, together with cabaret, has always been a more subtle medium for articulating facets of gay life, whereas rock music has almost singularly advocated heterosexuality, and only at its most extreme has it flirted with androgynity through the likes of Bowie and Lou Reed. Almond has come closer than anyone to taking on unorthodoxy, not only in giving voice to gay ideals, but in singing for all those who differ on psychosexual planes. Divas don't necessarily affiliate with any category of sexual nomenclature, they are unassimilable with norms. The mystery is in imagining their sexual vocabulary.

Almond tells us that Virgin wouldn't extend the budget on his album of cover versions, and consequently he was unable to record

'Something's Gotten Hold Of My Heart', the Gene Pitney ballad which was to give him international success three years later. It's regrettable that the sessions for *A Woman's Story* didn't include the complement for a full album, but the singer's versions of Lee Hazelwood's 'For One Moment', and Peter Hammill's 'Just Good Friends', compensate for this omission by their sensitive depictions of loss, and the complex emotions attendant on betrayal and its accompanying loneliness. Almond has made song his study, and over the years his critical faculties have shown a selectivity of taste which has enabled him to diversify, and to maximise on his voice potential. 'I look for a song which sends a shiver down my spine', he tells us, alert as always to how the sensory interacts with the lyrical.

Totally against the grain of fashionable taste, and uncompromisingly individualistic, *A Woman's Story* was a clear pointer to Virgin that Almond had little intention of aspiring to immediate chart success. And when *Violent Silence* was released a few months later, the artist's integrity appeared self-immolative, and radically untangential to the sort of dance hit formula that Virgin may have conceived as the direction for their new artist. Almond had never appeared more defiantly eccentric.

Almond toured Japan and Europe in the spring of 1986, his performances at Studio 54 Barcelona on the 30th April, and in Madrid on 2nd May, being received with extraordinary Latin enthusiasm. In the previous weeks he had played at Florence, Bologna, and Torino, to corresponding Italian adulation. Always better received where emotive passion is integrated into life and song, his generous embodiment of lyric decadence is ideally suited to a European cultural sensibility, rather than to the pronounced reservations of British realism. And back in Britain, Almond was to begin work on the *Mother Fist And Her Five Daughters* sessions, and to record the highly controversial 'Ruby Red' single which was set for October release. Almond, who had spent much of the year living in Barcelona, injected something of its torrid ambience into his newly written material. 'I wanted to reflect some of the smell of the streets, the warmth of the place, and its smoky atmosphere in the music. Quite exotic, frayed around the edges, a decaying splendour – that's how I find Barcelona. And the colour of the characters as well. I've always liked writing about characters, whether it's me or a fantasy of myself... Soaking up these atmospheres has been a very creative experience for the new album.'

Almond's return to a starkly acoustic sound, drums, piano, and trumpet, was in sharp contrast to the guitar and keyboard orientated music of *Stories Of Johnny*, and as such was inflammably antagonistic to his record company. 'Ruby Red' which was to be the first single released from the sessions was the only compromise towards a more instant commercial appeal, although the song's imagery and accompanying video contrived to have it banned.

'Ruby Red' was melodic enough to have gone to the top of the charts, if the lyrics hadn't been considered morally offensive. References to wrapping a heart up in a *"bouquet of barbed wire"*, and to a red light shining on a boy's bed, stated an obvious homoerotic union. And yet the song contains lines as sensual and pure as any of Lorca's ballads, and it's Almond's adopted Spanish influences that are most pronounced in the writing: *"It was as red as the sun in the evening sky/It was as red as the fire in a panther's eye/It was as red as the rose under the summer sun/Like the fire from a killer's gun."* Lyrics as passionately informed as these don't often find their way into chart music, and Almond was to meet with incontestable media opposition to the inspired duende informing his lyrics. Outwardly, the song appeared to have greater commercial potential than anything he had released since 'Torch', but the supporting video was considered sexually shocking, and was edited for restricted release. The increasing intolerance of Thatcher's despotism towards every form of cultural minority was beginning to have serious effects on individual liberty by the mid-eighties. An avaricious materialism founded on brute insensitivity had permeated almost every sector of the British public, and the recriminative measures directed towards the gay community were beginning to make inroads into Almond's creative expression. Commenting on the blacklisting of his video, Almond said, 'I fear it is the usual homophobic paranoia. If the video contained scenes of near naked women then that would make it acceptable. As it is, men's buttocks have been around for a long time and we must learn to live with them... It's the usual worrying about the usual things in an increasingly conservative climate.'

It was the new militantly unimaginative regime which was to consign Almond, and representatives in all of the arts to an enforced void throughout the tyrannical years of the Thatcher dictatorship. British art, whether it is poetry, song, or painting, has become under Tory aculturalism a medium that does little more than observe and comment on social realism. Almond's art, which belongs to an imaginatively emotive evaluation of life has suffered as music becomes a media commodity. By 1986 the rot was endemic. The release of 'Ruby Red' was a decisive factor in the rift between Marc

Almond and Virgin. The latter were even unhappier at the commercial prospects of the *Mother Fist And Her Five Daughters* album, which was not to be released until April of the following year. With the title track having overt references to masturbation and covert ones to fist-fucking, Virgin sensed the rigid censorship likely to surround the album's release. The anonymous reviewer of 'Ruby Red' for the *Newcastle Journal* sounded the pulse of Almonds predicament when he wrote: "There's surely a limit to how long Marc can continue to be so wonderful without the slightest twitch from the sleeping public."

Hot on the trail of the objurgation surrounding 'Ruby Red', Almond was in October to star as the headline of the Soho Jazz Festival at The London Palladium. A tribute to his vocal prowess, he was to return to the same venue for a solo concert in December, the singer appeared backed only by piano and drums and Enrico Tomasso on trumpet. His performance brooked no argument, it was an impassioned delivery of material as diverse as Juliette Greco's 'Undress Me', Eartha Kitt's 'The Heel', a first airing of 'St. Judy', his sleaze homage to Judy Garland, the melancholy investing 'When I Was A Young Man', and the fragile poignancy of two other songs he has never released in recorded form, 'Under The Neon Moon' and 'When A Girl Loves A Girl'. With his head shaved, and a single mohican strip of hair partly visible beneath a white sailor's hat, Almond looked every bit the most exotic anomaly to have appeared in the history of this prestigious festival. His exhibitionistic theatricality was ideally suited to the Palladium, and the sparse musical accompaniment assisted without detracting from his poetic narratives of flawed or broken love. Will Smith reporting the occasion for *Melody Maker* was ambivalently disparaging and admiring of Almond's performance. Entering into the torrid atmospherics of the occasion, Smith wrote of Almond as "Theatrically articulate, although in vocal possession of an unremarkable starting point in pitch and tone, he summons a tremulous lung power and emotion to his aid for the worrying, luckless images of suffering and fate, inherently obsessive in 'St. Judy' and the suspiciously autobiographical 'The Champ'. Dark, mysterious, but somehow beckoning, the surrounding arrangements of songs are constructions of suspense which writhe, painfully, evocatively, with the fall and rise of a tattooed arm or searing note."

The occasion was an extravagant triumph for the singer, it represented still another tangent of remove from the pop ethos in which he had begun his career, and into which he would continue to make periodic forays, not so much out of choice, but by subverting the medium to his own needs.

The year was to end on an additional note of triumph for Almond, who performed a Sunday night at The London Palladium on 23rd November, thereby joining the pantheon of elite vocalists who receive this invitation. And for Almond, who was only just 30, it was a considerable distinction to bring his own individualised blend of torch music to such a prestigious occasion.

Dancing on stage and breaking into a verse of Judy Garland's 'Somewhere Over The Rainbow', Almond's demonstrably luxurious vocal embellishments carried the night through a contrasting mix of camp joie de vivre, and brooding torch ballads, 'St. Judy' had never sounded better or more apposite, and the inclusion of the spicily Barcelonian 'Anarcoma' and 'Jackal Jackal' gave an emotive Spanish tang to the performance. And as always there was a generous selection of new material including 'The Stars We Are', as an appropriate opener to the show, a version that differs lyrically from the song that was to become the title track of the album of that name in 1988. Almond introduced songs that were to form the nucleus of the *Mother Fist And Her Five Daughters* LP, 'There Is A Bed', 'Ruby Red', 'Mother Fist', 'The Champ', and the valedictorially beautiful 'The River', as well as basking in the gin-sodden, red light ruination ballads of broken femme fatales, 'St. Judy' and 'A Woman's Story', and the quixotically florid 'Melancholy Rose'. Almond's stage dynamics and authoritative diva tones were to win the night, and to suggest that torch-cabaret would comprise an undisputed future for a burlesque performer with a voice aspiring to untutored operatics.

Press reception to the concert was almost unanimous in generating ubiquitous praise, although reservations were expressed in certain quarters about the accent on sleaze that predominated, and what was thought to be the division between the artist and the persona he adopted. Reporting on the concert for the *NME*, Jane Solanas expressed the conviction that Almond was clearly quite different from the image he projected through the use of fictional characters. "Almond revels in the concept of sin as liberation", she writes, "he likes to come across as a dirty little sod who inhabits a world totally committed to depravity, but the songs are obvious fantasies. The people Almond sings about (or role-plays) are stock characters from literature and cinema: the whore with the golden heart, the man-eating femme fatale, the homosexual hustler, the lonely old queen..."

The putative dichotomy between artist and his work, and the separation of experiential and fictional contents, is a subject that has been endlessly debated, and largely pivots on the concept of empathy. To empathise with something is to embody it as an imaginative reality, and most good writing is a mixture of real and imagined experience. Everything gets textured into the creative canvas, and it's often hard for the artist to know where imagination and reality separate.

Censored by the media, and in the process of disaffection from his record company, Almond collected gold laurels for his two Palladium performances, but entered 1987 with his new LP *Mother Fist And Her Five Daughters* subject to endless delay before finally finding release in April of that year.

Mother Fist And Her Five Daughters, an acoustic suite of songs vibrant with Almond's obsessive preoccupations was a synthesis of the diverse strands of music he had been pursuing since his experimental work with the Mambas. Its note of seriousness, and its rich lyric content were in contradistinction to its more dance-orientated predecessor *Stories Of Johnny*. Virgin had been unhappy all along about paeans to onanism, twisted love stories about rent boys, hustlers and the societal victims who occupy Almond's pantheon of heroes, and the two singles released from the album 'Melancholy Rose', and 'Mother Fist', both denied airplay and promotion, were portentous indicators of the album's commercial failure.

In songs that smouldered with emotive coloratura, Almond's vocal assemblage meditated on diva passions, sicknesses, and habits that belonged to the edge. Completely outside the parameters of British conservatism, his mordant floridity had never appeared odder in its romantic celebration of the individual at the expense of the mob. His courageous flying of colours at a time of collective greyness, fully supported Jean Cocteau's dictum: "That with which the public reproaches you, cultivate it: it is you." In his field, Almond has maintained an uncompromising individuality at the price of marginalised commercial appeal. *Mother Fist And Her Five Daughters* epitomises his belief in art rather than product.

Almond's mixture of flamenco, torch song and Brel style ballad was compounded on this album into a state of passionate loss, and in the song 'St. Judy' his morbid wit found a perfect target in the fictionalised creation of the Judy Garland legend. *"And if I die before*

I wake up/I pray the Lord don't smudge my make-up", he sings, lines as memorable as *"A diva a day/Keeps the boredom away"* from the same song. Of its genre 'St. Judy' is a classically written song, and bears no loss in its comparisons to Brel. Almond's vocal feeds into the melodramatic tragedy: *"Well they may find me on a hotel floor/High heels and a pool of gore"*, and the voice asks that we consider the reality of a diva's self-destructive ruin. The stereotypical legend surrounding a star's suicide ideation doesn't in any way mitigate human suffering, although it may reaffirm public conviction that death is a just reward for those who differ. Artists are expected to die for their sins; the proletariat want blood if they are to afford posthumous acclaim to those who live outside their strictures. 'St. Judy' takes up most of Almond's causes, and it's the pivotal song on which the album hinges. A defiant lyric that vindicates the torch singer's wounded sensibility, Almond's sense of empathy for his subject, and her excesses, has him declare *"I've wanted to do it for years."* And *Mother Fist And Her Five Daughters* was very much the LP that Almond had been waiting to make for years, even if it cost him his record label. Accompanied by accordion, piano, violin, Spanish guitar, and sparsely intermittent trumpet, Almond coaxed his poetic obsessions into lyric autobiography. Each of the songs contains the sultry glower of a concealed jewel worn at the waist, and the refined ode to masturbation is a paean to onanism not so dissimilar to Jean Genet's ecstatic evocation of masturbation in *Notre Dame Des Fleurs*. "If you are looking for bold gestures and a camp theatrical flourish, then Marc Almond is your man", extolled *The Times*, praising what they considered to be his compassionate insights into modern romance. At last someone had the courage to devote a song to the solitary pleasures of masturbation. It was Oscar Wilde who in *The Picture Of Dorian Grey*, propounded his belief that all original creativity goes counter to the morals of its age. "I consider" wrote Wilde, "that for any man of culture to accept the standard of his age is a form of the grossest immorality." All good art subscribes to that dictum, and Almond's work in its exploratory excursions into the shadow side of life has consistently upended the sort of otiose morals by which the status quo approves its own hypocrisy.

'People keep using the same words to describe my life and my work', he considered at the time of the album's release. 'Camp, squalid, a gutter queen, a dog from Leeds, flippant and lurid, obsessive, sleazy, tacky, melodramatic, nostalgic, cherubic, seedy and sinful.' And while some of these words were applied to *Mother Fist And Her Five Daughters*, the overall critical reception afforded the album's virtues was one of praise for the vocal finesse and carefully structured lyrics.

The two fine songs reconciling love and death 'There Is A Bed', and 'The Room Below', both expound death as we know it through desire and physical dissolution. Bed is the arena of pleasure and pain, we learn in that place the resourceful joys of sex, the dream-life generated by sleep, and the pain associated with illness and death. Almond moves effortlessly between these experiential states, and in doing so manifests all that he has learnt from French song. *"There is a bed that is my sanctuary/A bed where I can end my days"*, he sings, giving us the metaphor of a bed as a ship, a vessel that negotiates the dark waters of the underworld. Don't we often wake up out at sea, no land in sight, minatory birds with red eyes flapping over in the dark, and with the sound of water leaking through a drifting wreck? 'The Room Below', and 'There Is A Bed', are essentially companion pieces in which the traumatic impact of ruinous love is counterbalanced by attraction to death. The two songs are essentially novellas, and their minimal compression would have pleased Truman Capote to whom Almond dedicated the album. 'Capote said, "I'm a homosexual, I'm a drug addict, I'm an alcoholic, I'm a genius." Well, I'd just like to say that I identify with him almost completely. The only difference is that I'm not an alcoholic', Almond was to tell John Wilde in an interview for *Blitz*.

The songs on *Mother Fist And Her Five Daughters* form an integrated whole. The two definite mood uplifters 'Ruby Red', and 'The River', being offset by 'Mother Fist', and 'Melancholy Rose'. 'The Champ', and 'The Hustler', are sensitive portraits of outsiders, while 'The Sea Says', and 'Mr Sad', are moody melancholy ballads, and 'Angel In Her Kiss', links with the slightly upbeat 'Ruby Red' and 'The River'.

It must have been the album's anti-commercial slant that appealed to reviewers, for the record failed to sell outside the fanatical circle of Almond devotees. Singling out Almond's exceptional qualities as a lyricist, Tony Mitchell praised what he thought to be the artistic durability of the material. "Even the simplest of songs here", he wrote, "has more lyrical worth than pop's undemanding nursery rhyme standards dictate. The tracks on *Mother Fist* can be delved into time and time again, if only for the pleasures words bring in the mouth of a skilled raconteur. Don't look for clever synth patches, searing sampled sounds or blistering solos. Look for heart, soul and sympathy – and find it. Marc Almond – a difficult artist, thank God."

With the release of *Mother Fist And Her Five Daughters* Almond had once again narrowed the gap between poetry and song, the dense prosodic texture of his lyrics establishing a genre that was as individual as it was new. 'I became the antichrist, the bad influence on kids', he recollects. 'There was quite a lot of homoerotic imagery on *Mother Fist*, and that was quite intentional. It was completely wrong for the time, completely against the prevailing wave of homophobia, and it took about three years for people to start playing me again as a reaction against the bland pop ethos – so I became the acceptable face of odd.'

Mother Fist as an album is a sumptuously voluptuous liturgy to decadent hedonism, a celebration of sailors, tattoo, muscle, a rent boy spread across the bed, pills, death, and the eschatological extremes of heaven and hell. The extended mix of 'Ruby Red' makes the homoerotic intimations vitally explicit, and is the better song for the inclusion of *"You're coming on down like a sledgehammer baby/The woman in me's tired/Memory full of squirming eels/And a belly full of fire"*; and for the livid sexual image *"Ruby red all over the bed."* With the video to the single version of 'Ruby Red' censored by Virgin for its cavorting red devils, and the song receiving only a token two plays on Radio 1, there was all the more reason to offer the unedited song to serious fans.

Mother Fist was originally intended as a double album, and a variety of outstanding material recorded during the sessions was released on EPs which grew to mini-albums, before finding release in its own right on the two volumes of Virgin retrospective *A Virgin's Story*. Among these songs were 'Jackal Jackal', 'Anarcoma', 'Broken Hearted And Beautiful', 'I'm Sick Of You Tasting Of Somebody Else', 'Two Sailors On A Beach', 'Gyp The Blood', 'Black Lullabye', 'A World Full Of People', the two Brecht songs 'Pirate Jenny', and 'Surabaya Johnny', and two neglected masterpieces recorded for *Sounds* and *Melody Maker* compilations, 'Oily Black Limousine', and 'Indigo Blue'. The last two songs, the former a superb Almond composition phrased like a jazz singer to minimal accompaniment, and the latter a full fledged ballad given a big sound, remain uncollected, and yet are indispensable to any serious study of his work. 'Indigo Blue' with its vibrant colour imagery is ideally suited to Almond's voice, and was given a live airing in a number of 1988 concerts; and 'Oily Black Limousine' was presented live at the Zap Club, Brighton in a March 1986 acoustic set, but has otherwise been conspicuously absent from his live and recorded repertoire.

Mother Fist and *Violent Silence* presented the least compromising of Almond's creative facets, and while they accrued critical success, both albums were considered hermetic, distasteful, and uncommercially orientated by Virgin. Paul Mather writing for *Melody Maker* considered *Mother Fist* to be "Marc's finest moment yet, a black, silky moment, 12 songs long and devoid of any of the unnecessarily melodramatic hokum that's dragged a lot of his previous work out of the glamorous gutter and into the sixth form essay writing competition."

But it was an achievement on which to meditate, for Almond was soon to find himself in a void without a record label, but not before he had undertaken recording another ambitious project, the double album that was to have been called *Absinthe Stardust Opium And Lust*, and which, given a vote of no confidence by Virgin, was to appear in different versions and revised recordings as *Jacques*, and *Absinthe*, the respective 1989 and 1993 LPs of French songs put out by Some Bizzare. These illustriously masterful recordings of Brel and other French song writers are the subject of another chapter, but demonstrate how fertile and prolific a recording artist Almond was in his Virgin years.

Mother Fist marked the end of a period of manic and licentious recording for Almond, and no matter his justified contentions with Virgin, their reasonably flexible hegemony did allow the artist to get a lot done. 'It isn't a concept album but it is very reflective', Almond commented at the time, 'looking back over a certain period of my life. I think you go through an astrological state called Saturn Return, where you transcend from a young adult to a full adult. You find yourself looking back on your life in a very nostalgic manner, while also contemplating the future.'

Mother Fist registered Almond's youthful maturity, and in a less homophobic society the LP would have been accorded the egregious distinctions it richly deserved. As it was the record magnified Almond's cult status, and the degree of ostracism to which he was consigned outside the circle of his devotees. For the next eighteen months Almond dipped out of public attention, a pariah consigned to the marginalised parameters of a decadent cult, whose epigoni wore dagger-through-the-heart tattoos, and dressed in black. But Almond was planning sweet revenge, and just by believing in his talents as a singer he was able to stand back and wait for the break. It was agonizingly slow in coming, but was in time to affect radical changes in the direction of his future.

photo: Helen Ayer

photo: Nick Timms

photo: Ben Thornbury

photo: Nick Timms

photo: Ben Thornbury

photo: Helen Ayer

photo: Andrew Catlin

WHEN I WAS A YOUNG MAN

Just before the release of *Mother Fist And Her Five Daughters* in April 1987, Almond undertook two concerts for International AIDS Day, one at the Hackney Empire and the other at the Royalty Theatre. Originally intended to be staged over three nights at the Donmar Warehouse, both performances drew on an expansively enlarged repertoire, and spotlighted Almond as a virtuoso maverick integrating European song into his vocabulary of torch ballads. These two concerts, and the preceding month's Convention at Busby's, when he had introduced Brel songs like 'The Town Fell Asleep', and 'The Devil (Okay)', into his live performance, were a heterogeneous summation of his career to date, a young man's achievements arrested a moment in time before the artist entered another phase in his career. Certainly the generous diversity of material, and the uncompromising way in which it was presented suggested an artist balanced on a creative zenith. Almond had created his own myth: all the masks, sailor's hats, bleeding heart tattoos, toreador's jackets, rhinestone embellishments, Soho alleys, rent boys at Piccadilly, tequila, decadent poems written in the late hours, angels in attendance, the whole mosaic of associations had come together in his Saturn Return period to find him at his creative best; but paradoxically without a record company or an audience outside his own devoted nucleus of fans. Nobody else would have risked incorporating poems by Baudelaire and Verlaine into a London concert, or would have dared revive an old folk ballad 'When I Was A Young Man', or come up with five Jacques Brel songs, as well as a suitably camp rendition of Juliette Greco's 'Undress Me', and presented this to an audience whose knowledge of chanson was at best partial. And it was natural that Almond should gravitate towards French song with its emphasis on the poetic lyric, the resonant image, and its special flavour of bittersweet romance. French singers and lyricists like Jacques Brel, Léo Ferré, and Serge Gainsbourg have consistently made song an inalienable extension of poetry, rather than have it devolve into a lesser, but more popular mode of expression. Almond's own lyrics are in the tradition of French songwriting, and by 1987 his European sensibility seemed better accommodated anywhere other than in a conservatively uninspired Britain.

There was a valedictory air to the two International AIDS Day concerts, as though the singer was the young man moving away from performance, and the whole Gutterhearts zeitgeist over which he had presided. By the end of the year, and most notably by the time of his 'The Stars We Are' concerts in the autumn 1988, Almond had gained a degree of removal from his audience, and had instated professionalism at the expense of intimate collaboration with his devotees. He was to become more conscious of the need to separate elements of his private life from the integral components of his career. In short, he was to cultivate the mystique that has become synonymous with his person throughout the late eighties and increasingly so in the first half of the nineties.

The working title for Almond's interpretations of French songs *Baudelaire Meets Brel*, encapsulated the isolated nature of his work at the time, an artist at odds with the musical and sexual politics of a nation sold into contempt for culture. Charles Baudelaire has for long epitomised the ideal of the suffering artist, the poet who was outlawed by his contemporaries, prosecuted for what were considered to be obscenities in *Les Fleurs Du Mal*, impoverished by his family's stranglehold on his trust, eroded by years of syphilitic deterioration, and finally dying in his mid-forties in a state of nervous paralysis. Baudelaire's name is inseparably associated with opium, prostitutes, and the dream of sybaritic decadence. And Jacques Brel, the Belgian born and fevered raconteur of lyrics that combine the personal and political in one impassioned sweep, and who rose to fame in French café life in the fifties, gave a revolutionary voice to a post-war youth. Baudelaire's introspective lyrics are complemented by Brel's socio-political concerns, although the latter too always returns to the great themes of love and death, and it is these two opposite but reconciled poets who came to assert an influence on Almond's work of this period. It was also a time of considerable self-reflection. 'It got to the point', he commented at the time, 'where I was reading things people had written about me and thinking well, I'm not really like that and then wondering whether perhaps I was. Over the last few years I've been trying to find myself; trying to come to that place in my life where I could gather everything around me and say "This is me, this is what I've learnt and this is who I am."'

With his contract with Virgin dissolved, 1987, with the exception of two European tours, one in the spring and one later in the year, was a low-key time for the singer. But a surprise single, the duet with Sally Timms, 'This House Is A House Of Troubles', an Almond composition tied to a volatile domestic melodrama, was issued to considerable critical acclaim, although the eminently saleable release failed to make any bite on the commercial market. 'This House Is A House Of Troubles' followed in the tradition of hermetic recordings that Almond has put out over the years. There was 'Skin' released in 1984 under the name of The Burmoe Brothers, his contributions to 'Guiltless' and 'Stolen Kisses' from the Psychic TV album *Force The Hand Of Chance*, 'The Hungry Years' which he had recorded with Andi Sex Gang for a compilation *The Whip*, his work with Clint Ruin on the little known 'Flesh Volcano' EP, and a whole listing of discographic rarities.

By the time Almond made his next British appearances at the Astoria Theatre, London on December 13th, and 14th, a one off pacifier to his British admirers extended to a second show by popular demand, he had disbanded The Willing Sinners. He was now backed by La Magia, comprising Annie Hogan, Billy McGee, and Steve Humphries, a minimal unit who were to remain with him until their dispersal in 1989. Almond's two shows at the Astoria were positive energy displays in which new songs like 'The Sensualist', 'Tears Run Rings', and 'King Of The Fools' were offered an introductory profile, and so was Gene Pitney's 'Something's Gotten Hold Of My Heart', an encore premonitory of the massive solo hit the song was later to prove. These were difficult times for Almond, and despite the prominence of video cameras recording the shows for Japanese television, his position as an outsider had never been more pronounced. 'People always expect the worst from me,' he commented later, 'and when they do, I'll always come along with something to overthrow their expectations. When the Virgin deal broke down, and I was offered a contract with EMI, the mischief in me said, Right! Let's do something that's really accessible now.'

The two Astoria nights were confirmation of the artist's protean versatility. Almond on stage with his hair gelled to resemble Elvis Presley's indomitable quiff, and dressed in a simple black leather jacket and jeans, played the role of a diva to his front row admirers. There were hints of change in the air, and the introductory song, 'The Stars We Are' with its nostalgic look back to childhood, and the evocation of autumn implied by those *"hazy amber days"* set the tone for a transitional concert. The singer, using his past as a reference point, was clearly more occupied with looking to the future and the new songs which he was to preview. In an enthusiastic review of the concert Louise Gray endorsed everyone's feelings when she noted: "Almond's characteristic is the accessibility, the personalisation of emotion, so open-hearted, you'd have to be dead to be unmoved... This is a rare talent, and I imagine that if he worked anywhere less stiff-lipped than Britain, Almond would have already been recognised for the star he undoubtedly is."

There was to be a long interval before the autumn 1988 release of *The Stars We Are* LP, with its corresponding European tour; and denied the creative latitude he had enjoyed at Virgin, Almond was held to considerable commercial pressure by EMI. The latter were anxious that their newly signed artist shouldn't jeopardise his commercial potential by aberrant lapses into homoerotic imagery, or by writing about subjects likely to be outlawed by the media. Almond's career as a recording artist depended on his realising a successful album for EMI, and to a certain degree on reacquiring a redemptive public image after the black halo that had surrounded him during his Virgin years.

The eighteen months that existed between the release of *Mother Fist And Her Five Daughters* and *The Stars We Are* were broken in March 1988 by the publication of Marc Almond's book of poems *The Angel Of Death In The Adonis Lounge*. Brought out by a small independent publisher, The Gay Men's Press, the book attracted considerable attention, and its controversial melange of themes were characteristically infused with its author's obsessions: love, sex, and death. Evoking a pre-AIDS world of New York backroom bars, and twisting a knife into the pains of unrequited or impossible love, Almond explored avenues already made familiar by his song lyrics, but given a greater confessional honesty by the freedom from media censorship, and the emotional density that the printed word affords. The poems and lyrics collected in *The Angel Of Death In The Adonis Lounge* provide an autobiographical itinerary of Almond's salient preoccupations. The writing belongs to the night side of life, the cultic tilt towards underworlds, the Crowleyan celebration of sex as illuminative magic. Almond's lyrics are a form of alchemy, they transmute base or black matter into gold, they discover the rubies in the gutter, and the angel inside the rent boy. There is of course a difference in our response to a word held for the prolongation of a note, and the sensory assimilation of that same word on the page; but Almond's art as a lyricist is inseparable from his virtues as a poet. His essentially romantic sensibility puts him directly in line with Jacques

Brel, in that both men incorporate poetry into their lyrics, a quality that distinguishes both of them from most other contemporary lyricists. Almond's poetry like Brel's has a particular flavour, one that smells of dead roses, ports, the sexual aftermath, rain as it opens old wounds, crinkled leather and burnt sugar. Every form of love is the same love in its human and spiritual aspirations, and even if Almond and Brel differ in their sexual polarities, the intense passion that both convey towards the impossibility of a romantic ideal marks them with a particular brand of tormented genius.

Right from the book's opening poem 'Lonely, Lonely' a theme is found that proves constant, the loneliness of the sexual hunter or outsider in his nocturnal journey through the city. The poem's shock juxtaposition between an imaginary blue dahlia and an image of lubricious sleaze sounds a note of immediate surprise. *"Send me blue dahlias:/A bucket of spit/To moisten the slick of your thighs."* Most of the poems are night poems: they accentuate what we do on the reverse side of the day, they talk of loneliness, insomnia, masturbation, the sublimation of sexual fantasies, and the adventurer out in the night in search of someone or something to alter his life. The angel of death as it features in the book's title poem has *"Rock black nipples/And thick black prick."* His function is ambivalently cast between retribution and redemption. This angel is *"as rich as hashish"*, but he is also deadly in the way that Rilke tells us in the first of the 'Duino Elegies', "Every angel is terrible." Angels feature strongly in Almond's songs, both as an incitement to death through lust, and as beneficent guardians who are invoked to help the desperate lover. 'Who if I cried would hear me?' Rilke questions, and in deep pain we hope and expect to be heard. Exhausting our own sensory intervention, we look for divine mediators. Wim Wenders in his film *Wings Of Desire* brings the angel vitally alive to a modern ethos. The angelic walk-ins retain human characteristics, but possess divinized qualities that allow them to act as visible and invisible agents. A singer should be able to suggest an ambience in which there are propitiatory angels, be they black or white.

Most of Almond's poems could readily become lyrics for song, and its the interchangeability of the two that gives all of his work the integral feel of poetry. It's in 'The New York Poems' that his life as a decadently hedonistic sensualist, and as a sensitive observer of a backroom bar scene in which crack and fistfucking predominate, comes lividly to the foreground. The sequence portrays every club fetish, drag queens like The Crimson Diva, Puerto Rican boys on the make, Magda-Sade blowing twenty young men at the Hellfire Club, a locker room party in which there are *"Tubs of grease/And paper towels/In the warmth/Of New York's bowels"*, gay sex on Christopher Street Pier, and the whole desperate charge and hyped thrill of anonymous sex as Almond describes it in a pre-plague New York. Some of these poems link up directly with songs like 'Disease And Desire' and 'Ruby Red'. Almond's perception finds the exact lean metaphors to describe a scene which is beautiful for its anomalies. There are pre-op transsexuals, greatly prized for the dichotomy of possessing female breasts and a penis. One is encountered on Christopher Street Pier: *"There's a great pair of tits/On view,/And cocks the American way/Real big and thick and cut."* Almond encounters in the real, a world as exotic as that about which de Sade and Genet fantasise in their novels. The latter two writers created a compensatory world for their sexual frustration, and dreamt of a retributive sex which would shock all social conventions. Almond's New York is the materialisation of Sadean fantasies, and one admires the courage needed to externalise a world of coded initiates through the medium of poetry. Clubs represent stations of the cross to their devotees. Members enter hermetic orders and emerge at dawn as the sky begins to redden, their leather costumes serving as the only clue to identity. Almond's poems evoke something of that sense of nocturnal excess and orgy. They are like torches pulled from the fire and carried out to the light. The song 'Vaudeville And Burlesque' on *Tenement Symphony* vindicates the reckless lives of those who have taken *"Every powder every pill"* and are still here to vindicate their actions.

In a 1988 interview, Almond was to comment on the relationship between seeing and doing, voyeur and participant, and the link between secrecy and exposure, and his views are directly pertinent to an understanding of his poems and songs. 'I think I'm usually a participant as well as a voyeur' he told John Wilde. 'I'll always be a voyeur in the sense that I look at things, take them in, write about them. But I've always been right in there as well. It's like getting the keys to the city. I'm always trying to discover worlds behind locked doors, secret places. I'm totally involved but, at the same time, I'm separate and apart from it all. It's great to have that control. When you can dip a toe in and retreat if it's too cold. But you can stick your whole body in if you want to.' This ambivalence towards role taking is very much a part of diva mystique. The dual possibilities surrounding any diva action allow for its various construement, and are usually a comment on equally unresolved gender. Is it a man or woman who operates in this instance, and so the mystery remains.

In the poem 'Star II' Almond writes of how *"In the circus/In the square/We are part/Of a cryptic ritual."* This ritual is part possession and part exorcism. The poet is both fascinated and repelled by evil, but he will attract black angels in order to realise the beauty in that darkness. The song 'Real Evil', the B-side to the remixed single version of 'Only The Moment', gives voice to a similar dilemma, the power authorised by evil and the heightened sense of innocence that its use instates. It was a subject that preoccupied Baudelaire in all of his writings, and Huysmans in his two great psychological studies of decadence, *La Bas* and *A Rebours*. Almond has taken up the theme and translated the dilemma into song. Part of the opposition to his work is that he chooses to explore areas of life in song that involve painful honesty and self-reflection, subjects which find little sympathy with a materialistic public. If Baudelaire had chosen to be a mid-nineteenth century tenor, he would arguably have sung about themes every bit as controversial as Marc Almond's lyrics.

The poems in *The Angel Of Death In The Adonis Lounge* explore intense recurring obsessions, and there's little room outside these preoccupations for an alternative world. It's a poetry that looks at the great metaphysical absolutes through experiential values. The poet in search of the midnight sun, or the perfect stranger with gold in his eyes. The Adonis Lounge Almond reminds us is for the terminal and the lonely, with the emphasis on the latter.

Marc Almond's first single for EMI 'Tears Run Rings' was released in August of the same year as a precursor to *The Stars We Are* album. A return to a more recognisably commercial formula, and backed by a record company anxious to have Almond chart, the single skirted the edges of the Top Twenty proving once again that Almond could effortlessly slip in and out of cult and commercial profiles. While the song lacked overt homoerotic imagery, there were buried references to the gay predicament under Thatcher: *"They're bringing back the old rules/To please the few."* A melodically optimistic song, the lyrics were nonetheless infused with the sadness that characterises most of Almond's work; but the opening lines are glorious, *"On heavenly rain/You came into my life"*, with its mythic connotations of the god Zeus impregnating Danae with his golden shower. Angels and children enter the lyrics as components of innocence, those omniscient angels who are the light-givers in Marc Almond's lyrics.

Given that Almond's three previous singles had been denied air-play, and that suspicion of his work was at its highest amongst media censors, it was a considerable achievement to have ressurected his career in this way. Both EMI and their recording artist were determined to come up with a sound that would be more immediately accessible to the public, yet Almond was to express displeasure at being placed in a small recording studio in North London for *The Stars We Are* sessions. And while there's little artistic compromise in Almond's broodingly despairing lyrics, the more densely layered musical texture and the inclusion of a number of catchy up-beat songs like 'Tears Run Rings', 'Bitter Sweet', and 'Something's Gotten Hold Of My Heart' ensured that the album would prove more marketable than the acoustic *Mother Fist And Her Five Daughters*.

Almond was prolific with interviews to support his new creative venture, and was certainly no stranger to the recurring pattern in his career of rebirth or realignment. He was being given another chance and he rose to it tenaciously. He spoke not only of the current metamorphosis that his music and person were undergoing, but also of love, sainthood, evil, guilt, and being a star. He talked of AIDS and the neurotic fear of being infected, and also of an accreting S&M violence that had invaded the gay scene. He spoke of how 'In New York the ultimate act was starting to happen – killing someone through pleasure and pain. Bodies were found in a club called The Mineshaft. At that point the whole scene started to get very creepy.'

These certainly weren't the subjects that orthodox singers discussed in music interviews, and Almond's deep knowledge of arcane, nocturnal sexual lore increased his status as angel and devil inhabiting the same body. This conflict apparent in all his best material was to be reflected in his new set of songs, and to remain the contentious metaphysical gristle of his subsequent thought and writings. And in the same interview Almond was to side with the reverse side of anonymous sex, and to talk about the need for a greater closeness in gay love. 'So in a way I welcome the return to sensuality and erotica – closer experiences – rather than pure animalism. It's just unfortunate that an unpleasant disease had to come along to turn things round.'

Difficult for Marc Almond was the need to maintain a tenuous balance between his private and public worlds. Journalists anticipating sensationalism gravitate to his person hoping for confessional salicity; but Almond will only be drawn so far before rightly retreating into privacy. But there's a very real sense when he comes on stage that he inhabits a private world very different to that of his audience.

Almond spoke too of his inner debate with the concept of evil, and as an extension to it, his attraction to flawed beauty. 'Well sometimes I sit down and wonder how evil I've been in my life. I always come to the conclusion that I'm not an evil person... Making records is my confession box, a chance and an excuse to exorcise the demons inside me.' And of deformed beauty, the characteristic most often described by decadent literature with its aesthetic fascination with vice and sleaze, Almond expressed a strong standpoint. 'Beauty can floor me, leave me weak, ruin me. I can become a slave to it. But the people I'm attracted to usually have something ugly or deformed about them. I like beauty that's flawed. I find bland beauty very unsensual. It doesn't interest me at all. A flawed beauty seems more vulnerable and accessible. It's more dangerous in a way.'

The Stars We Are is a work of measured vocal achievement, and the tumultuous strings, horns, tympani, and piano provide the full complement to his voice that the singer needed in order to contend for commercial success. And that voice had once again improved, paradoxically having reviewers claim that a consummate technique had done away with the communicating passion of his earlier work. They demanded the untamed bruising of notes, rather than the balladeer's tenor pitch. But no matter, the album was a fine one, and the singer's preoccupations were taken up in the title track, a melancholy, poignant look back at childhood innocence, the 'reckless immaturity' that creates beds out of floors, disrespect for adults, and the whole paradisiacally exclusive kingdom that childhood seems to offer. We can't go back to that state but we can retrieve it through memory associations. Time recalled is time recreated, for we transpose the past to the present, we bring a mature set of experiences to bear on what at the time were spontaneous values. The lyric simplicity of 'The Stars We Are' is ideally suited to the reflective theme, and the song is accented by the disquieting image of loneliness: *"And to sit in the dark/Of my lonely room/Made it all seem so cruelly real."* The notions of illusion and loss, pain and redemption, love and rejection, good and evil, all the conflicting opposites that make up the contrariness of life, Almond himself being no stranger to the practise of strangulating happiness, are the resiliently emotive themes that run through the lyrics. And what has them live is the passionate honesty of the voice; it's impossible to listen to Marc Almond without situating him direct in one's living room, so close is the sense of communication afforded by his compassionate tone. Each time we listen to a Marc Almond record it's the equivalent of a private concert. His work gives no least impression that he is situated in a recording studio, or separate from the listener. His music is an endearing consoler, an intimate friend which becomes a constant support in life.

'Bitter Sweet', the second single to be released from the album was an up-beat bite at the paradox, a song that savoured of citric and sweet tangs, and formidably incorporated Houdini and Byron into its cast, with Almond maintaining a belief in illusion, and the moon living in his head as a symbol of inner space. Pleasure and pain, hope and dejection, love and hate, all these components come together in 'Bitter Sweet'. Almond was unconditionally articulate about his method: 'What I like to do with words, what I find myself doing with words, is to use an over-romantic image (something so sweet it's almost sickly) and stick it next to something that's dirty or brutal. So that it seems to cut through... It's beautiful brutality that I aim at. You lull people into a sense of sweetness and hit them with something that jars.'

Beautiful brutality was later to be the theme of 'Beautiful Brutal Thing' on *Tenement Symphony*, an album in which the cutting edge is much closer to gay experience, than the more buried form of homosexuality consistent on *The Stars We Are*. Songs like 'Your Kisses Burn', 'The Sensualist', and 'The Very Last Pearl', all explore the relationship between having and losing, reality and illusion.

There was considerable optimism surrounding the album's release, and barring Simon Reynolds' dismissal of it in *Melody Maker*, on grounds that smacked of personal dislike rather than objective critical assessment, *The Stars We Are* was well received and praised for its accessibility. Reviewing the LP for the *NME*, William Smith was generous in his praise that Almond had finally secured a sound which "while satisfying every record company's dream of unique commerciality, actually boasts the cinematic songs that suit his grandiose aspirations." Smith went on to conclude that Almond's work provides, "a perfect antidote to a pop world inhabited by singers curiously bereft of voices, songs which surrender to their mechanical treatment, and musicians served with redundancy notices by automatons."

Sounds called the album "a refreshing and convincing testament to a revitalised star," and viewed Almond's achievement as a dignified compromise in which the singer had returned to an idiosyncratic blend of pop music. If this was the case, then Almond's lyrics seemed glaringly incompatible with anti-literate trends in commercial music. He was once again out on a long limb, attempting to melodically insinuate his way into the charts, while lyrically remaining integral to the poetics of *chanson*. This dichotomy was evident in the titles of songs like 'The Very Last Pearl', and 'She Took My Soul In Istanbul'. The sensual, sultry poetry that infused the lyrics was little likely to appeal to a popular market. There was a bite of green poison circulating in all the songs, and none seemed more autobiographical than 'The Sensualist', in which the protagonist has known a surfeit of sensuality, and yet is still vampirical for sanguine experience. Almond had first introduced the song at his December 1987 London Astoria concerts, and his role in extolling erotomania as ecstasy seemed a natural extension of his sensual life. The need for sexual experience can grow to a desperate addiction, the hunter out in the night searching for bodies. Sex is the most elusive of all habits for it can never be properly satisfied, and so we return to it again and again on a psychophysical plane, the need to engage our obsessive fantasies often taking predominance over the physical act itself. Sublimation is never complete. The sensualist of Almond's song can never find appeasement. His gratification comes through the masochistic impulse to savour near asphyxiation, and to know through fear *"A kiss tastes sweeter on the brink of life."* It's this pushing out to a dangerous edge which affords the song its particular twist.

Almond had originally intended the album to comprise a series of duets, and something of his original intention surfaced in Nico's contribution to 'Your Kisses Burn', Suraya Ahmed's vocals to 'Istanbul', and Agnes Bernelle's duet on 'Kept Boy'. 'Your Kisses Burn' was made with reluctance on Nico's part, and she was to die soon after recording the song, but the lyrics manifest the familiar contention in Almond's songs of love turning to hate, and fire to ice. Passion is met with vicious disdain, and the fire fuelling love becomes all consuming: *"I'll kill you/With this final fire/And lead you to/Your funeral pyre"*, Nico sings in a chilling gothic tone, against Almond's equally portentous threats. The song seems a macabre litany to love as destruction.

Although it took EMI nearly six months to realise the latent commercial appeal inherent in Almond reviving the old Gene Pitney ballad, 'Something's Gotten Hold Of My Heart', there seemed little doubt on first hearing that the Greenaway/Cook song was ideally suited to Marc Almond's voice, and to chart approval. The song's passionately overwrought importunacy, and its use of the colour symbolism blue, scarlet, and grey, all fitted with Almond's own preoccupations and imagery. When the song featuring contributions from Gene Pitney was finally released in January 1989, it went to the top of the British charts and stayed there for a month, in addition to becoming a major international hit. And while for Almond, success was an act of justified revenge on his detractors, it was disappointing to his devotees that accolades should come through a cover version, and not through the singer's own compositions, a pattern that has been steadily repeated throughout his subsequent solo career.

One of the album's underrated successes seems to me to be the fragile elegy, 'The Frost Comes Tomorrow', a plaintive song which employs dream imagery, a symbolic *"white house of dreams"* and the metaphoric association of birds with angels. An incredibly delicate song, and sung with a gossamer sensitivity, it's one that has rarely been submitted to live performance, but should be included in any compendium of the singer's elegies. Dreams are important to Marc Almond's lyric impulse, and in an interview given at the time of the release of *The Stars We Are* he talked of one recurring nightmare. 'There was one nightmare I used to have all the time. In it a big cage or dome was coming over the bed and it was closing in and confining me in a little space. In the dream I get up on the bed and bang on the dome trying to get out. Then I'd wake up and I'd be over the other side of the bedroom. Things would be knocked all over the floor, my legs would be all cut, and I'd be banging on the bedroom door. I'm claustrophobic anyway and the dream has some sort of womb-like association with claustrophobia.'

Some of Almond's acute anxiety attacks, claustrophobia, and fear of crowds, all subjects that he had talked about in the mid-eighties, were of course triggered by the use of Valium. Almost all long term users of benzodiazepines suffer claustrophobic or agoraphobic symptoms, as well as related anxiety attacks, and while this particular type of tranquilliser is prescribed precisely to allay these symptoms, they do over sustained use magnify secondary symptoms. They generate panic. To Almond, like so many others, Valium had become a way of life in the attempt to insulate himself from potential anxiety.

There were other courageous admissions to the press at the time like, 'I think you could safely assume I'm bisexual. I don't shout it from the rooftops, I just am and it just is.' It was the album's deeply subjective contents, *"And if one day I don't wake up/Remember I was good upon reflection"*, which disturbed the less emotionally generous, like the sceptical Simon Reynolds. The Thatcher/Major era of conformism has been brutally antagonistic to writers, singers and artists who have the temerity to risk a personal vision. Distrustful of the decadent hero, the outré raconteur of confessional vice, the voice up-front backed by grandiose strings, Reynolds complained that, "His work is like some exhaustive and public diary, all bald depiction and slightly naff fantasy ('She Stole My Heart In Istanbul'). The insatiable quest for self-knowledge that can drive someone to rewrite a diary from two years back, in order to include the insights of hindsight, can be touching in a friend. Certainly, it's better than being in poor contact with your heart of hearts. But is Almond's relentless self-scrutiny turning up anything worth bringing to public attention? I fear not."

The reaction typified the anti-romanticism of a dead generation's belief in materialism. Pearls, angels, Istanbul, the scarlet city, banners of love, the scent of Turkish oil, and a love that entertained death as its catharsis, were little in tune with prevailing beliefs.

As part of the drive to promote his resurrected career, Almond undertook his first full scale British tour for three years, taking in on the way dates at Glasgow Barrowlands, Newcastle City Hall, Nottingham Rock City, Manchester Ritz, Liverpool Royal Court, Leeds University, Birmingham Powerhouse, Bristol Studio, Portsmouth Guildhall, and two nights at the London Victoria Palace.

The tour was also to extend that autumn to dates in Germany, Holland, and Austria. Performing generous two hour shows, Almond interspersed material from his new album with a solid nucleus of old songs, a number of Jacques Brel ones which were to include a moving a cappella version of 'The Lockman', a revamped version of 'Traumas', an acutely sensitive version of 'When A Girl Loves A Girl', the exotically phrased psychodramas lived out in 'Melancholy Rose', 'Anarcoma', and 'Ruby Red', the sensual flirtation of 'In Your Bed', the moribundly evocative 'There Is A Bed', and glances back to the past with the elegiac 'I Who Never', and 'Tenderness Is A Weakness.'

Almond brought an additional authority to the stage for 'The Stars We Are' tour, his manner being less concessionary to audience repartee, and his determination to prove himself to a new record company pronounced through a thoroughly professional and dynamized stage act. Pared down to the three piece musical accompaniment of La Magia, the voice benefited by being brought right up front in all its nuances of emotive passion, although overstated percussion sometimes tore across the singer's phrasing, as well as the tendency for La Magia to play songs too fast. There was an over-rushed nervousness to some of the arrangements which didn't allow the voice to properly warm.

A marginally disenchanted Alastair McKay reporting on the Glasgow Barrowlands concert described the stage set as "anchored by a candlelit Hammer Horror throne", and props that served as "a suitable backdrop for Almond's lurches into amateur dramatics. Inevitably the stage is awash with red light and star-chasing spotlights. Equally inevitably Almond eventually slides into his throne, leaving only his face illuminated in time honoured schlock horror tradition."

Ideally suited to the gothic stage set was Almond's atmospheric rendition of Baudelaire's 'Remorse Of The Dead', one of the highpoints of his 1988 concerts, sung over staccato percussion and piano. Audiences attending these shows could have no idea that they would be virtually the last full-scale concerts that the artist would perform for four years. And what emerged from 'The Stars We Are' concerts was a greater sense of detachment on Almond's part, there was a standing back from direct commitment as though he was trying to create a persona for the songs rather than an absolute identification with the material.

Almond's commercial profile seemed to have receded again after his autumn tour, and then suddenly after years of releasing exemplary singles which were never taken up outside his cult, he blazed a meteoric trail to the top of the charts in January 1989, with the Gene Pitney duet, 'Something's Gotten Hold Of My Heart'. I personally feel the song loses by Pitney's intrusion, his limited pitch and flawed vibrato cutting right across the exuberant lift that Almond's voice afforded the song. 'It's weird', Almond commented at the time, 'His sons have got some of my records, and I've got 10 or 12 of his. He's always been one of my favourite singers. He had so many great songs, and I always thought he was cool. And I sent him a tape of my version of the song, and he said yes.' The result was a single almost unbalancing in its ubiquitous success, and the meteoric rise in chart status was greeted suspiciously by Almond's closest fans. There was the feeling that Almond was being sold short, and that the general public were buying this song irrespective of his past achievements, and with little acknowledgement of the album from which it came. And the success proved to be one that suspended Almond in the void, it was an instant supernova that left a trail of cooling stardust. But for Almond, the collaboration proved to be one of personal satisfaction. 'It was the perfect meeting – he had his limo and I had mine, and we recorded the video at three o'clock in the morning in the freezing cold in a neon junkyard in Las Vegas. It was surreal. I kept thinking back to when I was young, seeing Gene Pitney on *Ready, Steady, Go*. And then X years later there I was singing a song that Pitney had made into a hit years before, and realising that he was here because of me.'

A few months prior to his abrupt glory trail, Almond in a 'Material World' feature for the *NME* had given a brief biography of personal likes and dislikes. It's interesting to quote some of his preferences by way of clues to his inner map at the time. Amongst his favourite things he listed "New York taxi rides, petrol, Triumph Bonnevilles, Angels (Hell's and Heaven's), tattoos, borscht, absinthe, amyl, the sea and its fruits, flamenco, passion, sensitivity, sense of humour, string sections, discretion." And pertinent to our study he named amongst his favourite music, "Jacques Brel, Les Baxter, John Barry, Arabic, Flamenco, Big '60s Pop (especially The Walker Brothers and Gene Pitney), Bhangra, Léo Ferré, Lee Hazelwood, Brecht and Weil, Country." And as a guide to his reading tastes, he included amongst his favourite books, "Huysmans' *Against Nature*, Ray Bradbury's *Something Wicked This Way Comes*, Gustav Davidson's *A Dictionary Of Angels*, Samuel R Delany's *Tides Of Lust*, Truman Capote's *In Cold Blood*, and Paul Verlaine's *Hommes Et Femmes*."

This exotically flavoured cocktail of personal obsessions seems consonant with the infrastructure of Almond's work with its feverish blend of romance, decadence, diva conduct, and street glitter. And it was something of these ingredients which suffused Almond's next single, an extended version of 'Only The Moment', from *The Stars We Are* LP, backed by an exquisitely sultry remix of 'She Took My Soul In Istanbul' – The Blue Mosque mix, and the threateningly incisive 'Real Evil', delivered in a mean whisper to the accompaniment of a Hammond organ. But there was to be no immediate return to chart glamour, and this fine self-penned song was to return to the court of Almond's devotees, rather than to the public who had ephemerally courted 'Something's Gotten Hold Of My Heart'.

The spectacular zenith achieved by the singer at the beginning of 1989, was as the year wore on to result in a partial eclipse. The singer was badly received at the Pink Pop Festival in Laandgraaf Holland in May, the out of doors festival proving unsuited to the intimate narration of his songs. Using reverb on most songs, Almond bravely attempted the impossible and won his way through a set undermined by a partly unsympathetic audience.

For the remainder of 1989 Almond dipped out of public attention. He wasn't to play live again until the end of the year, when he undertook a powerful performance of Brel songs at La Cigale in Paris, and a handful of acoustic concerts to promote his *Jacques* LP in Europe, Britain being signally ignored due to its unsympathetic response to the album of Brel songs. And with the defection and disbandonment of La Magia, Almond was accompanied at these acoustic concerts by Martin Watkins on piano, the beginnings of a collaboration which has helped inspire Marc Almond not only to a sympathetic reappraisal of old songs, but to some of his most sensitive vocal performances. Martin Watkins is in no manner a mere substitute for Annie Hogan, he is an accomplished classically trained pianist, whose inspired arrangements have allowed Almond's voice to warm to an increased vocal pitch. He has been instrumental in assisting Almond reach vocal maturity, and in helping him establish the seriousness of that claim in select European venues, and in Russia. In the summer prior to becoming a largely acoustic artist, Almond had reached exhaustion in attempting to play to audiences attuned to rock music. His last stab at that arena had been as a support act to The Cure. 'We survived the ordeal,' he remembers, 'but our inexperience in supporting another band and choosing songs for huge audiences really showed... We kept shortening the set, but people would chuck rocks at us. It became a case of survival. Am I going to live through this night?'

For the better part of a decade Marc Almond had been incorporating Jacques Brel songs into his live repertoire, and Brel songs had turned up on his first two solo LPs with the Mambas. And before leaving Virgin he had laid down in the studio most of the material which in a revised fashion was to appear on *Jacques* and its successor *Absinthe*, the two French albums. Assisted by new versions of Brel's original lyrics, as well as keeping to some of the fine Mort Schuman translations of the songs, versions which Scott Walker had used before him, Almond largely at his own expense, worked on the songs between 1986-89 at Milo Studios, and won the significant approval of Jacques Brel's widow for his passionately tragic identification with the Belgian poet's lyric intentions. Brel's own combination of evocative poetics and a coarse-grained sanguine reality, fitted directly with Almond's own lyric characteristics and untamed manner of singing. Something of Brel's agonised intensity can often be heard in Almond's desperate search to find the impossibly wounded note. It's the cry of the beast inside the angel's mouth. Both men sound like they are caressing silk before furiously slashing it with a knife.

The expectation of Almond releasing a Brel album had been riding high over the years, but in Britain there was a muted critical reception offered *Jacques*, and the feeling that Almond had not delivered to form. *Jacques* was to appear with low-key publicity from Some Bizzare at the end of 1989, almost a year after the surprise chart success of 'Something's Gotten Hold Of My Heart'.

Jacques is an album of unrelieved gravity, it's a journey that takes in dream states, vulnerability, love and its counterpart death, and the whole emotional spectrum implied by solitude. The songs demand that the singer lays himself bare, and adopts the honesty of someone engaged in self-confession while waiting for the executioner's bullet. In Brel, as in Almond, it's the immediate which is emphasised: the moment we hold back before losing it to flux, the sensation so intense that we ask it lasts for a lifetime. The songs record those moments in which pleasure can't be separated from pain, and into which we enter so intensely that the memory of the experience becomes constellated as poetic image. It's now and it's always, and rather than lose the sensation we take refuge in the idea of death as a consoling angel or lover. We would die from one love into another.

It's such a note that Almond achieves in 'I'm Coming' (*J'Arrive*), the most passionately assimilated of his Brel renditions, in which the offering of chrysanthemums afforded the dead in French cemeteries is linked also to a journey towards the lover. Almond steps direct into this narrative of an encounter between love and death, the self and the other. The song is one of the finest of his released studio recordings, and I think, a more emotively challenging response to the song than Juliette Greco's interpretation. Almond is lifted up by the song, he moves towards the *dénouement* with a lover or death as though he is on a train taking him to nowhere other than the solitary space in which he can be alone. His voice is like a summons to the living and the dead, it pleads to be heard in the great silence surrounding our inner actions, and in the ineffable mystery associated with death. Voice should be about extending communication to the dead. "Almond has been known to sing as if singing changed the world", wrote John Wilde in his review of *Jacques*, before finding fault with what he considered to be Almond's inability to locate the heart of Brel's work, and to deliver in accordance with his usual innate passion. Wilde's criticism was founded on what he felt to be Almond's detachment from the originals. "It is as though he has fallen into these songs and found himself unable to fill them out, as though he has been unable to locate the heart of Brel's work. Marc sounds strangely underwhelmed."

There is a legitimate criticism here from one of Almond's loyal sympathisers, in that his versions of 'If You Go Away', and 'My

Death', songs which have cried in his arms on stage, are strangely understated in their appearance on *Jacques*. It may be also that Almond was trying to distinguish his versions from Scott Walker's versions of these two songs, and that he felt that a slight remove of the emotional drive of Walker's phasing would allow the songs a new reading in English.

Listening to Almond's heartbreaking a cappella version of 'The Lockman' (*L'Eclusier*), we are made aware not only of the intensity of his rendition, but also of how hard it is to put poetry into song. The fragility of his version, and he had first aired this song at the Amsterdam Brel Festival in 1987, hangs on the thread between life and death which is very much the theme of the song, with the lockman discovering the drowned, which are, metaphorically, the dark chimeras of his unconscious. Almond's version trembles in its phrased delicacy, and we feel the thanatic bite of Brel's original in his poignant reaching to communicate with the individual death inside himself, as well as the collective dead. Interpretation depends on magic quite independent of voice training, and it's this faculty which Almond brings to song, as though he lifted the veil surrounding words and disclosed the concealed mystery. Singers need to be connected with magic in the same manner as poets sensitise that psychic force in their situation of the image on the page. "It is necessary to admit that a common denominator unites the sorcerer, the poet and the madman which is none other than magic. It is the flesh and blood of poetry." This truth articulated by the surrealist poet Benjamin Peret, also holds good with singers. The resonating timbre of an individual voice is made distinctive by the way in which it communicates inner with outer. Almond sings to establish a bridge between inner disquiet and its attempted exorcism through voice. The particle X involved is magic. So many singers fail to fit their songs, there's a measurable gap between voice and lyrics, and Almond's own definition of a torch singer as 'someone who burns a torch for loss, unrequited love and heartache in his or her songs' gives some notion of his passionate commitment. 'The songs burn with passion like a flaming torch' he stresses.

The overall mood of *Jacques* is sombre and autumnal. Brel's songs offer no resolutions to the dilemmas they engage, and are founded on paradoxical tensions. Love, even if it is won, is threatened by death or the solitary vacuum within the lover. There is nothing popular about Brel's songs in the way that lyricists so often attempt narrative conclusions to their songs. Almond, who is close to Brel in his own writing methods, perfectly takes up the Belgian singer's preoccupation with inner discord being reflected in political tensions. The anarchic themes expressed in 'The Devil (Okay)' (*Le Diable*), and in 'Never To Be Next' (*Au Suivant*), are acerbically subversive in their undermining of ideological structures, and the songs provide ideal personae for Almond to adopt. Almond has always been willing to adopt a satanic role in songs, and 'The Devil (Okay)', provides him with the chance to bring the devil above ground. And anyone who has witnessed his castanet-like heels-clicking live performances of 'Next', will know how deeply he empathises with a song that spits disrespect at the military, and recounts the experiences of a soldier undergoing his next dose of gonorrhoea, and one who is slapped on the ass by the lieutenant, thus invoking the homoeroticism implied by uniforms and male corporates.

Given that Almond is not only singing lyrics written for another language, but is also taking on another culture, he succeeds remarkably well in bringing these difficult songs alive. If some of the versions on *Jacques* seem to lack the driving commitment that he gives the songs in live performance, it's because some of the difficulties inherent in Brel's work are being overcome in the process of singing the songs in the studio. And there are real successes in the fine readings of 'Litany For A Return' (*Litane Pour Un Retour*), and 'The Town Fell Asleep' (*La Ville S'Endormait*), in which a lyrical tenderness pervades an elegiac theme. A song from Brel's last years, Almond had first sung 'The Town Fell Asleep' at the 1987 Convention, and the lyric simplicity of town, sky and stream come together within a poignantly observational context to afford moments of despairing gentleness.

Some of Almond's own writing, particularly the songs on *Mother Fist And Her Five Daughters* and *Enchanted*, seems to have learnt much from Brel's abilities to unify love and death, and in a later interview Almond was to expand on the importance of Brel to his own career. 'He was a huge influence on my work, a person writing about sex and death, and life and grit, characters from the street, prostitutes, outsiders. But at the same time he was very romantic. And I've always understood why he has such a big gay audience, even though he was a womaniser, and all his songs are about women. It's because his settings are so often the brothel, the bedroom, and the bar, places a lot of gay people know very well. So I related to his work, and I felt I had a right to, and it was part of my inheritance to sing his songs. *Jacques* was laughed at in this country, whereas in Europe it was the most acclaimed album I have ever recorded, and it brought out a whole new interest in Brel.'

Jacques is in some ways a lesser album than its opulent counterpart *Absinthe*, but the aura of loneliness surrounding the tautly apprehensive lyrics invests the songs as a whole with an agonizing sense of unrest, as though Brel's demons have likewise been summoned into attendance by Almond, and won't easily slink back to their abyssal underworld. These songs are like ghosts somatised by Almond's voice; presences who stare out of the mirror with blank eyes, the *doppelgänger* encountered in a railway carriage, the chuckle that hits your back in an empty alley, the words you never thought you would hear, but were there all along hidden in the deepest recess of your mind.

Jacques and *Absinthe*, or what are known as the French sessions, were the last recordings on which Almond was accompanied by his old nucleus of musicians, Annie Hogan, Billy McGee, Steven Humpheys, and Martin McCarrick. By the time of *Enchanted*, his second album for EMI, Almond was without a band, and has remained without one up until the time of writing. *Jacques* is a stripped down acoustic album, in the manner of *Mother Fist And Her Five Daughters*, and Almond's vocal approach to the songs is remarkably direct and lacking in the baroque flourishes which surface in his duende inspired singing, when florid embellishments aggrandise his gloriously liturgical notes.

The absence of publicity surrounding the British release of *Jacques* was a further comment still on the political ethos, with its material roots dug deep into concrete. Poetry that takes as its subject anything but social realism has gone underground, but only to burn brighter in the cult surrounding the imagination. In terms of durable and eventually posthumous recognition, Almond's two French albums are likely to remain high in the canon of his achievements as a singer.

Almond was gratified by the high praise accorded his album by Jacques Brel's widow, who wrote to him remarking on his songs being amongst the best interpretations of her dead husband's work. And there seems little point in comparing them to Scott Walker's, or Juliette Greco's renditions of individual songs, Almond has put his own idiosyncratic stamp on the material, and even if at times the album suffers from under-delivery, there's a solid nucleus of real successes to redress the songs which appear to lack this singer's passionate commitment.

By the time of releasing *Jacques*, Almond had grown sufficiently philosophic to be objective about public deprecation of introspectively structured songs. No longer seething with venomous recriminations against individual reviewers, his manner of approach had grown big enough to believe in serious work quite independent of its reception. 'You can never fulfil other people's expectations,' he was to comment, 'Whatever I do I can't win because it never matches up to what people expect. They want you to be the pervert prince of pop, the king of sleaze or the gothic romantic.'

It was once again a transitional time for Marc Almond. The opulent orchestration and accessibility of *The Stars We Are* album had been followed by the poetic lyricism of *Jacques*, and without a band or any immediate plans to tour it looked as if his career would be jeopardized by lack of immediate focus. But Almond's talent is indomitably resilient, and having broken with his past, and established himself as a European singer with the poetically resonant *Jacques*, he was to change direction yet again in the nineties, and to quickly re-establish himself as the only voice.

ORPHEUS IN RED VELVET

In keeping with his mastery of reconciling opposites, and his particular gift to move from profound cultic shadow back to the brutal scrutiny of the public spotlight, Almond followed up the tenebrously low-key *Jacques* with a more commercially polarised single 'A Lover Spurned' in February 1990. He had incorporated the latter song into his stage repertoire at both of his London Astoria concerts in December 1987, but rather surprisingly the song had been omitted from *The Stars We Are* LP. A melodramatic narrative about a lover seeking revenge for having been rejected, there's a characteristic element of overstated grandiosity given to lyrics which are quite fragile, but redeemed by a venomous injection of poison into the song's retributive theme. What should have been a midsummer release, given the song's passionate contents, was instead brought out in a cold, blue February, the cover boasting a Pierre et Gilles photograph of Almond, in which the intended object of his disquiet, a voluptuously miniaturized Marie France, stares out of the glass he is holding in his hand. The element of camp pastiche surrounding the record's visuals was not lost on Almond's admirers, and the single received its fair quota of mainstream play, the lyrics suggesting to a superficial listener that the contentious scene described is between a heterosexual couple. Produced by Stephen Hague, the single charted respectably in the twenties, but failed to make the corresponding commercial strides of his duet with Gene Pitney. This song, together with his next single 'The Desperate Hours', were to comprise the singles preceding the release of *Enchanted*, his second album for EMI. And perhaps what was missing from 'A Lover Spurned' was the passionate intimacy that informs Almond's timbre, Hague's production was too impersonally cold, and too public a statement for the register of passion in Almond's voice. There was a feeling amongst the more sensitive of Almond's devotees that EMI were discrediting his creative originality, and pushing him to undermine his virtuoso genius by compromising with technical productions for what remained romantic torch songs. It was the sense of alienation between lyric and music, and voice and production, human and inhuman, which gave 'A Lover Spurned' the feeling that the production team had never read the singer's lyrics. The song burns with the troubled apprehension of guilt, and in an interview given at the time Almond spoke of the prominence of this particular psychological state in his life. 'My major problem is guilt. I always wished I'd been brought up a Catholic, because then I could reason it out and blame it on my upbringing. I like symbolism and ritual, and Catholicism has plenty of that. Instead, I suffer guilt about everything. I feel guilty about being selfish and guilty about being mean.' Almond went on to reflect on his volatile temper, and the unpredictability of his frustrated rage at being unable to achieve the ultimate song. 'I've got such a bad temper. I used to shout all the time through frustration and when I couldn't communicate the sort of song I wanted to create. I always try and grab for things beyond my reach, or express things that can't properly be expressed, and create the perfect song that will encapsulate everything about my life. When it doesn't happen, which it never does, I take out my anger on someone else.'

Creativity is dependant not on the artist realising total vision, but rather approximating to that state, and the degree of incompletion manifested by the work is in turn the inspiration to renew that impulse. The romantic quest is always one of overload, the artist risking death in the process of aspiring to vision. The superhuman overreach to be found in the romantic sensibilities of Wagner and Mahler, the raid on the empyrean city evinced in the poetry of Blake, Shelley, Hölderlin, Rimbaud, and Lautréamont, are all tangents of that trajectory which reaches for the stars. The work is about getting there, the individual advancing universal consciousness by his or her unsparing efforts. Critics who write pejoratively of Marc Almond's overstrained reaching for the impossible in song, usually do so with scepticism rather than praise for the committed risk involved in the act.

Another attempt to breach the singles chart before the release of *Enchanted* was made with the romantic, flamenco-graced ballad, 'The Desperate Hours'. The song's portentous title had the listener anticipate the sort of extrapolated neuroses that Almond had delivered on *Torment and Toreros*, but the song proved to be objectively narrated, and without any saturation of pessimism. A melancholy ballad with a dramatic chorus, the song's eloquent romanticism was pitched to the right degree of sadness, and Almond was in fine voice to carry the theme with conviction. Like 'A Lover

Spurned', the song was eminently acceptable to the media, partly because it involved a boy/girl relationship, and partly for its accessibility as a love song. Avoiding all the usual clichés that categorize romance in lyric, Almond evokes an inner and outer landscape, a seascape with wind and shimmering stars, and a skull-faced moon, and a dream-like interior in which the lover's face is seen as the embodiment of an inner ideal. The song accommodates the androgyne, or the conception of bisexual consciousness, it's the feminine here who presents the masculine with flowers, and he who lives with their scent in his room. 'The Desperate Hours' made a smaller chart impact than 'A Lover Spurned'. I prefer the twelve inch mixes of both songs with their extended lyrics and instrumentation, but both singles introduced Almond to a wider public, in that they were given mainstream air-play, and secured video release on *Top Of The Pops*. EMI seemed determined to polish Almond's image, to have him conceal his mosaic of tattoos, to dress him in suits and frilly shirts, and to present him as a singer of poetic, but uncontroversial songs. But the commercial hype surrounding 'Something's Gotten Hold Of My Heart', was to prove an unrepeatable formula, and Almond genuinely risked alienating his hardcore fans by accepting the minor compromises dictated by his record company.

Almond's break with La Magia, excepting Billy McGee, meant that *Enchanted* was strictly a studio album, and not one that he would be able to promote through live performance. But the songs in their textural richness, and in their expansion of themes are amongst his finest, for he had assimilated Brel's art of objectifying the personal, and of writing through the medium of personae, rather than through continual first person confession. His new material proved indubitably that he has no British equal as a contemporary songwriter, and in an interview given as a preview to *Enchanted*, he spoke not only of his indebtedness to Brel, but of his wish to write of a world independent of his own life experience. 'I got very afraid of being too introspective in songs. I was writing about myself too much. My traumas had become a bit of a cliché. I used to deliberately search for adventure to take myself out of the boundaries of the ordinary in order to write something. There are times when I still need to do that. One of the reasons I like Jacques Brel is because he was brought up in a middle-class background, but tried to create a life that was an escape from those bourgeois roots. To an extent, I wanted to escape from my normal middle-class background, as I needed something more out of life, something else.'

What seemed to have arrived in Almond's life by the time of

recording *Enchanted*, was an element of greater detachment in his writing technique, and a removal from being the pressurized, street-harrassed Soho anomaly that he had been in the early to mid-eighties, with disaffected teenagers and weirdos turning up on his doorstep in Brewer Street. Mascara and eyeliner were still a feature of his appearance, but they had been thinned, and while the tattoos had expanded to an eschatological graffiti on his arms and shoulders, his small, nervous body was easily assimilated with the London crowds, and he seemed now in his early thirties to have acquired a considerable degree of self-knowledge, and to be more concentrated on the quality of his work rather than the presentation of self-image. The inflammatory side of him was also in check, and he no longer saw it as a mission of personal revenge to verbally castigate those with whom his work found little favour.

Enchanted suffers from a cold studio overproduction, and working for the first time without his familiar complement of musicians, Almond seems to have found an unsympathetic producer in Bob Kraushaar, whose Fairlight programming of instruments worked in contradistinction to the singer's emotively charged voice. An exotic and eclectic group of songs, *Enchanted* seemed a distillation of Almond's predominant musical concerns: French romantic chanson, Spanish flamenco, Arabic melodies, torch ballads, hypnotic dance music, and aspiring diva operatics. I find it the richest and most consummately lyrical of his albums, there's a sparkle to the poetry and a sense of Europeanism which places it quite outside of British limitations. That it should have been a taut acoustic album is no reflection on the quality of the songs. Some of the material on *Enchanted* was to find its way into the piano concerts that Almond staged in the early nineties, and there the songs take dramatic colouring from the acoustic arrangements.

By the time *Enchanted* was released in June 1990, the rift between Almond's predominantly European influences and the bland formula of British dance automatism had never been wider. His acoustic concerts had all been staged outside Britain, and *Enchanted* is in some ways the product of the artist's isolation. A courageous set of quixotic, exotic, lyrically inspired songs, *Enchanted*, despite the artist's subsequent criticism of it, is not any the less a sparkling achievement. It's customary for artists to praise their work in hand, and to consider the current project superior to the individual work which has preceded it, and then in retrospect to re-evaluate its meaning. Almond is no stranger to adopting this strategy, and has spoken of his disillusionment with the overall feel of *Enchanted*. 'It was a battle between me and the producer, me wishing to use real instruments and him wanting to programme it all into the Fairlight. It was too produced, and some of the heart and soul was taken out of the songs, and it really was the first time I hadn't enjoyed making an album.'

Enchanted was released without any plans on the artist's part to tour, and without the demonstrative publicity campaign surrounding the promotion of *The Stars We Are*. EMI clearly weren't going to push hard on this one, and the album was released to a favourable but unimpassioned critical response by the British press. The general reception was that Almond was repeating obsessive themes without placing new colours in the mosaic. Reviewers failed altogether to connect with the quality of the lyrics, and to recognise the significant expansion of subject matter which was in evidence on the new album. Inapposite references to Almond emulating Scott Walker, Edith Piaf, and Jacques Brel, had by now become critical cliché, and were as inappropriate as ever in their association with so individualistic an artist. We learn from our mentors in order to heighten our own potential, and creative awareness, we assimilate influences in order to compound our originality, and part of Almond's maturity on *Enchanted* is to have found a singular strength from the diverse singers who have explored a dramatic torch and cabaret genre of singing. Far from representing an aural collage of Almond's thematic idiosyncrasies, *Enchanted* seems to me to manifest an opening out of the artist's creative sensibility, his lyric impulse having never been wider or more generously focused. There were outstanding new compositions like 'Death's Diary', 'Toreador In The Rain', and 'Orpheus In Red Velvet'. The sumptuous imagery employed in these songs, and the paradoxical tension between good and evil as metaphysical absolutes, which they explore, gives them a visionary tone more in keeping with Brel than any other songwriter, but at the same time distinctly informed by Almond's own love of sensual imagery. 'Death's Diary', which I hope we will hear the singer perform live, adopts the panoramic awareness of death as the omnipotent confiscator of life. The demonic impishness that Almond often plays with as a stage persona finds its correlative in a song in which the satanic aspect of death is characterised through havoc and devastation. *"On Saturday night I took a country/Praying for the rain/Parched throats and swollen lips/Without a harvest grain/And I wiped out generations/And I'd do it all again."*

The whole dimensional sweep of a song like this, in which Almond has mastered the art of writing other than through directly personal experience, marked an important breakthrough with his work. His richly subjective material had always been projected through 'I', and it was the minute neurotic bibliographies of singers' lives which had led to Simon Reynolds protesting about what he considered to be an over-emphasis on private neuroses manifest in *The Stars We Are*. It's a problem of which Almond's not unaware, and in an interview given in 1990 he spoke precisely of the egomania which dominates so many recording artists' personalities. 'The whole music scene is a very selfish business. It's self-indulgent – you spend most of your life writing about yourself or singing about yourself, and when you're not doing that, you're talking about yourself in interviews... Also, everyone in this business is overpaid. When I was doing videos I used to think, "This is costing a fortune, and it's never even going to be shown on the television. Not if it's one of mine."'

It's this sort of ruthless honesty, together with an uncompromising perspective on the things that really do count – life, love, and death, which has kept Almond true to his own committed vision, rather than commercially manipulable as an image primed to sing hit material. There is an inexhaustable inventory of cover songs which Almond could convert into respectable successes, but he has rightly chosen only to cover songs which are directly linked to his own preoccupations. That same principle of integrity is applied to *Enchanted*, for the songs, no matter their slick technical production, are not popular pieces, and their lyrical vision directs them towards the province of poetry. There's an exhilaration too in songs like 'Carnival Of Life', and 'The Sea Still Sings', which had been absent from the singer's earlier work, and suggested that something of his own detraumatization was finding its way into the songs. 'Toreador In The Rain' is a colourful evocation of a favourite Marc Almond theme: the street boy who defies social redemption and chooses his own ruined end. The boy is to be found *"Dancing along/Using his dirty red coat as a cape."* The youthful toreador's aspirations are more exotically placed than his counterparts, the urban rent boys who chase in and out of 'Waifs And Strays.' The toreador is like a kid out of a Genet novel: *"Sad little boy of the street/Hands of a thief/With the mind of a dreamer."* The conflict in life is invariably one between inner and outer values, our dreams are invalidated by the social ethos, and the command is that we should give them a secondary place, and conform to the material dictates of living. There are boys in every city, outcasts who sell their bodies in order to live or feed a habit, street kids on the make, or those who are genuinely gay and in search of social elevation. Almond's first really autobiographical song 'Fun City', dealt with his confusion in running away to London and consorting with a rent boy street scene, and it's a theme which has placed a consistent colour in his work, the homoerotic attraction between innocence and experience, youth and age. The child anticipates its own state of future corruption in the adult's sexual advances, and is compelled to be the neophyte to sexual rites, which it may come one day to practise on youth itself. And so the interchangeable roles of innocence and experience are repeated. The relationship between good and evil is beautifully evoked in 'Toreador In The Rain': sex, the devil, and the arena coming together in an extended metaphor for corruption, *"He kneels and kisses the beast/Fearing the least/Knowing death will not find him/But maybe one day he will face/The Horns of the Devil/His childhood behind him."* The trial of innocence takes place every hour in big cities, where a youth either out of sexual curiosity, or driven by poverty to sell his body, encounters a sexually enquiring adult. The complex reciprocation in such a meeting can be viewed as initiative, exploitative, redemptive, transgressive, but essentially each meets the other in himself. The adult was the youth and in time the youth will become the adult. Time is the separator, and we give to it the name experience. In Barbara's 'Incestuous Love', one of the songs on *Absinthe*, the incestuous adult thanks the child for offering its twenty years to the other's superior forty. It takes compassionate empathy to bring the two together, and not the sort of paraphiliac disequilibrium suggested by the media.

If the toreador in Almond's song is also an angel who will fly with swifts around the cathedral, then the inhabitants of the song 'Waifs And Strays' are decidedly the city's rejects, the rent boys who hang around Piccadilly Circus, Pigalle, or Times Square, involved in rough trade or selling its reductive factor, meat. William Blake's poem 'A Little Boy Lost' from his *Songs Of Experience* has a leaning here into Almond's ethos. Blake writes, "And Father, how can I love you/Or any of my brothers more?/I love you like the little bird/That picks up crumbs around the door." The strays in Almond's song are looking to be found, they are waiting to be picked up, but they will give no love in return, they will leave as soon as the adult forms a sense of emotional attachment. *"In and out of life they wander/Little waifs and strays/They stay until you fall in love/That's when they slip away."* Their condition is not to be converted into adult values, they resist security and possessiveness, for secretly these boys are looking for the perfect stranger, the one who never arrives, but remains the reason for their street search. And what if he came in a scarlet robe, dispensing riches and liturgical benedictions, would they kneel at his boots, or reject him as the wrong one, and retreat back into an alley where Verlaine might have pissed his absinthe-tinctured urine against a blindside wall? Almond's song is motivated more by the adult's feelings of unassuagable loneliness, the need to be loved and the feeling of separation that the incongruous relationship brings about. Resting from the excesses of the night, the adult is sleeping while the child slips away into the busy day. There's a courageous explicitness in the confession, couched indirectly, *"You go out every evening/ Collecting waifs and strays."* Blake's poem, with its spiritual allegory is more sadistically punitive than Almond's connection to the stray in his lyric. Blake's little boy becomes the sacrificial victim: "The weeping child could not be heard,/The weeping parents wept in vain;/They strip'd him to his little shirt,/And bound him in an iron chain." Of his Soho years, Almond recalls, 'I had a police watch on my house and there was all sorts of strange characters coming and going. They always asked me questions and made it their business to know everything. This isn't my paranoia. There were cameras up on Brewer Street and Wardour Street and the police continually used to stop and search me. It got really infuriating.'

Almond's intrinsic relationship with good and evil, a rose and a knife in alternate hands, link his work to the way those concepts are expressed in a long tradition of literature that includes the writings of de Sade, Blake, Baudelaire, Wilde, Genet, and Bataille. If success has changed his life, and sent him imaginatively searching for his escaped innocence, then the contradictory tension needed to reconcile opposites was always a part of his character and creative expression. Songs like 'Toreador In The Rain', 'Waifs And Strays', and 'Death's Diary', brilliantly exemplify this mode of expression, and make *Enchanted* into his roundest lyric achievement.

Reviewing the album for the *NME*, Stephen Dalton was anxious to note the undertones of sleaze that lined the glossier surface to the songs. He also commented on Almond's "decadent orchestral majesty, low-life Latin struts, gay disco gallops and transsexual trawls through every camp cabaret act in European history." Reviewers are always careful to remind Almond of his origins, but there's an expansion on *Enchanted*, an enrichment of text which suggests in songs like 'Madame De La Luna', that the singer has learnt from Lorca's passionate lyricism, and has channelled compatible Latin characteristics into his own songwriting abilities. 'Madame De La Luna', the name of a Spanish drag bar, is one of the most ambitious of Marc Almond's compositions, its diva-operatic leitmotif of gender change, together with its allowance for his full vocal pitch, make it a song which rivals 'L'Esqualita' as an evocation of drag in a transvestite bar. A song of purple passages which leap from the immediate to the richly sensual, 'Madame De La Luna' is nonetheless a blazing torch song. Its emphasis is on the various metamorphoses that gender undergoes. *"Adrift on a sea of indigo silk/Passionate like an Arabian torch/Enticing two lovers to jump off a bridge/Changing the man into the wolf"*, Almond sings, as an enticement to go the whole way and marry extremes. La Luna alternates between male and female identities, she is a transvestite diva, and her ambivalent role is to switch sexes, her allurement as a woman being all the more enticing because she is a man. Marc Almond's love of transvestites is the inspiration behind much of his writing, and even in songs which appear to incorporate a masculine/feminine theme, the 'she' is easily interchangeable with a male transvestite. In the song 'A Lover Spurned', the vicious recriminations carried out by the avenging party in the affair are not usually associated with women. This could only be a gay relationship, with Almond singing, *"She'll tell her friends to treat you rough"*.

Having released *Enchanted* to the immediate commercial bite of Marc Almond's devotees, EMI found themselves with a dormant record and an artist unable to promote his new material, for lack of musical accompaniment. Almond was to play two low-key acoustic concerts in November 1990. One at the Brixton Academy as part of a benefit for the Terrence Higgins Trust, where accompanied by Martin Watkins on piano he resurrected a few Soft Cell numbers, 'Youth', 'Where The Heart Is', and 'Say Hello Wave Goodbye', as well as giving us a flourishing rendition of 'Toreador In The Rain' and 'Waifs And Strays'. The other concert played in November 1990, was the 5th Convention staged at Heaven, where again accompanied by Martin Watkins, Almond performed much the same set as at the Brixton Academy, Agnes Bernelle joining him on stage for the duet 'Kept Boy'. The poetic sensitivity of both concerts emphasised how well Almond had warmed to his voice potential, but his future as a performing artist seemed to hang suspended, and still searching for an elusive hit from *Enchanted*, EMI decided to release a remixed version of 'Waifs And Strays' as he third single from the album. The Grid, comprising Almond's old Soft Cell partner Dave Ball, and Richard Norris, were responsible for the remix, Ball having originally contacted Almond about the song and having expressed interest in its studio production. Applying an industrial synth alienation as a mix to 'Waifs And Strays', hardly seemed a formula for success; and to Almond's following the single's real value lay in the new songs released as B-sides: 'Old Jack's Charm', and 'City Of Nights'. From a record company's point of view, Almond's continued association with

The Grid has arguably modernised his sound, but on the negative side it has subverted the meaning of voice, and has placed emotive passion in direct conflict with automated music. Without it being an attempt to recreate Soft Cell, there's a danger once again of the singer becoming subordinate to bland instrumentation.

'Waifs And Strays', no matter the Grid remix, wasn't the single to raise Almond's commercial stature, and at the end of 1990 with Almond due to fly to L.A. to perform a number of acoustic concerts to promote *Enchanted* in America, and with EMI unhappy about the sales of *Enchanted* and offering to extend the artist's contract only on reduced terms, Almond took up an option with Warner Brothers, and was almost immediately signed to WEA. It was a risk on both sides, for Warner Brothers insisted that Almond should tour to promote his next album, and that of course he should prove himself commercially. Without a band, and reliant on his hardcore following to keep him respectably placed in terms of sales, Almond was faced once again with having to prove himself to a new record emporium. And it was a new decade, a decade in which lyrics have become increasingly deleted by sampling and ambient strains, and not one best suited to the singer of poetic lyrics. That said, 1991 was to prove a surprisingly successful year for Marc Almond, a year in which he was to score a solo hit with 'Jacky', and to take 'Tainted Love' back into the Top Five for the second time. In retrospect he would probably see the arrangements given to both songs as a serious compromise, but their successes provided a necessary alert to his continuing influence as an adaptable and serious voice, and to a talent resilient enough to ride the changes.

When a single by Marc Almond proves commercially successful, it means that a sector of the public in addition to his devotees have bought the record. And for that sector of the public to buy the record it has to be either infectiously danceable or targeted at mainstream interests. Almond's first hit for his new label was an extraordinarily dance-orientated, fully orchestrated version of Brel's 'Jacky', one of the Brel songs he had oddly omitted from his *Jacques* album, and a song with which Scott Walker had scored a similar success in his equally fluctuating career as a solo artist. Produced by Trevor Horn, and sung in the same Mort Schuman translation that Scott Walker had used, Almond's 'Jacky' is grandiosely camp, although it is not the voice but the fanatically epic production which deserves that epithet. Horn's big gestured pop sound applied to Brel's cynical anthem to lowlife created an oddity calculated to assure commercial success. Almond's approach to 'Jacky' is so far removed from the way he was to address the Belgian poet's lyrics on *Jacques*, that the song sits securely in the pop end of his spectrum. An unnervingly bizarre swipe at the Top Ten which succeeded in getting there, 'Jacky' pointed once again to the facility with which Marc Almond is able to resurrect his career at times when he appears to have dipped into obscurity.

Two particularly fine songs, 'Deep Night', and 'A Love Outgrown', found their way on to the various formats in which the single was released, and for those who revere Almond as an incurably melancholic torch singer, these proved fine substance for that insatiable need. 'Deep Night' takes up the singer's perennial writing theme of dream and reality, illusion and its counterpart, and the issue of loneliness as it is felt in the night. While 'A Love Outgrown', a plaintive ballad about growing up misunderstood in Southport, and having to escape regional boundaries in order to preserve sanity, rates with the best of Almond's autobiographical compositions.

Almond's pop reorientation in 1991 was consolidated by the release of the *Memorabilia* compilation, a selection of Soft Cell and solo hits, including remixed versions of 'Tainted Love', 'Memorabilia', and 'Say Hello Wave Goodbye', the singer adding new vocals for the latter take. 'Tainted Love '91' pursued a meteoric trajectory to No.4 in the charts, and *Memorabilia* proved to be a considerable commercial success, given that neither of the earlier Soft Cell or Marc Almond singles compilations had made any significant register in terms of sales. And having spent the better part of a decade discrediting his techno-pop associations with Soft Cell, and talking of a psychological allergy induced even by hearing 'Tainted Love', Almond seemed confident to re-evaluate his past free of the traumatic turbulence that had conditioned his years of early success. Authors come to be embarrassed by their early work, as do all creative artists, and with Almond's voice being far too superior for orthodox pop, he had grown to dissociate from the formula which had instated his iconic status in early eighties pop. And without doubt, 'Tainted Love' a second time round was the chance to capitalise on its commercial merits. 'I could have sold my soul a million times, but that is not to say I wouldn't: in this exterior of integrity beats the heart of a prostitute,' he commented at the time. 'But there are times when I could have taken the money and run, if that's all it meant to me. I was offered £10,000 to do a NatWest bank advert – I could have blown that on a weekend in Bangkok.'

Part of Almond's anguish when it is centred in the merits or defects of pop achievements, as distinct from his genuinely poetic concerns as an artist, is the fact that pop records grow so quickly to be disposable ephemera. We forget all too soon the countless transient modes of expression that enforce attention on the charts for a week, a month, or a year, a condition that allows for little matrix of past achievements, even in those who endure. And so the need to keep on again and again restating oneself is the disquieting quandary at the heart of all pop contenders. The need to satisfy a record company is not the only fuelling source to Almond's recurrent raids on commercial success, it's also got to do with the psychological motivation not to be forgotten or disinherited from a particular role associated with public attention. There is no other art expression which demands the degree of public exposure given to popular singers. Most poets, painters, novelists, and classical musicians work privately and with little degree of media recognition, whereas the pop side of Almond has been ruthlessly exposed and so often at the expense of his more serious contributions to song. 'I still find pop music a real challenge,' he expressed in the months preceding the release of *Tenement Symphony.* 'When people tell me I'm not part of pop music any more I want to fight back. Although my influences have been people like Brel in the past, the inspirations here are more people like Dollar and Madonna. Ten years ago you had to apologise for being pop, and now you do an interview with *NME* and pop is credible.'

In October 1991, at the time of releasing the Trevor Horn produced *Tenement Symphony,* the most overproduced of all his studio albums, Almond was busy contradicting the techno-ethos by playing a series of strictly acoustic concerts: voice and grand piano. In August 1991, and in support of the successful *Memorabilia* retrospective, he had undertaken a short Japanese tour, playing a number of dates in Osaka and Tokyo, most of which have been captured on audience tapes. Almond played a characteristic set opening with a melancholy 'Fun City' and incorporating a sprinkling of Soft Cell numbers including the diva-pastiche 'L'Esqualita', as well as revived numbers like 'In My Room', and 'A Woman's Story', the more recent 'Toreador In The Rain', and 'Waifs And Strays', and Almond's favourite Brel number for live performance, 'If You Go Away'. A surprise and welcome inclusion to his acoustic repertoire was 'Broken Hearted And Beautiful', a moving and neglected B-side to his 1986 single 'Ruby Red.' 'Stories Of Johnny', and 'Mr Sad', were also lifted from his archives, but it was the sensitive recasting of his old Soft Cell song 'Youth', which accented his increased vocal prowess. 'Youth', now interpreted as a sparse elegy, and 'Torch', benefiting greatly from the acoustic arrangement given it, were the highlights of what appeared to be Almond's finest vocal concerts to date.

In October 1991 Almond was to perform acoustic concerts in an Athens ampitheatre, and at Kreutzberg's Passion Kirche in Berlin, a liturgical venue ideally suited to his torch theatricals. Dressed in a gold lamé shirt beneath a rhinestone-studded toreador's jacket, Almond performed in front of an altar decorated with scarlet roses. Staying at the Palast Hotel prior to his two concerts at the Passion Kirche, Almond was willing to expatiate on the merits of making Brel's 'Jacky' into a successful pop single. 'I just try to make records that stand out, records that make everything else seem dull by comparison. The pop music I have enjoyed has always been, you know, flash, slightly gaudy, a touch pretentious. Big gestures. A pop single, to me, should be a big gesture. Why make a little gesture?'

With the church altar illuminated by a bank of red bulbs on lighting rigs, and with a dry ice screen periodically enveloping his corscatingly studded jacket, Almond's histrionic gestures were ideally suited to his ecclesiastic role as purveyor of torch cabaret in a house of prayer. And with the audience standing in wooden pews, and throwing red roses at the singer, Almond proved he had come into his own. 'Just me naked', as he told the audience, the voice creating the organic symbiosis with language which is the mark of a singer. A remarkably relaxed Almond, no longer rushing the first three songs from compulsive anxiety, but warming to the occasion with consummate finesse, was in fine voice. Opening with an empathetically rendered and piano-rich 'Fun City', Almond was from the first note one with his extraordinary surroundings. All of the luciferian iconography inherent in his songs, the sexual angelology in his imagery, and the messianic aspirations of his diva rituals were afforded the right context in this red brick church packed with an exaltedly enthusiastic audience. Singing much the same set of songs as he had employed for his Japanese concerts a month earlier, that is a mixture of acoustically arranged Soft Cell numbers, older consistent favourites from his solo career, and a number of new songs from *Enchanted*, Almond used the altar as a charged backdrop to his gestural theatre. Dropping to his knees in the course of singing the opulently elegiac 'Orpheus In Red Velvet', the emphasised *"Take me through hell 'cos I deserve it"* jumped out of the song as a spiritual reality. A heart-wrung version of 'Torch', the relentless self-exposure implied by 'Youth', and the transsexual paean 'L'Esqualita', all given a rich piano treatment, demonstrated how the songs acquire stature through acoustic renditions. 'A Man', later to appear on *Absinthe*, was brought into the repertoire, Agnes Bernelle accompanied Almond on 'Kept Boy', and 'Say Hello Wave Goodbye' served as a valedictory gesture to a ceremonial concert.

Back at his hotel Almond discoursed on the importance of the right venue to his work, and on the significance of Berlin to his life. 'Berlin has always been a sort of island, a special place with its own tension. If you try to do things a little bit different the people here seem really to appreciate it, and with all the religious iconography and the spiritual element in my songs, this church is a great setting. I hate normal rock venues – all that wheel them in and wheel them out; a place like this makes a concert more of an event. Over the past couple of years it's been the fashion to go for the rock spectacular. I'd love to compete with that, but I can't, so I go for the other extreme, which really tests me as a performer. It's hard work, but it's rewarding.' In the select few acoustic concerts that Almond staged in 1991, he reached maturity as a vocalist.

Hot on the heels of the success scored by 'Jacky', and 'Tainted Love '91', WEA released Almond's new studio album *Tenement Symphony*, a collection of new songs produced by Trevor Horn in a manner that clashed stormily with the acoustic genre that Almond had adopted for recent concerts. After the cold sound surrounding *Enchanted*, and the new intimacy of performance, it came as a shock to be presented with another slab of studio alienation, in the sense that the voice is diminished on *Tenement Symphony* at the expense of overproduction. With three of the songs co-written with The Grid, and with Dave Ball responsible for synthesizers and programming, the new album was aimed at consolidating the singer's place in a new decade. Almond said at the time that no-one needed another Marc Almond album, what they required was *the* Marc Almond album, and *Tenement Symphony* was a shot at attempting to realise this search for ultimate diva recognition. Interviewed at the time of the album's release, Almond spoke eloquently about the definition of a star. 'All fact becomes blurred with fiction and nobody really cares, that's what makes a true star', he told Stephen Dalton, and in response to the question of why people need stars, he was equally perceptive. 'They want somebody to live out the pains and fantasies for them, to take them into taboo areas denied them by their lives, and to suffer on the cross. You could look on it as sad, but it's just part of life. If everybody could get what they want, and everybody could be stars, then what?' Never a careerist, Marc Almond nonetheless understands to a profound psychological degree the distinctions which make him a star. 'My heart is a socialist, my wallet is a capitalist', he declared in the same interview, again proving the paradoxical tensions which are at the roots of his creativity. Being a star is a calculating profession, and it's one that Almond has carried well, allowing his public just sufficient insight into his privacy to have them want to know more. And it's the nature of his work to suggest that an unlimited decadence also applies to his life. It's why he provokes fascination in his fans, and then retreats into a guarded mystique.

As with the release of *Enchanted*, there was to be no tour in support of *Tenement Symphony*, and Almond's career as a live performer appeared once again to be at risk. Living in a mews flat off Portobello Road, there were no longer the dispersed Gutterhearts to question the singer's privacy, and the music outlined by *Tenement Symphony* suggested that his career was temporarily confined to the studio. And clues as to his personal state of survival were to be found in his new lyrics: *"Look at me, do you see a man against the world?/But don't look at me and see an unhappy man/With some powder and some paint/And the patience of a saint/I'm still here."*

The new songs, and particularly those which engaged on an autobiographical level, 'Meet Me In My Dreams', 'I've Never Seen Your Face', and 'Vaudeville And Burlesque', were all songs about the desperate resilience needed to survive pain and the consequences of sexual difference. But there's a feeling throughout of the artist being marginally out of touch with his work. 'I'd started recording songs with Billy McGee and I'd felt *Enchanted* was happening all over again,' he tells us. 'I was there with a programmer and a computer, so I went to my recording company with the twelve songs I had recorded and they said, "Yes, well it can be another Marc Almond album, and it can be another good Marc Almond album, but you've really got to try something that's different and special."' The result was to be a fully orchestrated record with Trevor Horn at the controls. 'We worked together on "Jacky", "What Is Love?", "The Days Of Pearly Spencer", and "My Hand Over My Heart". Unrelated songs, but pulled together by an imaginary symphony. The effect was meant to be like looking through the windows of this tenement building and seeing the characters and their individual lives. There's the megalomaniacal "Jacky", the guy who has it all, like Citizen Kane, but really he just wants his childhood back, the pure and simple things. I really related to that. And then it became a whole project, taking the whole production thing that started with *Enchanted* to extremes with a 40 piece orchestra, Trevor Horn, and five studios on the go. I could finally tie off the orchestral, camp dramatics, and finish with that whole period.'

Almond's commentary on the making of *Tenement Symphony* was made at a time when he was still contracted to Warners, and he has subsequently, since the termination of his contract with that company, spoken about his extreme dissatisfaction with the way in which his creative individuality was undetermined in the studio. But for all the artist's confessed disapproval of the production given his songs, *Tenement Symphony* has its real successes, and the stark minimalism of 'Champagne', the elegy for a dancer of that name who worked at the Show Palace Theatre on 8th Avenue in New York, is a triumph of composed melancholic sentiments. The sweepingly balladic 'My Hand Over My Heart' has Almond reaching towards the one impossible love that lights the stars, and the emotive importunacy in his voice has the song dramatically mount the highest stair in its search for truth. The song came to be released as the second single taken from the album, and it was a measure of great personal sadness to the singer that it failed to make the impact on the charts he had anticipated. It may also have been the fact that the song was written in collaboration with Dave Ball, that had Almond aspire to a renaissance of their songwriting partnership. 'My Hand Over My Heart' disappeared as a single, although it did offer B-sides which were not included on the album, 'Deadly Serenade', 'Money For Love', and the hauntingly moving 'Night And No Morning', one of the best of Almond's nocturnal songs, a lament that the night journey, with all its sexual hunger, should be overtaken by the day.

The explicitly gay song, 'I've Never Seen Your Face', the lyrics recounting anonymous sex in the dark, the no-contact world of numbers on the heath or in the park, risked a statement that Warners were clearly willing to let ride. Almond tells of the partner's indiscernible features: *"I've never seen your face/But I'm longing for the time/When we don't have to hide/Anymore."* Incorporating an unspoken protest against the political Clauses (28,25) that limit the legality of homosexual behaviour, the song conjures up the illicit and covert night world of gay outlaws fired by the risk of apprehension. *"In threat of law/In sweat of fear/I'd risk it all/To have you near."* The opulence and sexual edge to the songs, conveyed more by delivery than the lyrics, won the album favourable notices. The *NME* issued enthusiastic praise: "It's hard not to love Marc Almond. His extravagance, his operatic gestures, his sordid past, his guilt, his glitter – he's the sort of romantic for whom the adjective 'hopeless' was created. And even if part of it is affectation (he is after all, a born performer), his desire to make a big gaudy splash in the still waters of pop is, despite all odds, still thrilling. *Tenement Symphony* is a gorgeous piece of indulgence."

But for all the injected modernity into the production, and for all the mixing-desk flourishes by Trevor Horn and Julian Mendelsohn, the lyrics are simple old-fashioned love songs, speaking of pain, and an often brutal pain, cutting across the expectations of pleasure, and death extracting the loved one from life. And with three of the songs not written by Almond, the lyric texture of *Tenement Symphony* never lives up to the exotic imagery employed in the writing of *Enchanted*. One can't help feeling in retrospect that the sweepingly melodic 'Meet Me In My Dreams', or 'Beautiful Brutal Thing' would have been better placed as singles than 'My Hand Over My Heart'; but the success had already been scored through 'Jacky', and was to be repeated the following year with 'The Days Of Pearly Spencer', Almond's idiosyncratic reading of David McWilliams' old hit from the sixties.

Grit, glitter, brash Las Vegas aspirations, a look towards the classical with the Debussy extract 'Trois Chansons de Bilitis', sung by Sally Bradshaw, supernally emotive ballads, the driving Eurobeat applied to Brel's 'Jacky', the return to simple pop melodies in the collaborative work with Dave Ball, *Tenement Symphony* is a montage of diverse musical formulae aimed at commercial success. *Tenement Symphony* was also the germinating idea behind Marc Almond's Royal Albert Hall concert the following year, the orchestral extravaganza which dictated his evaluation of twelve years of song.

On its intial release the album sold no more or less than any other Marc Almond album, and the photograph of the singer on the cover, wearing a black tuxedo and a white dress shirt, his conducting baton comprising a thorny rose branch, did however suggest still another change in the singer's chameleonic adoption of identities. Almond had entered the nineties under Warner Brothers' aegis, and there was an air of commercial qualification about the project, even if it wasn't fully realised in terms of sales.

Particularly disappointing for Almond at the time was that WEA rejected most of the darker, more confessionally informed songs that he wished to include on *Tenement Symphony*, the material about addiction, and psychological and sexual extremes. Interviewed in 1994, and after the termination of his contract with WEA, Almond spoke of the creative alienation he had experienced in the making of *Tenement Symphony*. 'I know a lot of people felt that my heart wasn't in it, and in a way they were right. It was a totally manufactured record – great slabs of kitsch which were all wonderful and fabulous just so long as you didn't mind the fact that you couldn't find me in them. Creatively speaking, *Tenement Symphony* was a completely barren experience for me. Especially with the whole Trevor Horn thing, basically I became a guest on my own record. And then of course I had to promote something I didn't believe in.'

Almond raises here the whole human issue of what part does a singer have in the making of albums which grow progressively more contingent on studio production. And what has this got to do with being a singer? If we separate the vocal takes from the multitextured sampling, then the singer's creative input is small by comparison, and yet is the pivot on which the production rests. The singer grows increasingly isolated on records given formidably expensive technical production. He becomes the ghost in the machine.

Suffering at the time of making *Tenement Symphony* from addictive drug problems, which included the prescribed drugs Valium and Halycon, Almond claims he felt too dispirited to fight the manipulative spirit of his record company. 'I love "Jacky", and I adore "My Hand Over My Heart", but it didn't all add up. At that time I really needed a lifting experience. It didn't lift me. I felt that I'd compromised, sold out. There were songs I really needed to get out at the time, songs that expressed how I was feeling and what I was going through, and they were dropped or relegated to B-sides. And I didn't have it in me to fight back.'

After the relative chart failure of 'My Hand Over My Heart', WEA released 'The Days Of Pearly Spencer' as a single in April 1992, and the song rapidly ascended to the Top Five, giving Almond his second major single success for WEA. Again, it came from a cover version, but it was a means for the singer to retain a public image, and to confirm his continuing presence as a chart contender. Opulently orchestrated, and sensitively modulated in terms of melancholy, 'The Days Of Pearly Spencer' tells the story of someone born into a tenement ethos, a loser engaged with attempting to elevate himself from the grey side of life. Almond tells us, 'I first heard it on Radio Caroline, and it's stayed with me all these years. I like the lyrics, they're strong and dark. I like songs about characters, about characters that tell stories, but I always felt the song was so short, it was incomplete. The original was quite despairing, so old sentimentalist that I am, I added an extra verse to help the character find peace. Whether it's in death, or by simply lifting himself out of the gutter, it's not clear.'

The slightly elevated, transcendent note that Almond gives the song, does lift it from the socially despairing matrix in which the original was couched. But it was a record bought by a different public to the Almond aficionados who would have preferred one of his own controversially tinged compositions to have achieved high chart placing.

The summer of 1992 brought news of the first British concerts Almond would have staged for four years. There was to be a celebratory visual extravaganza at the Royal Albert Hall, preceded by a show at the Royal Concert Hall in Nottingham. But before these September dates, and some would argue superior in quality to both of the 'Twelve Years Of Tears' concerts, came an emotively charged acoustic show on 12th June at the Philharmonic Hall, Liverpool. Incongruously part of Liverpool's Festival Of Comedy, this one-off concert was the first time Almond's British fans were to be given the chance to see the acoustic show he had presented in Japan and Europe the preceding year. Accompanied by Martin Watkins on piano, and occasionally electric keyboard, Almond dressed in a red suit and white shirt was at his spectacular best. I would argue that this particular concert represents his singularly most distinguished vocal performance, a perfectly balanced set is afforded a mastery of phrasing and impassioned delivery. There's not a note out of place, and the piano enriched suite of songs begs release as a live album.

Performing 25 songs over the better part of two hours, there were to be new inclusions to the repertoire, 'Meet Me In My Dreams', and 'Champagne', both from *Tenement Symphony*, the Peter Hammill song 'Vision' was recast for acoustic rendition, there was a desparingly beautiful new Almond composition 'Amnesia Nights', and a first live performance of the Charles Aznavour song 'What Makes A Man A Man'. These songs augmented the mixture of Soft Cell and solo material that Almond had worked into the texture of his live performances the preceding year. It was the richest of his concerts, and one that served as an evaluative compendium of the songs dearest to him. His reading of the anonymous folk ballad 'When I Was A Young Man' was a cathartically heart-wrung identification with the uncompromisingly dissolute who die young, and set the tone for two other moving elegies: 'Amnesia Nights', and 'Champagne'. 'Amnesia Nights' continues with the theme of visionary or idealised love that had been sounded in some of the songs on *Tenement Symphony* like 'Meet Me In My Dreams', and 'Champagne'. It's also close to 'Deep Night' in its placing dream and hallucination, the oneiric and the autonomously imagined, over and above reality.

Heaven is recognised as being *here*, as an intrinsic and psychic state, and yet so often in life we look to the external for support rather than find it within. 'Amnesia Nights', 'Champagne', 'Youth', and 'There Is A Bed', formed a consolidated elegiac core to the concert, a lamenting valediction to youth, and an acceptance that death is the ultimate poetic mystery, a mystery which should be the companionable acquaintance of song, as much as it is that of poetry. Superb renderings of 'In My Room', 'Torch', 'Orpheus In Red Velvet', and 'What Makes A Man A Man', were only some of the blazing highpoints to a concert that had Almond distributing red roses to the front rows by way of a triumphant encore appropriately structured around 'Say Hello Wave Goodbye'.

photo: Della Grace

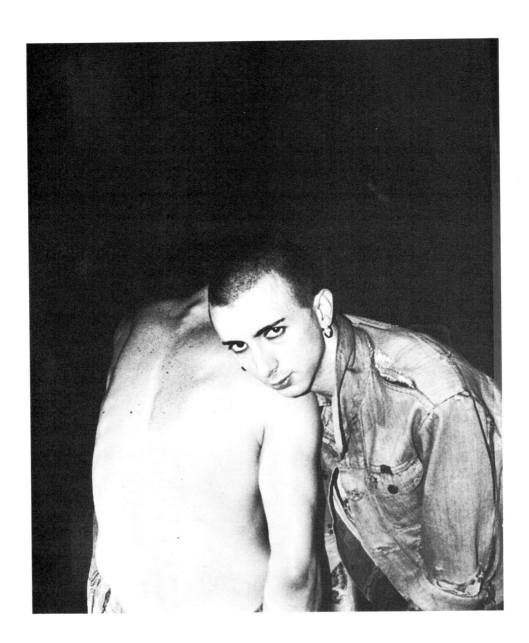

photo: Piers Allardyce

photo: Piers Allardyce

photo: Derek Ridgers

photo: Zoe Jones

MY FINAL AUTUMN PERHAPS

The late summer and early autumn of 1992 were to be industriously busy times for Marc Almond's career, 'Twelve Years Of Tears' was to be the live retrospective evaluation of his diversely faceted career, and to tie in with his raised commercial status, Virgin brought out *A Virgin's Tale*, two separate CD volumes collecting the prolific range of B-sides and EP tracks he had released during his time with that company. Much of this material had been recorded with the idea in mind that *Mother Fist And Her Five Daughters* should be a double album, and welcome inclusions on this compilation are the two Brecht songs 'Pirate Jenny', and 'Surabaya Johnny', the songs from the two mini-albums *A Woman's Story* and *Stained* EP, the Westminster Choir arrangements of 'Stories Of Johnny' and 'Love Letter', the punchily squalid 'Blond Boy', and the fragilely lilting 'Two Sailors On A Beach'. Complete with inadequate and shoddy liner notes, this valuable collection of controversial, misanthropic, bruisingly balladic, exemplarily diva-motivated songs allowed fans to have most of the material for the first time on CD. Sadly missing from the compilation was *Violent Silence*, a set of songs which are still at the time of writing awaiting re-release. The selection also omitted the songs 'Indigo Blue', and 'Oily Black Limousine', two of the finest of Marc Almond's uncollected rarities.

October was to bring the video release *Marc Almond Live In Concert*, a video only representation of his December 1987 Astoria concerts. Competently and atmospherically filmed, the video proved to be a welcome artifact to fans who had been denied all commercial vestige of the singer's outstanding live performances over the better part of a decade. A much needed addition to his recorded oeuvre *Marc Almond Live In Concert* captured the singer at an experimental phase of his career, airing new songs, performing an urgent tap-dancing version of Brel's 'Next', and completing the show with the directional ambivalence of 'The River', before delivering 'Something's Gotten

Hold Of My Heart' as an achingly balladic finale.

I wrote earlier that on the days on which Marc Almond is due to play in London, the carnations at the flower-seller's stall appear redder. There's a sense of apprehension in the air, one's memories are sharper in their abrupt visual flashbacks, and a little alley in Soho is remembered for having first been seen on a foggy day in October. One expects to find rubies or emeralds in the gutter, and for sequins to fall with the rain. All day we are waiting for dark and the advent of the show. We are remembering other concerts, his appearance at the London Palladium in 1986, the Royalty Theatre and the Astoria in 1987, the Victoria Palace Theatre in 1988, and now far more grandiose than those other prestigious venues, Almond is to be located on Wednesday 30th September, 1992, at the Royal Albert Hall. A concert that is to prove a festive extravaganza, a retrospective evaluation of his career over twelve metamorphic years of committed devotion to the art of song. Given the title 'Twelve Years Of Tears', the coming show has been previewed at the Royal Concert Hall, Nottingham, two days earlier on the 28th September, and given the almost total absence of concerts in Europe for the past four years, fans have arrived from every country to celebrate the singer's triumphant assessment of the songs he has most valued over the years. He is described in the catalogue as combining "the spirit of Aznavour, Presley, Bolan, Orbison, and Johnny Ray, with the entire chorus of the Folies Bergères; his spiritual home." We are also told that he has been called the "Judy Garland of the garbage heap, the Prince of Sleaze, an acid-house Aznavour, the Jim Reeves of the bedsit generation and the Perverse Pixie of Pop."

And 'Twelve Years Of Tears' with its extravagant costume changes, dancers, orchestra, band, and pyrotechnic theatricals, proved to be just such an amalgam of reworked pop influences and romantically opulent torch ballads. Right from his dramatic entry in a long sequinned gown, which might have jumped out of Judy Garland's stage wardrobe, the singer proved to be ideally matched to his surroundings. He began on a note of optimistic survival, both creative and physical, by commencing with 'Vaudeville And Burlesque', followed by another four songs from *Tenement Symphony*, material charged with the knife-edge tension between life and death which characterises so much of Marc Almond's writing. By beginning with the present, and so putting current work up front, Almond was able to warm to past legends, and to work his way to his own interior, signposting it with songs from almost every phase of his career. An acoustic re-reading of seven of his favourite songs, with Martin

Watkins on piano, 'Stories Of Johnny', 'Tenderness Is A Weakness', 'Black Heart', 'Vision', 'Mr. Sad', 'There Is A Bed', and a poignantly searching 'Youth' brought the singer's poetic sensitivity into emotive focus. There were the Soft Cell revivals, 'Torch', 'Bedsitter', and a declaratively affirmative 'Soul Inside', the latter two songs coming as shock tactics to the audience. There was the homage to Brel in stylised renditions of 'Jacky', and 'If You Go Away'. There were the voluminous Almond ballads 'The Desperate Hours', 'A Lover Spurned', and 'My Hand Over My Heart', the instantly retrievable 'Something's Gotten Hold Of My Heart', the tragically confessional statement implicit in the Charles Aznavour song 'What Makes A Man A Man'. And the biggest surprise of them all, a blisteringly felicitous version of 'Tainted Love', the first time Almond had performed the song for ten years, then by way of an appropriate encore 'Say Hello Wave Goodbye', while a cascade of pink balloons descended on the ecstatic audience.

In this three hour spectacular being filmed for television and video, and being recorded for the release of the live album *Twelve Years Of Tears*, Almond, in periodic costume changes, appeared in a cascade of diversely coloured sequins as he lived out the role of polymorphic diva to his adoring fans. With Warner Brothers having put a reputed quarter of a million pounds into the staging of the show, the concert was to prove Marc Almond's most memorably extravagant venture into the public eye, and to serve as confirmation that his star's qualities had weathered the years of indifference and public neglect to combust in a meteoric trail across this theatricalised spectacular. Almond had gained his nemesis; the concert was a vindication of his virtuoso finesse as a singer, and was an act of retributive vengeance on critics who had earlier on written off his career.

Particularly outstanding in the night's repertoire was an acoustic rendition of Charles Aznavour's 'What Makes A Man A Man', a song which narrates the life of a drag queen who works as a strip-artist at night, and who as a victim of societal homophobia, and who declares *"I know my life is not a crime/I'm just a victim of my time"*. The questioning evaluation of gender which the song provokes, and the poignancy implicit in the lyrics were heartbreakingly evoked by Almond's reading of one of the great torch songs used in drag cabaret. The standing ovation he received for this song was proof of the profound sympathies his audience nurture for his sexual propensities. It's hard to think of anyone attending a Marc Almond concert who is not in love with drag. And of the feminisation realised through the creative act the Austrian poet Rainer Maria Rilke has written: "The deepest experience of the creative artist is feminine, for it is an experience of conceiving and giving birth. The poet Obstfelder once wrote, speaking of the face of a stranger: 'When he began to speak, it was as though a woman had taken a seat within him.' It seems to me that every poet has had this experience in beginning to speak."

The Royal Albert Hall concert was well received by the national and music press. Almond was viewed as a chameleon adept at fluently exchanging the roles of pop and torch singer, and bringing to both expressions a unique artistry. The concert was by no means his best vocal performance, but it comprised a brilliant retrospective, and one which alerted his fans to the diverse facets of a twelve year career. Only Marc Almond could have followed on from Charles Aznavour's 'What makes A Man A Man' with the Northern Soul number 'Tainted Love'. The incongruous juxtaposition was superb.

Reporting on the show, *Melody Maker* proclaimed, "Marc Almond is the pop Nick Cave. Both thrive on a certain ruined glamour, and a romanticism that grows less, not more, cynical with every passing year. Both inhabit self-created worlds that are easy to scorn from the outside. But once you're in, critical perception is corroded beyond repair." The comparison between Almond and Cave is a tenuous one, but both are survivors who have never relinquished a tenacious self-integrity.

Despite rumours of the show going to Europe, a procedure which would have proved far too costly, the Royal Albert Hall concert turned out to be a one-off, and the proposed touring assemblage was dismantled. And 'Twelve Years Of Tears' was best kept as a luminous memory. Writing the show up for *The Evening Standard*, Max Bell discerningly commented: "Narrative singing has long been Almond's forte; his deceptive expressionism matched to an ambition that made a nonsense of his linear vocal style. Liza Minnelli couldn't have done material like 'Jacky' or 'If You Go Away' better. It was a concert that excelled at all the sequinned showbiz glamour necessary to spotlight a star." And voicing the opinion that 'Twelve Years Of Tears' was "the year's most brilliantly realised pop extravaganza", *The Independent On Sunday* drew attention to how "The show changes gear effortlessly down and up through tortured torch songs at the piano to ancient pop monuments like 'Bedsitter' and on to the second half's grand orchestral epics such as 'The Days Of Pearly Spencer'."

Almond had talked of a ten date tour of Germany in February of the next year, retaining the band with whom he had worked at the Royal Albert Hall, and having the strings on keyboards, but the concerts were sadly never to materialize. Warners promised a live album and video release of the concert for April 1993, and the singer's next engagement was at the sixth official Marc Almond convention held at the Astoria theatre on 18th October 1992. A low-key, but passionately informed set of songs, with Martin Watkins on keyboards, was made memorable by the inclusion of a number of new songs, including 'Amnesia Nights', a song he'd written for Marie France 'The Flame', 'Lost Paradise' which was from the still unreleased French album 'Absinthe', and 'Like A Prayer', the Madonna song he had originally recorded for the compilation *Ruby Trax*. The additional songs were: 'Champagne', 'Black Heart', 'In Your Bed', and 'Vision'.

After the monumentally apexical 'Twelve Years Of Tears' concert, Almond seemed undecided about a direction for the future. What looked like the secure professionalism of a mature singer, who had realised both the commercial and cult status to which he aspired, and who had recently returned to prominence in the public eye, was something of a contrived illusion. In truth, he was lacking the musicians and support around him to set him on a new direction. As always he had an abundance of songs to take into the studio, but the making of *Tenement Symphony* had been a disorientating and unnerving experience, and for the first time in his life he showed no alacrity to be at work on a projected album.

With the idea of maintaining his success as a singles artist, Warners considered releasing 'What Makes A Man A Man' in both live and studio versions in January 1993. Undoubtedly the best appreciated of the songs Marc Almond had delivered at the Royal Albert Hall, and with the lyrics ideally accommodating his personal obsessions, there seemed little doubt on an artistic level that the Charles Aznavour song was perfectly suited to his voice and image. But there were commercial reservations at Warners about the expediency of this move. The consequences of releasing a single which narrates the life of a drag artist who changes his sex each night, and with lyrics which included the lines *"So many times we have to pay/For having fun and being gay"*, would have been to place Marc Almond back on the rota of blacklisted artists at the BBC. Aware of the media prohibitions likely to be placed on the song, the single's release date was delayed until 15th March, as a clearly unenthusiastic record label waited to register the song's predicted failure as a commercial release. The song was released on two separate CD volumes. The first containing the live version of the song backed by 'Torch', and 'The Stars We Are', as they were recorded at the Royal Albert Hall. The second CD issued a week later contained a live and studio version of the song, backed by 'Tainted Love', 'Vision', and 'Only The Moment' from the same concert. Shamefully lacking any record company promotion, almost unreviewed due to the uncoordinated release dates, and denied all mainstream airplay, the single sunk without a trace in the lower parts of the Top Sixty. What was arguably the best single Almond had ever released, as well as being a positive statement for transvestites and drag artists dipped into oblivion without any proper notification that it had been released. The media repression of the song was another sad indicator that Britain in the conformist nineties is still predominantly a homophobic nation. Every Almond devotee would like to have seen him take this controversial and emotively cathartic song to the top of the charts. As such, it was his first singles failure with a cover version.

March also brought with it a secret concert at Kensington Roof Gardens in London; the singer, encumbered by a debilitating flu, performed a showcase acoustic concert to the press and a hundred of his most loyal fans. This acoustic formula which had been preceded by similar concerts at small venues in Madrid, Paris, and Milan, was ostensibly to promote the forthcoming *Twelve Years Of Tears* CD and its companion video of the Royal Albert Hall concert. It was an extraordinarily underprofiled publicity campaign to celebrate a live retrospective of his career. A heavily made up Almond performed on a small stage containing the piano and two candelabra supported on columns strategically placed one at each end of the stage. Performing much the same acoustic set as he had at the Royal Albert Hall, Almond opened the concert with a powerfully spirited version of 'Jacky', before launching into the sustained bittersweet melancholy of 'Tenderness Is A Weakness', 'Stories Of Johnny', 'There Is A Bed', 'Black Heart', 'Vision', 'Mr. Sad', 'If You Go Away', 'Youth', the highly pertinent 'What Makes A Man A Man', before introducing a new song, a breathtakingly sensitive colouring of Charles Aznavour's 'Yesterday When I Was Young'. This was arguably the emotional highpoint of a thirty minute set which the singer concluded with the appositely memorable 'Say Hello Wave Goodbye'. The intimacy of the venue and the courageously anti-commercial stance implied by a clandestine show were reminders that the singer still nurtured his status of being a cult artist. And if Almond had chosen to play a venue smaller than the location of any of the six official Conventions, then the defiance implied by this act seemed to presage lack of record company cooperation for the release of the *Twelve Years Of Tears* package, which in all attracted the same lack of critical attention as the single which had preceded it. There was an uncharacteristic lack of vivacity on the artist's part in not being directly engaged with the recording of new material, and the edited and selected highlights of the concert made available on the *Twelve Years Of Tears* CD were something of a disappointment to fans who had been waiting a decade for the commercial release of a live album. Nor was the concert necessarily Almond at his best. There had been so many intensely atmospheric shows over the years, such an abundance of diva agonies in the living out of songs on stage, such a plethora of operatic denouements of the moment, that *Twelve Years Of Tears* seemed an attempt to sell the artist short. Disappointing art work in a tasteless combination of colours didn't help the album's sales, and it was clear at this point that there were little connective sympathies between the artist and his label.

The Independent On Sunday ran a feature 'The Boy Who Came Back' focusing on *Twelve Years Of Tears* and on Almond's position as a enduring icon of contemporary music. There was critical generosity at work in the assessment that "His willingness to be difficult – to drop out of the mainstream while he works on a new direction – might not have gone down well with some of his shorter-suffering record labels, but it has played a vital part in sustaining him as one of the most enduring of British pop icons." In a form of journalism not easily given to praise, the same writer continued, "How many other stars of the past decade could hold their own with Gene Pitney? When Almond first turned to the songs of Jacques Brel, people laughed, but over the years his voice has matured into a surprisingly expressive instrument. Nowadays he can carry off the gleeful sado-disco symphony of 'Jacky' and the florid melodrama of 'If You Go Away' with equal aplomb."

Still critically undervalued and seriously underrated as the consummate master of a genre conflating torch cabaret with an angularly controversial pop, Almond seemed little fêted for this live encapsulation of representative songs. The album was hardly noticed on its release, and the singer took off at the end of April for a two week tour of Russia, the desire to explore Eastern Europe seeming eccentric and self-punitive, given his continuing abstention from performing for his popular European fan-base. Something of the practical vicissitudes and glorious celebrations of the Russian concerts were noted in the diary extracts Almond made available for his fans in Issue 5 of *Vaudeville And Burlesque*, the official Marc Almond fanzine. Undeterred by appallingly inefficient travel, bureaucratic authoritarianism, food which proved antipathetic to vegetarian needs,

---

salty water instead of the preferred Evian, faulty sound-systems, undemonstrative but highly appreciative audiences, vodka-stoned people wandering onto the stage, and uncomfortable hotel facilities, Almond, accompanied by his pianist Martin Watkins persevered. And so he took sequins and torch songs to Russia, and through the message implicit in his lyrics, was able to speak for tolerance to gay people. By performing 'What Makes A Man A Man', and by coming into the audience to do so, Almond made good his message without any need for propaganda. Only in his last concert staged in a spectacularly baroque theatre in St. Petersburg, and filmed for Russian television on Monday 10th May, did the singer make any overt reference to gay rights. Wearing a holographic sequinned suit, and by way of prefacing 'What Makes A Man A Man', Almond made a statement that was translated into Russian: 'This is for all the gay people in Russia and my wish is for a Russian society which fully tolerates those with different ideas, styles, views, and sexualities, all of them contributing to the greatness of the Russian people.'

Reporting on Almond's courageously grandiose concert in St. Petersburg, an acoustic and part a cappella show, and of the explicitly gay life depicted in 'What Makes A Man A Man', *The Times* spoke of his liberating gesture towards decriminalisation: "Before he is even a verse into its depiction of a lonely cabaret artist, the first young male fan has pushed forward to hug him and give flowers. Others follow, and the resultant demonstrations of devotion to an openly gay British artist might cause some activists at home who deem Almond insufficiently strident to pause for thought. Although it is no soft option to preach political correctness back in Britain, it suddenly seems far braver to descend from the stage and embrace a star-struck Russian before this cross-section of his fellow citizens."

The concert at St. Petersburg introduced two new songs into the repertoire, 'Amnesia Nights', and 'Nothing Ever Changes'. It took place in a rococo theatre, a vast mirrored room painted ice-blue and white with an abundance of scarlet and ormolu decoration, this fantastic edifice having been designed by the architect Alexander Schtakenaneider. Almond's audio-visual facilities comprised an ancient microphone, a single spotlight operated manually with various different coloured plastic filters, and the accompanying gesture of Martin Watkins' piano. Again we come back to the communicative instrument of his voice, and the naked emotional charge which it conveys. Marc Almond's Russian concerts were renewed proof that his voice alone had grown into the pivotal instrument on which his future would depend.

By the early summer, news had infiltrated to the phalanx of Almond devotees that his long overdue French album, originally recorded in 1986, was due to have an autumn release date, although the project was still without a confirmed title. Almond spoke of having a new song, 'Absinthe', awaiting release, and also of having recorded the two songs he had performed on *Viva Cabaret*, 'Life Is A Lonely Drag', and 'Yesterday When I Was Young'. There was news of him being approached to take the part of Paul Verlaine in a film being made about Rimbaud and Verlaine, but Almond's career seemed to be without a positive direction. Although the singer was to re-record and remix much of the material on *Absinthe* in the summer of 1993, he was to neither promote nor publicise this album. And so, *Absinthe*, which to my mind is his greatest achievement to date, was to come out as an underworld release; almost unreviewed in Britain, and orientated solely towards the cult side of Marc Almond's oeuvre.

Continuing a seemingly increasing preoccupation to play short sets at relatively obscure venues, Almond took up an option to perform a half hour set to backing tapes on the 18th July at a small club in Krefeld, near Düsseldorf, close to the Dutch/German border. There at the Königsburg club, and dressed in a red sequinned shirt and leather trousers, Almond performed a spirited suite of songs which included 'I've Never Seen Your Face', 'The Desperate Hours', 'Beautiful Brutal Thing', 'My Hand Over My Heart', and as a fitting tribute to a gay icon, his version of Madonna's 'Like A Prayer'.

Given his developing predilection for recondite performance, the singer was to appear on the 27th August as the star attraction at the Sopot Forest Opera Festival in Poland. A gravely introspective acoustic concert played out of doors, and in a drivingly cold wind, the show which was filmed for Polish television found a harrowingly skeletal singer performing in best voice. Hauntingly autumnal, right from the extemporised opening bars of 'Amnesia Nights', through to the sustained funeral rites of 'Black Heart', 'There Is A Bed', 'Mr. Sad', 'Vision', and 'Youth', the inflected sadness in Almond's voice seemed appropriate to the forest surroundings. The resonating chord struck by the singer's voice was one of inner pain finding its modulated release through breath. Dressed unadventurously, but sensibly, in a leather jacket and jeans, and with a bunch of red roses placed on the piano-top, Almond faced the same problems as he had previously experienced in Russia. In particular, that of an undemonstrative and repressed audience who found it hard to show their genuine register of enthusiasm. Stopping the show at one point, in mid-passage with 'Jacky', Almond demonstrated his displeasure at the contained applause, expressively throwing the roses stem by stem over his shoulder to indicate what he felt to be a lack of audience appreciation. Events weren't helped by much of the audience drifting away during the performance, but Almond's vocalisation of a short suite of painfully sensitive elegies, broken by stridently vigorous renditions of 'Mother Fist', 'Toreador In The Rain', and 'Jacky', constituted one of his finest concerts; comparable in its moody, autumnal atmospherics to the *Violent Silence* set of songs performed at the Bloomsbury Theatre in 1984.

The Sopot Forest Opera Festival was yet another diverse performance achievement for a singer whose work has taken him from theatres on Broadway, to clubs in Las Vegas, to department stores in Tokyo, go-go bars in Bangkok, strip joints in Hamburg, churches in Berlin, palatial theatres in Russia, the amphitheatre in Athens, and the prestigious London Palladium and The Royal Albert Hall.

Almond was to give a club performance in Potsdam in the suburbs of Berlin, a month later on 25th September, as part of a week long tribute to Derek Jarman. On stage at midnight in a drag bar warehouse called Waschaus, and constrained by the use of backing tapes, Almond was to deliver a surprise set of songs which included first ever live performances of 'A Love Outgrown', and 'The Slave', the latter song coming from the newly released *Absinthe* album. 'Deadly Serenade' was another unexpected inclusion in a brief repertoire which took in 'Tears Run Rings', 'I've Never Seen Your Face', 'A Man', 'Jacky', 'In Your Bed', and by way of an encore, 'The Desperate Hours'.

After an interminable wait of seven years, brought about by lack of record company interest in the material, and by difficulties connected with permissions, Some Bizzare finally released the companion album to *Jacques*, *Absinthe* in September 1993, although the singer was to offer the release no live support or interviews. As with *Jacques*, Europe offered a more enthusiastic reception to this finest and most serious suite of songs that the singer has released to date.

Absinthe arrived in the autumn, a season when one dreams of châteaux, burgundy coloured leaves flicking into dark moats, poems that instate a new imaginative reality, and of death which comes closer in its protean forms, death which might be at the interior of a forest, or beneath a lover's tongue, and is always there to complement love and desire. It's a time when we encounter the Marquis de Sade on the road to his ruined château at La Coste, and he is still wearing a grey coat and an orange silk shirt. There's a story how at the end of his life in confinement at Charenton he would order baskets of red roses, and then proceed to trample each flower underfoot as he found the realisation of beauty too intolerable. Autumn is like holding a glass of wine up to the sun before drinking that rich fire. It's a time when we take account of age, summer is for youth and white beaches, autumn is for reflection and deepening, it's a season in which to evaluate experience lived and known. We think of the mad poet Hölderlin watching the countryside turn red from his tower, and of Keats spitting blood around the time of writing his 'Ode To Autumn', of the Austrian poet Georg Trakl sleeping out in the woods and evoking autumn through his melancholy lyricism. We think of Rimbaud stepping out under the yellow chestnut leaves, his mind lit with vision, his breath smoking on the country road. Time seems to hang suspended, there's a stillness in the air, the days seem like a tableau of unrequited losses, and sometimes one can imagine a blue tear escaping from a statue's eye, or a great boar running through the forest with a girl's red scarf trailing from a tusk. In his *Memoirs* the Italian painter Giorgio de Chirico writes of autumn as "that ineffable melancholy, that strange, distant and profound poetry that Nietzsche discovered in the clear autumn afternoons, especially when they lie over certain Italian cities such as Turin." Autumn is what? A sunken lake, a red bonfire, a rusty key that no longer fits the heart, and its elegy, song, and Barbara's reflective question, "My final autumn perhaps?"

Absinthe is an infamously potent liqueur, 'the fairy with the green eyes' favoured by the decadent poets and artists of the 1890's. Oscar Wilde drank copious amounts of it at the Café Royal, Paul Verlaine developed DTs from its consumption, and until its manufacture was actually prohibited by law in 1907 it continued to be the green drink favoured by degenerates and bohemians. An inclination for the forbidden and the decadently taboo has always been one of Marc Almond's most indelible characteristics, so *Absinthe* seemed an appropriate title to a selection of songs that took in lyrics by Charles Baudelaire, Arthur Rimbaud, and originally Paul Verlaine. Most of the songs on *Absinthe* went through two or three different stages of recording and completion, and work was begun as early as 1986 with the then Willing Sinners on versions which I prefer for their underproduction, and for their giving absolute emphasis to the sensitivity of the voice. Included in the original sessions were an exquisitely ethereal version of Barbara's 'Seul' (Alone), in which the voice floats in an aspiring falsetto over a plaintively buried piano, and a stridently sensitive reading of Paul Verlaine's '1,003'. These songs were omitted from the final release and replaced by the later additions 'The Slave', and 'Yesterday When I Was Young'.

Absinthe brings together songs which pursue the salient emotional preoccupations which have recurred in Marc Almond's work over a long and extraordinarily diverse career. They provide a framework in which to explore complex and extreme psychological states like incest, being a sex slave, and living constantly outside convention.

There is no precedent for *Absinthe* in English, any more than there was for *Jacques*, and French *chanson* with its emphasis on poetic lyric, and its demand for a phrasing which accentuates image, is an extraordinarily difficult medium to handle in English. There's the busy wordiness of the lyrics, and of course the gravity of tone implied by poetry, but for Almond it's the perfect dramatic genre, and one which allows full expression to the essentially tragic sensibility he projects through the medium of song. Taking colour from his impassioned sense of empathy with the originals, Almond succeeds in making the lyrics distinctly his own. The vocals are often more accomplished than those on *Jacques*, and the complex range of material covered allows for the exploration of a richer emotional field. From the playfully camp 'Undress Me', a song written by Robert Nyel for Juliette Greco, and Almond is the first male singer to add it to his repertoire, through to Aznavour's 'Yesterday When I Was Young', the album's predominant concerns are psychologically introspective. What's explored is an inner landscape, that prerogative of French poetry, for which there appears to be no identifiable terra firma, and which inhabits an obsessively imaginal universe.

Almond's version of the two Baudelaire lyrics, originally sung and arranged by Léo Ferré, one of the most prolific and engaging of French lyricists, are masterful renderings of the sombre, sin-orientated side of Baudelaire's death-obsessed poetics. Baudelaire's poetry, with its inexorable melancholy draped over each line like a mist on the river, inhabits a twilight world in which the neurotic take refuge from the ruthless psychological exposure the poet anticipates at death. A bohemian aesthete disinherited from family wealth, a syphilitic tormented by the inequalities of a ruinous love affair with a mulatto mistress, Jeanne Duval, Baudelaire who published his infamous collection of poems *Les Fleurs du Mal* in 1857, died at the age of 46 ten years later. Beleaguered by poverty, illness, and notoriety, and dependent for much of his life on opium, Baudelaire's decidedly modern sensibility was to highlight the predicament of the artist as outsider; the poet as social pariah who lives and dies for a commitment despised by the bourgeois. Baudelaire's life symbolises the wound, the psychological confessionalism of a voice reviled by reactionary bureaucrats in literature. It seemed more than appropriate that Marc Almond, an outsider to contemporary song, and a voice every bit as concerned as Baudelaire with poetic truth, should adopt the latter's despairing persona for the two songs 'Abel and Cain' and 'Remorse of The Dead', the second of the two songs resonating as a sparse elegy, a cry from the tomb as to the injustices suffered by the body's decay. The poem was originally written in strict sonnet form, and addressed to the eventual decomposition of Jeanne Duval. The poet seeks a compensating revenge in imagining his lover laid out in a black marble tomb, a prey to dissolution by worms. The poet has oracular knowledge of the dead, and feeds on the idea of this advantage over the insensible decay of his once voluptuous mistress. Almond's tone is perfect in its enquiry, and seeks an answer from the dead where none is found. The song is given the atmospherics of death-rites, and is executed with exemplary skill.

The two meditative elegies 'Lost Paradise', and 'Secret Child', the first written by Robert Nyel, and the second by Juliette Greco, are in their balladic form perfectly suited to Marc Almond's voice, and to his thematic pursuit of lost innocence as it occurs to adult experience. For Almond, innocence and childhood are characterised by a return to the sea, and 'Secret Child' evokes the image of retrieving a shell from the sand, and of keeping alive the secret child within one, as the source of generative creativity. Almond's own composition 'Youth', stands with these two songs in their fragile conjuration of childhood associations from which the adult is dispossessed.

Perhaps the most outstanding song on *Absinthe*, and as we know it, Marc Almond's favourite, is 'The Slave', a song written by Serge Lama and Yves Gilbert, and sung originally by Serge Lama, one of the most authoritative French singer/songwriters in the tradition of Jacques Brel. Lama's powerful voice and passionate performance attributes, make him very much into one of Marc Almond's integrated prototypes, and this decadently perverse lyric which recounts the desires of a sex-slave in a Byzantine harem, intent on being buggered in a cage, and imploring that he should become a real woman, is one of the most hauntingly bizarre of songs, and as such, a model of quintessential corruption. A litany to transsexuality, Almond's intimately confessional tone suffuses the song with anima, and the connotations of *"heavy black pearls"* and *"purple-blue eyelids"* enlist the image of a Byzantine ephebe, as well as that of a modern day initiate to an S&M dungeon. The song embraces the mysteries of life and death, in a way that is ideally suited to Almond's subjective preoccupations, his voice affirming the insoluble enigma surrounding both states, and the image of crawling naked on all fours across the floor as an act of prostrate self-debasement, is carried superbly by the sense of feminine importunacy in the voice. There are few moments more moving in Almond's recorded oeuvre than those at the end of 'The Slave' when he prays to God that he becomes a real woman.

'We need dreams and we need mysteries and we need the unexplained, and we need death as the biggest mystery of them all,' Almond had commented in a 1992 interview. The songs on *Absinthe*, particularly 'The Slave', 'Incestuous Love', and 'A Man', deal precisely with these themes, and the psychological evaluation of sex, gender, and experience in how they relate to life and death. One of the most mysterious of French singers, and one of the most poetically talented as a lyricist, Barbara, has been a legend in France since the sixties, and while her records have become fewer, live recordings of the annual series of concerts she performs each winter, have maintained her legendary and enigmatic status, her expressive voice and simple piano accompaniment evoking the poignantly moving and luminous grace of her lyric compositions. Almond's rendition of 'Incestuous Love', with its leanings towards falsetto, is an exquisitely sensitive one, his reading of the disparity in ages between the couple, one is forty and the other twenty, being mastered with the *"luminous tenderness"* which suffuses a song about a taboo subject. There's no English equivalent of 'Incestuous Love', and discussion of such a difficult area of sexual attraction could only be achieved by resonant lyricism. The song oscillates between temptation and consummation, death as *"my final autumn perhaps"*, and life as the opening up of a closed house in spring, and the letting go of the child love into the world. Again, the song is fragrantly autumnal, and one imagines the forbidden sex taking place in a château, the heavy red leaves falling outside, and the couple coming together in a high room by a massive open hearth. Almond's voice imparts just the right notion of secrecy to the idea of incestuous love, and the ethereal quality of his voice affords the song the notion of castrati singing in a ruined chapel.

The song that completes the trilogy of poetically decadent material on *Absinthe*, is Robert Nyel's composition 'A Man', another lyric which highlights the oppositional tensions between innocence and experience. Childhood and youth involve a dream of an indefinite future, the possibilities are as endless as they are unsublimated, but with the passage of years between youth and adulthood, boundaries become more defined, and there's a realisation that limitations are imposed by self and society, and the hardening is like the wolf in the song which scratches its nails on the heart. We grow into a personal destiny, *"I must postpone my Spanish château/dreams which befuddle like an old wine."* The voyage is towards masculine savagery, identification with the wolf, the cutting free from angelic protection, and the testing of experience on the pulses and the heart. A drivingly fast and impassioned song, Almond loses none of his articulacy in delivering this up-tempo song, a number which he had begun to include in the repertoire of his acoustic concerts in the early nineties.

There are other more marginal successes on *Absinthe*; a hauntingly sparse reading of 'Rue Des Blancs-Manteaux', the lyric which Jean Paul Sartre had written specifically for Juliette Greco, which with its executioner's guillotine sentiments is like a sharp bite at a green apple, and the delicately restrained 'In Your Bed', for a long time a favourite at Almond concerts, which by its suggestiveness and playful sexual ambiguity fits well with the singer's facility to adopt a female persona.

There's a fine attempt to master Arthur Rimbaud's poem 'My Little Lovers', which should have been complemented by his recording of Verlaine's '1,003', in order to bring out the dual hostilities of their relationship as homosexual lovers. Arthur Rimbaud, the schoolboy visionary from Charleville, who proposed a poetry constructed from "the systematic derangement of all the senses", and who propounded a belief in the poet as voyou and alchemist, believed in the state of hallucinated delirium as poetic truth. Perverse, emotionally cold and generously gifted with genius, Rimbaud gave up writing poetry at the age of 19, after altering its future as a consequence of his risk-taking imaginative experiments. He was to prove one of the prototypical inspirations behind surrealism, and André Breton was to include Rimbaud, Edgar Allan Poe, Gerard de Nerval and Lautréamont in his approved pantheon of surrealist heroes. Rimbaud's 'My Little Lovers' is expressive of the poet's youthful bohemianism, and the essential perversity of his sexual fantasies. He will whip his lover, and break his hips for having loins, rather than offer a sensual or erotic love. Rimbaud was known to slash Verlaine's palm with a knife, and to blow smoke into the nostrils of waiting horses, and his untamed sensibility is everywhere evident in 'My Little Lovers', with the poet's sneering irony finding uppermost voice in Almond's idiosyncratic colouring of the sadistic lyrics. Rimbaud too, is characterised by autumn, his heels kicking up leaves on the country roads between Charleville and the Belgian border, his voluntary pariahism and confrontational hostility to any form of institution, finding support in his return to nature, and eventually in his exile as a gunrunner in the Sahara. The most ferociously contemptuous of modern poets, Almond appears to find less empathy with 'My Little Lovers', than the two Baudelaire lyrics, but the song is still vitally construed, and lives as an important constituent to the overall feel of *Absinthe*.

One of the most beautiful songs on *Absinthe*, and a fitting coda to its lyricism is the smoky blue Charles Aznavour number 'Yesterday When I Was Young', a tear-jerking lament for vanished youth, and one in which the speed and recklessness of youth are counterbalanced against the retrospective experience implied by age. A pivotal song to Marc Almond's own advancing maturity, there are few more inspired openings to a song than *"Yesterday when I was young/the taste of life was sweet/As rain upon my tongue."* Almond commits his whole passionate being to the song, an emotionally charged heart-wrung elegy that reaches for the invisible stars, and it's a song to die for, one that might fittingly see the singer collapse into a pool of red roses on a darkened stage. A romantic elegy framed around the admission to age, *Absinthe* perhaps lacks the other Aznavour song that Almond was to release as his finest single to date, 'What Makes A Man A Man', but 'Yesterday When I Was Young' seems the fitting conclusion to the autumnal beauty and despair surrounding *Absinthe*.

December 1993 was to bring the 7th annual Convention at the opulently baroque Café de Paris at Leicester Square, Marc Almond delivering a short set of songs to the accompaniment of a backing tape, and inspired versions of 'Jacky' and 'A Man' were set against slower surprises like 'A Love Outgrown', and the sublime 'The Slave'. Offering little clue as to his direction for the future, and still without a new album or plans to tour, the Convention was nonetheless a generous affirmation that the singer was still alive and with us. Unrehearsed, and clearly tired, Almond gave a spirited display which was deeply appreciated by his loyal fans, and a week later he was to perform a short set on New Year's Eve at Astoria 2 for Jeremy Joseph's G.A.Y., a set which incorporated 'Tainted Love', and 'The Days Of Pearly Spencer'.

News of the continuous delay involved in the recording of his new album, and the severance of his contract with Warners in the process of work on a new studio album in New York, have all added fears to the penumbra surrounding Marc Almond's future. Known for his chameleonic and regenerative abilities to come back, to surprise the opposition just when his chances appear at their lowest, the four years which have elapsed since the release of *Tenement Symphony* are the longest period in his career that he has been without a new studio album. He has spoken in a recent interview in *Attitude* of problems with agoraphobia and memory loss due to tranquilliser addiction as being responsible for the absence of concerts over the past four years; the forgetting of lines in songs having become a familiar eccentricity which characterises Marc Almond concerts. Benzodiazepines can contribute towards periodic memory loss, but now in the process of detoxification there's every reason to believe that Marc Almond will make a full recovery; and with news of a new recording contract with Mercury, and an album tentatively titled *The Fantastic Star* planned for release in autumn 1995, it is hoped he will quickly regain his status as the last and greatest star.

Autumn again. Perhaps it's always that season in one's heart, a red cloak draped over the poet's body, a copy of Jean Genet's *Our Lady Of The Flowers* open in the flowerseller's hand, a black boat putting out into the sea-fog, or it's Soho, the cries of the marketeers, the alleys echoing in the afternoons, the busy crowds coming and going down Wardour Street into Old Compton Street, and up Frith and Greek Street, carriers of hope and despair alive in the little moment in time which comprises life. And sometimes you'll see Marc Almond in those crowds, nervously preoccupied, or looking for a London taxi. Poetry is made of those moments. Turn a red leaf over and you may find the first line of a poem written on its veined underside. Marc Almond is a theatrically orphic voice, a man who lives in a converted church in Fulham, the light leaking through apocalyptically stained glass windows, the one who has taken up poetry and placed it in song, restored it to one of its most eloquent expressions. We may now and always place a crown of dark laurel leaves on his head.

POSTSCRIPT

This book was completed in March 1995, before Marc Almond's return to live performance, and before the release of the new single 'Adored And Explored'. It is intended that an expanded edition of this book will in time encompass his new recordings and touring projects.

—J. R.

DISCOGRAPHY

This discography spans Marc Almond's recorded musical career from 1980 to 1993. No claim is being made that the discography is definitive, merely that the compilers have done their very best to collate all available material.

All information relates to British releases, and no attempt has been made to cover white labels, foreign releases, promo copies, DJ releases, and unofficial recordings. Such information is outside the scope of this present book but may form part of a future edition.

If there are any inaccuracies or omissions or you have any additional information then please contact Vaudeville & Burlesque, the official Marc Almond fan club, whose address is at the back of this book.

This discography has been compiled by Peter Colebrook, and Michelle Robek from Vaudeville & Burlesque.

SOFT CELL

SINGLES

Sep 1980
Mutant Moments – 7″ EP, p/s with b&w postcard
Potential • *L.O.V.E. Feelings* • *Metro MR X* • *Frustration*

Big Frock ABF 1

Did not chart. The first ever Soft Cell release. Only 2000 pressed. Came with a postcard insert. Sleeve also credits Steven Griffith on visuals. Re-pressed by the Japanese Fan Club which is identical to the original apart from a printed matrix number on the run-out grooves.

Feb 1981
A Man Can Get Lost • *Memorabilia* – 7″, p/s
Some Bizzare HARD 1
Memorabilia (Long Version) • *Persuasion* – 12″, p/s

HARD 12

Did not chart. Produced by Daniel Miller who had been in The Normal and was the label boss at Mute Records. *A Man Can Get Lost* and *Persuasion* are both re-recordings of tracks from the original **Mutant Moments** sessions. The 12″ was reissued in 1990 on CD in Germany on **Phonogram 875 401-2.**

Jul 1981
Tainted Love • *Where Did Our Love Go* – 7″, p/s

Phonogram BZS 2
Tainted Love/Where Did Our Love Go • *Tainted Dub* – 12″, p/s

BZS 212

Aug 1981
Tainted Love • *Memorabilia* – 12″, p/s
BZS 212

Reached Number 1 and subsequently re-entered the chart on three seperate occasions. Produced by Mike Thorne.

Written by Ed Cobb who had been in the Four Preps and the Piltdown Men and originally recorded by Gloria Jones. The song was a much played classic on the Northern Soul scene. Both versions of the 12" contain the *Where Did Our Love Go* segue. *Where Did Our Love Go* was originally recorded by the Supremes and written by the Tamla Motown songwriting team of Brian Holland, Lamont Dozier and Edward Holland Jr. and reached Number 3 in September 1964. *Tainted Love • Where Did Our Love Go* was released as a 7" in Japan with a different sleeve in Japan on **7PP-57**. *Tainted Love* and *Memorabilia* was released as a 7" in USA on **49855**. The 12" was reissued in 1990 on CD in Germany on **Phonogram 875 401-2**.

Oct 1981
Bedsitter • Facility Girls – 7", p/s
Phonogram BZS 6
Bedsitter (Early Morning Dance Side) • *Facility Girls* (Late Night Listening Side) – 12", p/s
BZS 612
Reached Number 4. Produced by Mike Thorne. The 12" features extended versions of both tracks. The 12" was reissued in 1990 on CD in Germany on **Phonogram 880 743-2**.

Oct 1981
Metro MRX – 7", red flexi
Lyntone LYN 10410

Given away free with issue 12 of *Flexipop* magazine. There was also a very limited release on black vinyl. There were two tracks on the flexi, the other being *Remembrance Day* by B Movie.

Jan 1982
Say Hello Wave Goodbye • Say Hello Wave Goodbye Instrumental – 7", p/s
Phonogram BZS 7
Say Hello Wave Goodbye (Extended Version) • Fun City – 12", p/s
BZS 712

Reached Number 3. *Say Hello Wave Goodbye* was produced by Mike Thorne and featured Dave Tofani on clarinet. *Fun City* was recorded live, and is essentially a

Marc and the Mambas recording with Anne Hogan and Tim Taylor playing. *Say Hello Wave Goodbye* was backed with *Bedsitter* in some countries. The 12" was reissued in 1990 on CD in Germany on **Phonogram 875 403-2**.

Apr 1982
Torch • Insecure Me – 7", p/s
Phonogram BZS 9
Torch • Insecure Me – 12", p/s
BZS 912

Reached Number 2. Produced by Mike Thorne. Cindy Ecstasy provides voice on both tracks, John Gatchell played trumpet on *Torch*, and Dave Tofani played tenor sax on *Insecure Me*. The 12" features extended versions of both tracks. Came in a different sleeve in some countries. The 12" was reissued in 1990 on CD in Germany on **Phonogram 875 397-2**.

Jul 1982
What! • ....So – 7", p/s
Phonogram BZS 11
What! • ....So – 12", p/s
BZS 112

Reached Number 3. *What!* produced by Mike Thorne and *....So* produced by Dave Ball. *What!* was written by H B Barnum and originally recorded by Judy Clay, like *Tainted Love* it was another Northern Soul classic. The 12" features an extended version of both tracks. *....So* was written and performed by Dave Ball on his own. The 12" was reissued in 1990 on CD in Germany on **Phonogram 875 399-2**.

Nov 1982
Where The Heart Is • It's A Mugs Game – 7", p/s
Phonogram BZS 16
Where The Heart Is • It's A Mugs Game – 12", diff p/s
BZS 1612

Reached Number 21. Produced by Mike Thorne, John Gatchell plays trumpet. The 12" version features extended versions of both tracks. The 12" was reissued in 1990 on CD in Germany on **Phonogram 812 591-2**.

Dec 1982
The 12" Singles – 12" box set with colour brochure

Phonogram CEL BX 1

Box set containing the first six 12" singles.

Feb 1983
Numbers • Barriers – 7", p/s

Phonogram BZS 17
Numbers • Barriers – 12", p/s

BZS 1712

Reached Number 25. Produced by Soft Cell and Mike Thorne. The 12" features extended versions of both songs by Dave Ball assisted by Flood. This was released as a double A-sided single. Initial copies came shrink-wrapped together with a copy of *Tainted Love*. The 12" was reissued in 1990 on CD in Germany on **Phonogram 811 139-2**.

Mar 1983
Say Hello, Wave Goodbye – 7", light blue flexi

Live flexi available only to members of the Soul Mates Fan Club. Recorded at the Theatre Royal, Drury Lane on 5th December 1982.

Sep 1983
Soul Inside • You Only Live Twice – 7", p/s

Phonogram BZS 20
Soul Inside • You Only Live Twice • Loving You – Hating Me • Her Imagination – 7", p/s, limited edition double pack

BZS 2020
Soul Inside • Loving You – Hating Me (remix) • You Only Live Twice • 007 Theme – 12", diff p/s

BZS 2012

Reached Number 16. Produced by Soft Cell. The 12" features an extended version of *Soul Inside*, and the 7" double pack and 12" feature an extended version of *Loving You – Hating Me*, this was remixed by Soft Cell. *You Only Live Twice* written by John Barry and Leslie Bricusse and taken from the James Bond film **Thunderball**. *007 Theme* written by John Barry. *Her Imagination* was recorded for the David Jensen Show on BBC Radio 1 and produced by John Sparrow. The tracks on the 12"

were released on a cassette and as a mini LP in the USA. The 12" was reissued in 1990 on CD in Germany on **Phonogram 814 249-2**.

Feb 1984
Down In The Subway • Disease And Desire – 7", p/s

Phonogram BZS 22
Down In The Subway • Disease And Desire • Born To Lose – 12", p/s

BZS 2212
Mar 1984
Down in the Subway (Extended Remix) • Disease and Desire • Born to Lose – 12", diff p/s

BZSR 2212

Reached Number 24. Produced by Soft Cell. Gini Ball provides backing vocals, Gary Barnacle plays sax on *Disease And Desire*. The first Soft Cell 12" which did not feature extended versions. This was put right with the release of a second 12" a month later with a gold sleeve and black margin and contained an extended version of *Down In The Subway*. *Down In The Subway* was written by Jack Hammer. *Born To Lose* was written and originally recorded by Johnny Thunders and the Heartbreakers. The 12" was reissued in 1990 on CD in Germany on **Phonogram 818 437-2**.

Apr 1984
Ghostrider – 7", flexi

Live flexi. Originally written and recorded by seminal New York electropunk duo Suicide.

1990
Soft Cell CD Singles

Phonogram 878 241-2

This was a German CD box set containing all 10 Soft Cell 12" singles on separate CD's.

Mar 1991
Say Hello Wave Goodbye '91 • Memorabilia '91 – 7", p/s

Mercury SOFT 1
Say Hello Wave Goodbye '91 (The Long

Goodbye – Extended Mendelsohn Remix) •
Memorabilia '91 (Extended Grid Remix)
– 12", p/s
SOFT 112
Say Hello Wave Goodbye '91 •
Memorabilia '91 – cassette
SOFMC 1
Say Hello Wave Goodbye '91 • (The Long
Goodbye – Extended Mendelsohn Remix) •
Memorabilia '91 (Extended Grid Remix) – CD
SOFCD 1
Say Hello Wave Goodbye '91 • *Numbers*
(Original Version) • *Torch* (Original 12"
Version) – picture CD
SOFCP 1

Reached Number 38. *Say Hello Wave
Goodbye '91* was produced by Mike Thorne
and remixed by Julian Mendelsohn.
Memorabilia '91 was produced by Daniel
Miller and remixed by The Grid who
comprise Richard Norris and erstwhile Soft
Cell partner Dave Ball.

May 1991
Tainted Love (Original Version) • *Tainted
Love '91* – 7", p/s
Mercury SOFT 2
Tainted Love (Original 12" Version) •
Tainted Love '91 – 12", p/s
SOFT 212
Tainted Love (Original Version) • *Tainted
Love '91* – cassette
SOFMC 2
Tainted Love • *Where The Heart Is*
(Original 12" Version) • *Tainted Love*
(Original 12" Version) – CD, limited numbers
came in a leather wallet
SOFCD 2
Tainted Love • *Loving You Hating Me*
(Original 7" Version) • *Where The Heart Is*
– picture CD
SOFCP 2

Reached Number 5. Produced by Mike
Thorne. The '91 remix of *Tainted Love* was
by Julian Mendelsohn. There was an
advance DJ promo with different sleeve of
Tainted Love (The Mendelsohn Mix) •
Tainted Love (The Grid Remix) DJ on **SOFT
DJ 212**. Also released as *Tainted Love '91* •
Where The Heart Is in Australia in a card
sleeve on **848 426-2**.

1991

Bedsitter • *Torch*
Mercury SOFT 3
Bedsitter (Original 12") • *Bedsitter '91* •
You Only Live Twice
SOFT 313

Never released but was available as a
promo.

1991
Megamix '91: *Tainted Love/What/
Bedsitter/Torch* • *Bedsitter*
Mercury SOFT DJ 312

This was a DJ only release.

ALBUMS

Mar 1981
Some Bizzare Album – LP with inner bag
The Girl With The Patent Leather Face
Some Bizzare BZLP 1

Reached Number 58. A various artists
album that included one Soft Cell track.
Also released on cassette **Some Bizzare
BZMC 1** then re-released in **April 1992** on
Phonogram 5102974 and released on CD
on **5102972**.

Dec 1981
Non Stop Erotic Cabaret – LP with inner bag
lyric sheet
Frustration • *Tainted Love* • *Seedy Films* •
Youth • *Sex Dwarf* • *Entertain Me* • *Chips
On My Shoulder* • *Bedsitter* • *Secret Life* •
Say Hello, Wave Goodbye
Phonogram BZLP 2

Reached Number 25. Produced by Mike
Thorne, backing vocals provided by Vicious
Pink Phenomenon, Dave Tofani plays sax
on *Frustration* and clarinet on *Seedy Films*.
Also released on cassette **Phonogram BZMC
2**, then re-released in **April 1982** on
Phonogram 8000612 and released on CD
on **8000614**.

Jun 1982
Non Stop Ecstatic Dancing – LP
Memorabilia • *Where Did Our Love go* •
What • *A Man Could Get Lost* • *Chips On
My Shoulder* • *Sex Dwarf*
Phonogram BZX 1012

Reached Number 6. Mike Thorne produced, Cindy Ecstasy provides rap on *Memorabilia*, Dave Tofani plays tenor sax, John Gatchell plays trumpet and flugel horn. This is an album of specially remixed dance versions of Soft Cell songs. Also released on cassette **Phonogram BZM 1012** then re-released in **April 1992** on **Phonogram 510295-4** and released on CD **510295-2**.

Apr 1983
The Art Of Falling Apart – LP with inner bag and free 12" (see below)
Forever The Same • Where The Heart Is • Numbers • Heat • Kitchen Sink Drama • Baby Doll • Loving You, Hating Me • The Art Of Falling Apart

Phonogram BIZL 3

Reached Number 5. Produced by Mike Thorne and Soft Cell, John Gatchell plays trumpet. The 12" came with initial copies of the album and contained the tracks *Martin* and *Hendrix Medley* comprising the tracks *Hey Joe/Purple Haze/Voodoo Chile* and was given the separate catalogue number of **Apart 12** though it was never separately available. The original recording of *Hey Joe* is in some dispute but it is generally thought to have been by The Leaves though Jimi Hendrix was to make the song his own reaching Number 6 in Feb 1967; *Purple Haze* and *Voodoo Chile* were written and originally recorded by Hendrix reaching respectively Number 3 in May 1967 and Number 1 in Nov 1970. Also released on cassette **Phonogram BIZLC 3** with the extra tracks *Martin* and the *Hendrix Medley*, then re-released in **April 1992** on **Phonogram 510296-4** and released on CD **Phonogram 510 296-2** with the extra tracks.

May 1984
This Last Night In Sodom – LP with inner bag lyric sheet
Mr. Self Destruct • Slave To This • Little Rough Rhinestone • Meet Murder My Angel • The Best Way To Kill • L'Esqualita • Down In The Subway • Surrender (To A Stranger) • Soul Inside • Where Was Your Heart (When You Needed It Most)

Phonogram BIZL 6

Reached Number 12. Produced by Soft Cell assisted by Tim Dewey. Sister Celeste provided voice on *Slave To This*, Gary Barnacle played sax and Gini Ball provided vocals. Also released on cassette **Phonogram 818 436-1** then re-released in **April 1992** on **Phonogram 818436-4** and released on CD **818436-2**.

Dec 1986
Soft Cell – The Singles – LP
Memorabilia • Tainted Love • Bedsitter • Say Hello Wave Goodbye • Torch • What • Where The Heart Is • Numbers • Soul Inside • Down In The Subway

Phonogram BZLP 3

Reached Number 87. Also released on cassette **Phonogram BZMC 3**, then later released on CD **Phonogram 830708-2** with the extra track *Loving You, Hating Me*.

Apr 1991
Memorabilia – The Singles – LP
Memorabilia '91 • Tainted Love • Bedsitter • Torch • What • Say Hello Wave Goodbye '91 • Soul Inside • Where The Heart Is

Reached Number 8. The album is credited to Soft Cell/Marc Almond and also includes 4 Marc Almond tracks. Also released on cassette **Mercury 848 512-4** and on CD **Mercury 848 512-2** with the extra track *Say Hello Wave Goodbye* 12" (The Long Goodbye – Extended Mendelsohn Remix). The collection was also available on video.

Jun 1994
Down In The Subway – CD
Where Did Our Love Go • Memorabilia • Torch • Entertain Me • Fun City • Secret Life • Kitchen Sink Drama • Down In The Subway • Baby Doll • Where The Heart Is • Insecure Me • Seedy Films • Loving You, Hating Me • Soul Inside

Phonogram 550 189-2

Did not chart. Only released on CD. This was a budget priced release.

Phonogram BZS 2112

The Mambas were a loose collective of musicians who included: Annie Hogan – keyboards; Steve Sherlock – saxes and flutes; Lee Jenkinson – guitars, bass, drums; Gini Hewes – violin; Anne Stephenson – violin; Martin McCarrick – violin; Billy McGee – Double bass

SINGLES

Mar 1981
Sleaze (Take It, Shake It) • *Taking It And Shaking It* – 12˚, p/s
Some Bizzare BZS5 12

This was only available to members of the Gutter Hearts Fan Club. Produced by David Ball, Tim Taylor plays bass, and Dave Ball – credited as Lance Rock – plays drums and synth.

Nov 1982
Big Louise • *Empty Eyes* – 7˚, p/s
Phonogram BZS 15
Big Louise • *Empty Eyes* • *The Dirt Behind The Neon (Sleaze Revisited)* – 12˚, p/s
BZS 1512

Though shown in many discographies, including an official one included in the brochure that came with the Soft Cell **Twelve Inch Singles** box set which even showed picture sleeves, this single was never released and no copies exist.

Jun 1983
Black Heart • *Your Aura* – 7˚, p/s, with colour postcard
Phonogram BZS 19
Black Heart • *Your Aura* • *Mamba* – 12˚, p/s
BZS 1912

Reached Number 49. Produced by Flood and Marc. The 12" featured an extended mix of *Black Heart*. Matt Johnson plays guitar and provides backing vocals on *Black Heart*.

Nov 1983
Torment • *First Time* • *You'll Never See Me On A Sunday* • *Megamillionmania-Multimaniamix* – 12˚, p/s

Did not chart. *Megamillionmania-Multimaniamix* was produced by Flood, Jim Thirlwell – credited as Frank – and Marc, all other tracks by Marc and Flood. *Torment* was co-written with erstwhile Banshee Steve Severin, and is an extended version of the track on *Torment and Toreros*. *Megamillionmania-Multimaniamix* was co-written with Jim Thirlwell who plays all instruments and provides backing vocals - credited as Karl Satan and the Transvestites from Hell. This is an extended version of *A Million Mania's* from. *Torment and Toreros*. Only released as a 12˚, some discographies mention a 7˚, though this was never released.

Apr 1986
Your Aura – 7˚, one sided clear flexi

Given away free to members of Gutter Hearts Fan Club.

ALBUMS

Sept 1982
Untitled – LP and 12˚ with gatefold sleeve and inner bags
Untitled • *Empty Eyes* • *Angels* • *Big Louise* • *Caroline Says* • *Margaret* • *If You Go Away* • *Terrapin* • *Twilights & Lowlifes* • *Twilights & Lowlifes (Street Walking Soundtrack)*
Phonogram BZS 13

Reached Number 41. Produced by Marc and the Mambas (with special thanks to Steve Short and Flood). Matt Johnson co-wrote and plays all instruments on the track *Untitled* and guitar on *Angels*, he also plays on *Empty Eyes*, and *Twilights & Lowlifes*. Cindy Ecstasy provides backing vocals on *Empty Eyes*, *Terrapin* and *Twilights & Lowlifes*. Peter Ashworth provides percussion on both versions of *Twilights & Lowlifes*. *Big Louise* written and originally recorded by Scott Walker - credited under his real name of Scott Engel, *Caroline Says* written and originally recorded by Lou Reed, *If You Go Away* written and originally recorded (as *Ne Me Quitte Pas*) by Jacques Brel, *Terrapin* written and originally recorded by Syd Barrett. The two versions of *Twilights & Lowlifes* appear on the 12". *Margaret* was written and performed by Annie Hogan on her own. Also released on cassette **BZM 13** and re-released in **April 1992** on Phonogram **510 298-4** and released on CD **510 298-2**.

May 1984
Bite Black & Blues – LP
The Plague • *In My Room* • *Fun City* • *Gloomy Sunday* • *Switchblade Operator* • *Muleskinner Blues* • *Blue Prelude* • *Sleaze*
Gutter Hearts GH 1

A live album recorded at the Duke of York's Theatre on 18th December 1983. The band comprised Annie Hogan on piano and Farfisa, Richard Riley on guitars, Bill McGee on double bass, Martin McCarrick on cello, Audrey Riley on cello, Gary Barnacle on saxophones, Winston Detleir on guitar and bass, Jenny Benwell on violin, Nick Pendlebury on viola, Zeke Manyika on drums, and Nancy Peppers provides vocals on *Muleskinner Blues*. *The Plague* originally written and recorded by Scott Walker. The sleeve credits Raoul And The Ruined though this is *de facto* a Marc And The Mambas performance. Only ever available to members of the Gutter Hearts Fan Club.

Aug 1983
Torment And Toreros – double LP with gatefold sleeve and black inner bags
Intro • *Boss Cat* • *The Bulls* • *Catch A Fallen Star* • *The Animal In You* • *In My Room* • *First Time* • *(Your Love Is A) Lesion* • *My Former Self* • *Once Was* • *The Untouchable One* • *Blood Wedding* • *Black Heart* • *Medley: Narcissus/Gloomy Sunday/Vision* • *Torment* • *A Million Manias* • *My Little Book Of Sorrows* • *Beat Out That Rhythm On A Drum*
Phonogram BIZL 4

Reached Number 28. Produced by Flood and Marc. Jim Thirlwell – credited as Frank Want – plays drums on *Beat Out That Rhythm On A Drum*; and – credited as Jim Foetus And The Transvestites From Hell – co-wrote, plays all instruments and provides backing vocals on *A Million Manias*, Matt Johnson plays guitar on some tracks, Peter Ashworth plays drums and tymps on *Intro* and *My Little Book Of Sorrows*, and Lee Jenkinson provides backing vocals on *Boss Cat*. *The Bulls* written and originally recorded by Jacques Brel, *Blood Wedding* is a traditional Spanish song, *Gloomy Sunday* is a European song written in the 1930's by Lewis/Seress, it has been covered countless times including a version by Lydia Lunch, but most famously by Billie Holliday, *Vision* written and originally recorded by Peter Hammill, *Beat Out That Rhythm On A Drum* is a combination of *Carmen* written by Bizet and *Carmen Jones* by written by Rodgers and Hammerstein. The lyrics to *Boss Cat* were written by Anne Stephenson and Gini Hewes. Also released on cassette **BIZLC 4**, then re-released in **April 1992** on **Phonogram 812 872-4** and released on CD **812 872-2**.

MARC ALMOND AND THE WILLING SINNERS

The Willing Sinners included: Annie Hogan – Piano, Vibes, Marimbas, Pump Organ, Farfisa Organ, Synths and Vocals; Billy McGee – Electric Bass, Double Bass and Vocals; Martin McCarrick – Cello, Keyboards, Accordion, Yang T'Chin, Pump Organ and Vocals; Richard Riley – Acoustic and Electric Guitars and Vocals; Steven Humphreys – Drums and Percussion
with additionally
Gary Barnacle – Saxes; Enrico Tomaso – Trumpet and Flugal Horns; Gini Ball – Violin; Martin Ditchum – Tymps, Percussion; Audrey Riley – Vocals; Jane West – Vocals; Peter Thoms – Trombone; Nigel Eaton – Hurdy Gurdy; Spiros – Bazooki

SINGLES

May 1984
The Boy Who Came Back • *Joey Demento* – 7", p/s

Phonogram BZS 23
The Boy Who Came Back (Loud Cut) • *Joey Demento* (Extended Version) – 12", diff p/s

BZS 2312
The Boy Who Came Back (Loud Cut) • *Joey Demento* (Extended Version) – 10", diff p/s, with colour lyric sheet

BZS 2310

Reached Number 52. Produced by Mike Hedges. Nancy Peppers provides backing vocals on *The Boy Who Came Back*. The Loud Cut is an extended version.

Aug 1984
You Have • *Split Lip* – 7", p/s

Phonogram BZS 24
You Have (Long Version) • *Joey Demento* • *Split Lip* (Long Version) – 12", diff p/s

BZS 2412
You Have (Long Version) • *Black Mountain Blues* • *Split Lip* (Long Version) – 10", diff p/s, with colour lyric sheet

BZS 2410

Reached Number 57. Produced by Mike Hedges. Also released as a special 12" club promo with *Split Lip* • *You Have* (Long Version) • *Joey Demento* (Extended Version) on **BZCLB 2412**.

Nov 1984
Tenderness Is A Weakness • *Love For Sale* – 7", p/s

Phonogram BZS 25
Tenderness Is A Weakness (With Instrumental Overture) • *Love For Sale* • *Pink Shack Blues* • *The Heel* – 10", diff p/s, with lyric sheet

BZS 2510

Did not chart. Produced by Mike Hedges. There was no 12" version. *Love For Sale* was written by Cole Porter. *The Heel* was written by Robinson/Wilson/Ferre and was originally recorded by Eartha Kitt.

1985
Pink Shack Blues (Swing Version)

NME 014

A different mix to the song that appeared on the *Tenderness Is A Weakness* single and the **Vermin In Ermine** album. Appeared on a cassette only various artists release entitled **Raging Spool** and only sold through the NME. This version also appeared on a 12" four track promo advance album sampler for **Vermin In Ermine** together with *Crime Sublime* • *Gutter Hearts* • *Tenderness Is A Weakness* on **Phonogram MADOX 6**.

Aug 1985
Stories Of Johnny • *Stories Of Johnny* (With The Westminster City School Choir) – 7", p/s

Virgin BONK 1

Stories Of Johnny • *Stories Of Johnny* (With The Westminster City School Choir) • *Blond Boy* • *Take My Heart* – 7", p/s, limited edition double pack

BONK 1
Stories Of Johnny • *Blond Boy* • *Stories Of Johnny* (With The Westminster City School Choir) • *Take My Heart* – 12", p/s, with colour poster

BONK 1-12
Stories Of Johnny (Special Remix) • *Blond Boy* • *Stories Of Johnny* (With The Westminster City School Choir) • *Take My Heart* – 10", diff p/s, stickered sleeve

BONK 1-10

Reached Number 23. Produced by Mike Hedges. *Stories Of Johnny* was never backed with *Blond Boy* as a 7" though this is shown in some discographies. The Westminster City School Choir solo by Alexander Mason and the harp played by Julie Allis.

Oct 1985
Love Letter • *Love Letter* (With The Westminster City School Choir) – 7", p/s
Virgin BONK 2
Love Letter • *Love Letter* (With The Westminster City School Choir) – 7", diff p/s, with special full colour poster
BONK P2
Love Letter (Extra Mix) • *Love Letter* (With The Westminster City School Choir) – 12", diff p/s
BONK 2-12
Love Letter (Special Mix) • *Love Letter* (With The Westminster City School Choir) – 10", diff p/s, stickered
BONK 2-10

Reached Number 68. Produced by Mike Hedges. The harp on the Westminster City School Choir version is played by Julie Allis. *Love Letter* is subtitled *A Simple Message Of Undying Devotion*. *Love Letter* Special Mix on 10" is by Cabaret Voltaire.

Dec 1985
The House Is Haunted (By The Echo Of Your Last Goodbye) • *Broken Bracelets* • *Cara A Cara (Face To Face)* • *Medley: Unchain My Heart/Black Heart/Take My Heart* – 7", p/s, double pack, gatefold sleeve
GLOWD 1
The House Is Haunted (By The Echo Of Your Last Goodbye) (Ectoplasmix) • *Broken Bracelets* • *Cara A Cara (Face To Face)* • *Medley: Unchain My Heart/Black Heart/ Take My Heart* • *Burning Boats* – 12", p/s
GLOW 1-12

Reached Number 55. Produced by Mike Hedges. There was not an ordinary 7" release of this single though it is shown in some discographies. *The House Is Haunted (By The Echo Of Your Last Goodbye)* was written by Rose/Adlam and originally recorded by Mel Torme, *Cara A Cara* written by Manola Garcia. *Unchain My*

Heart written by Jones/James. The *Medley* was originally recorded for the Janice Long Show on BBC Radio 1 and produced by Barry Andrews. *Burning Boats* was produced by Jim Thirlwell – credited as Clint Ruin – and is taken from Annie Hogan's *Kickabye* 12" EP. There was a 7" promo with *The House Is Haunted* • *The House Is Haunted* (Time Expanded DJ version) on **GLOWDDJ 1**.

Feb 1986
Oily Black Limousine – 7" EP
MM Vinyl Conflict 1

Marc Almond provided one song on a four track EP given free with *The Melody Maker*

May 1986
A Woman's Story • *For One Moment* – 7", p/s
Virgin GLOW 2
A Woman's Story • *The Heel* • *A Salty Dog* • *The Plague* • *The Little White Cloud That Cried* • *For One Moment* • *Just Good Friends* – 12", p/s
GLOW 2-12
A Woman's Story • *The Heel* • *A Salty Dog* • *The Plague* • *The Little White Cloud That Cried* • *For One Moment* • *Just Good Friends* – 10", stickered clear vinyl sleeve, picture disc
GLOWY 2-10
A Woman's Story • *The Heel* • *A Salty Dog* • *The Plague* • *The Little White Cloud That Cried* • *For One Moment* • *Just Good Friends* – cassette
TGLOW 212

Reached Number 41. Subtitled *Some Songs To Take To The Tomb Compilation One*. Produced by Mike Hedges and Marc Almond. Julie Alis played harp and Roland Sutherland played flute on *Just Good Friends* and *A Salty Dog*. *A Woman's Story* was written by Nino Tempo, April Stevens and Phil Spector and originally recorded by Cher, *For One Moment* was written and originally recorded by Lee Hazelwood, *The Heel* was written by Robinson/Wilson/Ferre and originally recorded by Eartha Kitt, *A Salty Dog* was written by Gary Brooker and Keith Reid and originally recorded by Procul Harem reaching Number 44 in **June**

1969, *The Plague* was written and recorded by Scott Walker under his real name of Scott Engel. *The Little White Cloud That Cried* was written and originally recorded by Johnny Ray, *Just Good Friends* was written and originally recorded by Peter Hammill. It had been intended that the tracks on this would form part of a whole album of cover versions.

Oct 1986
Ruby Red • *I'm Sick Of You Tasting Of Somebody Else* – 7", p/s
Virgin GLOW 3
Ruby Red • *Anarcoma* • *I'm Sick Of You Tasting Of Somebody Else* • *Broken Hearted And Beautiful* • *Jackal Jackal (Mustapha Tomb Stone Teeth)* – 12", p/s
GLOW 3-12
Ruby Red (Special Re-recorded Extended Dance Mix) • *Ruby Red* (Instrumental) • *I'm Sick Of You Tasting Of Somebody Else* – 12", diff p/s
GLOW 3-13

Reached Number 47. Produced by Mike Hedges and Marc Almond. Subtitled the **Stained** EP. *Anarcoma* is based on a cartoon character by Nazario Barcelona, and special thanks is given to Tony Churracca for Spanish voice and translation. *Jackal Jackal* is dedicated to Sebastian Venebles (and Mohammed Jamal). Some copies of the Dance Mix play this mix a second time instead of the Instrumental.

Feb 1987
Melancholy Rose • *Gyp The Blood* – 7", p/s
Virgin GLOW 4
Melancholy Rose • *Gyp The Blood* • *Pirate Jenny* • *Surabaya Johnny* – 7", p/s, double pack gatefold sleeve
GLOWD 4
Melancholy Rose • *Gyp The Blood* • *A World Full Of People* • *Black Lullaby* – 12", p/s, with picture card containing details of Fourth Official Marc Almond Convention
GLOW 4-12

Reached Number 71. Produced by Mike Hedges/Marc Almond. Sally Timms provides backing vocals on all tracks except *Melancholy Rose*. *Pirate Jenny* and *Surabaya Johnny* were both written by

Bertolt Brecht and Kurt Weill. *Pirate Jenny* is sung by the character Polly Peacham in **The Threepenny Opera** and was first performed on stage by Roma Bahn.

Mar 1987
Mother Fist • *Two Sailors On The Beach* • *The Hustler* – 12", p/s
Virgin GLOW 5-12

Reached Number 93. Produced by Mike Hedges/Marc Almond. Words to *Two Sailors On The Beach* written by the poet Federico Garcia Lorca. Only ever released as a 12" though some discographies show a 7".

ALBUMS

Oct 1984
Vermin In Ermine – LP with inner bag and lyric sheet
Shining Sinners • *Hell Was A City* • *You Have* • *Crime Sublime* • *Gutter Hearts* • *Ugly Head* • *The Boy Who Came Back* • *Solo Adultos* • *Tenderness Is A Weakness*
Phonogram BIZL 8

Reached Number 36. Produced by Mike Hedges. Nancy Peppers provides backing vocals on *The Boy Who Came Back* and *Pink Shack Blues*. Zeke Manyika drums on *Ugly Head* and *Pink Shack Blues*. Also released on cassette **Phonogram BIZLC 8** and on CD **Phonogram 822 832-2** with two extra tracks *Split Lip* • *Pink Shack Blues*, then re-released in **April 1992** on **Phonogram 822 833-4**, and released on CD **822 833-2** with the two extra tracks plus *Joey Demento*. Also released in **1990** in Germany on CD **Phonogram 822 833-2** with just the LP tracks.

Sep 1985
Stories Of Johnny – LP with stickered sleeve, inner bag and lyric booklet
Traumas Traumas Traumas • *Stories Of Johnny* • *The House Is Haunted* • *Love Letter* • *The Flesh Is Willing* • *Always* • *Contempt* • *I Who Never* • *My Candle Burns* • *Love And Little White Lies*
Phonogram FAITH 1

Reached Number 22. Produced by Mike

Hedges. Also released on cassette **T FAITH 1** and on CD **CD FAITH 1** with two extra tracks *Stories Of Johnny* (With The Westminster School Choir) and *Love Letter* (With The Westminster School Choir).

Apr 1987
Mother Fist And Her Five Daughters
– LP with inner bag and lyric sheet
Mother Fist • There Is A Bed • Saint Judy • The Room Below • Angel In Her Kiss • The Hustler • Melancholy Rose • Mr Sad • The Sea Says • Champ • Ruby Red • The River
Phonogram FAITH 2

Reached Number 41. Produced by Mike Hedges/Marc Almond. The title is taken from **Nocturnal Turnings or How Siamese Twins Have Sex**, a short story by Truman Capote to whom the album is dedicated. Also released on cassette **TFAITH 2**, and on CD **CD FAITH 2**.

Nov 1987
Singles 1984–1987 – LP
The Boy Who Came Back • You Have • Tenderness Is A Weakness • Stories Of Johnny • Love Letter • The House Is Haunted (By The Echo Of Your Last Goodbye) • A Woman's Story • Ruby Red • Melancholy Rose • Mother Fist
Virgin FAITH 3

Reached Number 58. Also released on cassette **TFAITH 3** on CD **Virgin CD FAITH 3**.

Sep 1992
A Virgins Tale Volume I – CD
Stories Of Johnny (Featuring Westminster City Choir) • *Love Letter* (Featuring Westminster City Choir) • *Blond Boy • The House Is Haunted* (Ectoplasmix) • *Broken Bracelets • Cara A Cara • The Heel • A Salty Dog • The Plague • The Little White Crowd That Cried • For One Moment • Just Good Friends*
Virgin CDVM9010

Did not chart. Part one of a two volume set collecting together most of the B-sides and other rarities during Marc's tenure with Virgin Records. Also released on cassette **TCVM 9010**.

Sep 1992
A Virgin's Tale Volume II – CD
Gyp The Blood • A World Full Of People • Black Lullaby • Pirate Jenny • Surabaya Johnny • Two Sailors On The Beach • Anarcoma • Jackal Jackal • Broken Hearted And Beautiful • I'm Sick Of You Tasting Of Somebody Else
Virgin CDVM 9011

Did not chart. Part two of above collection. Also released on cassette **TCVM 9011**.

MARC ALMOND WITH LA MAGIA

La Magia were: Annie Hogan, Billy McGee and Steve Humphreys.

SINGLES

Tears Run Rings • *Everything I Wanted Love To Be* – 7", p/s

Parlophone R 6186

Tears Run Rings • *Everything I Wanted Love To Be* – 7", limited edition box set including two postcards, badge, booklet and record

RX 6186

Tears Run Rings (Extended) • *Tears Run Rings* (Seven Inch Mix) • *Everything I Wanted Love To Be* – 12", p/s

12R 6186

Tears Run Rings (Extended) • *Tears Run Rings* (Seven Inch Mix) • *Everything I Wanted Love To Be* – 12", p/s, special collectors edition etched disc

12RS 6186

Tears Run Rings (The Justin Strauss Mix) • *Tears Run Rings* (The La Magia Dance Mix) • *Everything I Wanted Love To Be* – 12", stickered sleeve

12RX 6186

Tears Run Rings (Extended) • *Tears Run Rings* (Seven Inch Mix) • *Everything I Wanted Love To Be* – CD

CDR 6194

Reached Number 26. Produced by Marc Almond, Annie Hogan and Billy McGee. The La Magia Dance Mix was remixed by Bob Kraushaar, the Justin Strauss Mix was remixed by Justin Strauss with Eric Kupper providing additional keyboards. A 3" CD with *Tears Run Rings* was given away free with *Offbeat* magazine in **May 1989** on **Offbeat 1**. There was a red vinyl 12" with a plain black and stickered sleeve released in Europe on **Parlophone 060 Y 20 3108 6** with the same tracks as UK 12" release. Also a US release on **Capitol V 15418** 12" with stickered sleeve and the following tracks: *Tears Run Rings* (The Just Rite Mix) • *Tears Run Rings* (The Just Rite Edit) • *Tears Run Rings* (Acid Tears Dub) • *Everything I Wanted Love To Be*, the remixes were by Justin Strauss.

Bitter Sweet • *King Of The Fools* – 7", p/s

Parlophone R 6194

Bitter Sweet • *King Of The Fools* – 7", p/s, gatefold sleeve

RG 6194

Bitter Sweet • *King Of The Fools* – 7", p/s, clear vinyl

RC 6194

Bitter Sweet • *King Of The Fools* • *Tears Run Rings* (The Justin Strauss Remix) – 12", p/s

12R 6194

Bitter Sweet • *King Of The Fools* • *Tears Run Rings* (The Justin Strauss Remix) – 12", p/s, limited edition gatefold sleeve

12RG 6194

Bitter Sweet • *King Of The Fools* • *Tears Run Rings* (The Justin Strauss Remix) – 12", p/s, limited edition etched disc

12RS 6194

Bitter Sweet (The Big Beat Mix) • *King Of The Fools* • *Tears Run Rings* (The Justin Strauss Remix) – 12", plain black stickered sleeve

12RX 6194

Bitter Sweet (The Big Beat Mix) • *King Of The Fools* • *Tears Run Rings* (The Justin Strauss Remix) – CD

CDR 6194

Reached Number 40. Produced by Marc Almond, Annie Hogan and Billy McGee, co-produced by Bob Kraushaar, the Justin Strauss Remix by Justin Strauss, the Big Beat Mix remixed by Extra Beat Boys.

Kept Boy – 7", one sided etched

Parlophone PSR 500

This was withdrawn from release but not before some copies found their way into the shops.

Something's Gotten Hold Of My Heart (With Special Guest Star Gene Pitney) • *Something's Gotten Hold Of My Heart* – 7", p/s

Parlophone R 6201

Something's Gotten Hold Of My Heart (With Special Guest Star Gene Pitney) • *Something's Gotten Hold Of My Heart* – 7" limited edition box set including 2 postcards, discography, badge & record.

RX 6201

Something's Gotten Hold Of My Heart (With Special Guest Star Gene Pitney) • *Something's Gotten Hold Of My Heart* • *The Frost Comes Tomorrow* – 12", p/s

12R 6201

Something's Gotten Hold Of My Heart (With Special Guest Star Gene Pitney) • *Something's Gotten Hold Of My Heart* • *The Frost Comes Tomorrow* – 12", p/s, limited edition etched disc

12RS 6201

Something's Gotten Hold Of My Heart (With Special Guest Star Gene Pitney • *Something's Gotten Hold Of My Heart* • *The Frost Comes Tomorrow* – CD

CDR 6201

Marc Almond returns to the Number 1 position he last occupied in July 1981. Produced by Bob Kraushaar except *The Frost Comes Tomorrow* produced by Marc Almond & La Magia. *Something's Gotten Hold Of My Heart* was written by Roger Cook and Roger Greenaway and was originally performed by Gene Pitney reaching Number 5 in **Dec 1965**. A Dutch 7" of *Something's Gotten Hold Of My Heart* • *King Of The Fools* was released in **Oct 1988** with a different sleeve on **006 20 3190 7**.

Mar 1989

Only The Moment • *Real Evil* – 7"

Parlophone R 6210

Only The Moment • *Real Evil* – 7", clear vinyl

RC 6210

Only The Moment (All The Time In The World Mix) • *She Took My Soul In Istanbul* (The Blue Mosque Mix) – 12", some copies with poster insert

12R 6210

Only The Moment (All The Time In The World Mix) • *She Took My Soul In Istanbul* (The Blue Mosque Mix) – 12" etched vinyl

12RS 6210

Only The Moment • *She Took My Soul In Istanbul* (The Blue Mosque Mix) • *Real Evil* – CD

CDR 6210

Reached Number 45. Produced by Marc Almond and La Magia except *Only The Moment* co-produced and mixed by Bob Kraushaar.

ALBUMS

Sep 1988

The Stars We Are – LP with inner bag lyric sheet
The Stars We Are • *These My Dreams Are Yours* • *Bitter Sweet* • *Only The Moment* • *Your Kisses Burn* • *The Very Last Pearl* • *Tears Run Rings* • *Something's Gotten Hold Of My Heart* • *The Sensualist* • *She Took My Soul In Istanbul*

Parlophone PCS 7324

Reached Number 41. Produced by Marc Almond, Annie Hogan, and Billy McGee, except *Something's Gotten Hold Of My Heart* produced by Bob Kraushaar. Nico provides vocal on *Your Kisses Burn*, Victoria Wilson-Jones provides vocal on *These My Dreams Are Yours*, Suraya Ahmed provides vocal on *She Took My Soul In Istanbul*, additional percussion by Bob Kraushaar, trumpet and flugal horn by Enrico Tomasso, oboe and cor anglais by Julia Girdwood, clarinet and bass clarinet by Derek Hanigan, strings by The False Harmonica. Released on cassette **Parlophone TPCS 7324** and on CD **Parlophone CDPCS 7324**, both with two extra tracks *The Frost Comes Tomorrow* • *Kept Boy*, Agnes Bernelle provides backing vocals on *Kept Boy*. After the success of the Gene Pitney duet on *Something's Gotten Hold Of My Heart* this was included on a re-issue on all formats, on LP **Parlophone PCSX 7324**, on cassette **Parlophone TCPCSX 7324**, and on CD **Parlophone CDPCSX 7324**.

MARC ALMOND SOLO

SINGLES

Feb 1990

A Lover Spurned (Full Length Version) •
Exotica Rose – 7", p/s
Parlophone R 6229

A Lover Spurned (Full Length Version New
Mix) • *Exotica Rose* – 7" square picture disc
R 6229

A Lover Spurned (Full Length Version) •
Exotica Rose – 7" stickered p/s
RPD 6229

A Lover Spurned (12" Version) • *A Lover
Spurned* (Full Length Version) • *Exotica
Rose* – 12" p/s
12R 6229

A Lover Spurned (Full Length Version) •
Exotica Rose – cassette
TCR 6229

A Lover Spurned (12" Version) • *A Lover
Spurned* (Radio Edit) • *Exotica Rose* – CD
CDR 6229

Reached Number 29. *A Lover Spurned*
produced by Stephen Hague and *Exotica
Rosa* produced by Billy McGee. Cover
features a photograph by Pierre et Gilles
featuring the model Marie France. Julie T
Wallace – the star of the television series
Life And Loves Of A She Devil – provides
backing vocals on *A Lover Spurned*. A 3"
CD of *A Lover Spurned* • *The Desperate
Hours* was released in Japan on **TOTDP-
2223**.

May 1990

The Desperate Hours • *The Gambler* – 7", p/s
Parlophone R 6252

The Desperate Hours (Extended Flamenco
Mix) • *The Desperate Hours* • *The Gambler*
– 12", p/s
12R 6252

The Desperate Hours (Extended Flamenco
Mix) • *The Desperate Hours* (Orchestral
Version) – 12" pic disc on clear vinyl
12RPD 6252

The Desperate Hours • *The Gambler*
– cassette
TCR 6252

The Desperate Hours (Extended Flamenco
Mix) • *The Desperate Hours* • *The Gambler*
– CD
CDR 6252

Reached Number 45. *The Desperate Hours*
produced by Bob Kraushaar, *The Gambler*
produced by Billy McGee. The cover
features a photograph of Marc Almond
taken by Brad Branson. A CD of *The
Desperate Hours* (12" Vocal Remix) • *The
Desperate Hours* (12" Dub Mix) • *The
Desperate Hours* (12" Alternative Dub Mix)
was released in Germany on **560-20 3949 2**.

Nov 1990

Waifs And Strays (The Grid Mix) • *Old
Jack's Charm* – 7", p/s
Parlophone R 6263

Waifs And Strays (The Grid Mix) • *Old
Jack's Charm* – 7", p/s with postcard
RX 6263

Waifs And Strays (The Grid Mix) • *Old
Jack's Charm* – cassette
TCR 6263

Waifs And Strays (12" Grid Mix) • *Waifs
And Strays* (Grid Twilight Mix) – 12", p/s
12R 6263

Waifs And Strays (The Grid Mix) • *Waifs
And Strays* (12" Grid Mix) • *City Of Nights*
– CD
CDR 6263

Did not chart. *Waifs And Strays* produced
by Bob Kraushaar and Gary Maughan with
the Grid Mix and Grid Twilight Mix by The
Grid. *Old Jack's Charm* produced by Billy
McGee and Nigel Hine.

Sep 1991

Jacky • *Deep Night* – 7", p/s
WEA YZ610

Jacky (12" Version) • *Jacky* (Alpine Dub) •
Deep Night (12" Version) – 12", p/s
YZ610T

Jacky • *Deep Night* – cassette
YZ610C

Jacky (7" Version) • *Deep Night* (12"
Version) • *A Love Outgrown* – CD
YZ610CD

Reached Number 17. *Jacky* originally
written by Jacques Brel and Gerard
Jouannest and originally recorded by
Jacques Brel, translation by Mort Shuman.
Also covered by Scott Walker (as *Jackie*)
who reached Number 22 in **Jan 1968**. *Jacky*

was produced by Trevor Horn with the Alpine Dub remixed by Youth, *Deep Night* by John Coxon, and *A Love Outgrown* by Marc Almond/Billy McGee/Nigel Hine. The rhythm track of *Jacky* is taken from *Red Summer* by Sun Electric. The US CD contained the following tracks: *Jacky* (Single Mix) • *Jacky* (Youth Remix) • *Deep Night* (12" Mix) • *Jacky* (Alpine Dub) • *A Love Outgrown*; and a Japanese CD contained *Jacky* (7" Version) • *Jacky* (Youth Remix) • *Jacky* (Alpine Dub) • *Deep Night* (12" Version) • *Deep Night* (7" Version) • *A Love Outgrown*, on **WMC5 462**.

Dec 1991
My Hand Over My Heart • *Deadly Serenade* – 7", p/s

WEA YZ633

My Hand Over My Heart (Grit And Glitter Mix) • *Money For Love* (Ennio Mix) • *Money For Love* (Fiddle Mix) – 12", p/s

YZ633TP

My Hand Over My Heart (Grit And Glitter Mix) • *Money For Love* (Ennio Mix) • *Money For Love* (Fiddle Mix) – 12", picture disc

YZ 633T

My Hand Over My Heart • *Deadly Serenade* – cassette

YZ633C

My Hand Over My Heart (Grit And Glitter Mix) • *Money For Love* (Ennio Mix) • *Money For Love* (Fiddle Mix) • *Night And No Morning* – CD

YZ633CD

Reached Number 33. *My Hand Over My Heart* was produced by Trevor Horn and the Grit and Glitter Mix was by The Grid, *Deadly Serenade* produced by John Coxon, *Money For Love* (Fiddle Mix) produced and mixed by John Coxon and the Ennio Mix was by Phil Harding, *Night And No Morning* produced by Marc Almond/Billy McGee/Nigel Hine. *My Hand Over My Heart* was written by Marc Almond and David Ball and Richard Norris of the Grid. This was the first Marc Almond written with Dave Ball song since Soft Cell. A CD was released in USA with *My Hand Over My Heart* (Grit And Glitter Mix) • *Money For Love* (Ennio Mix) • *Money For Love* (Fiddle Mix) • *Night And No Morning* • *Money For Love* (Ennio Mix) • *Deadly Serenade* on **9**

40367-2 with card sleeve.

Apr 1992
The Days Of Pearly Spencer • *Bruises* – 7", p/s

WEA YZ638C

The Days Of Pearly Spencer • *Bruises* – cassette

YZ638C

Extract From *Trois Chansons De Bilitis* • *The Days Of Pearly Spencer* • *Bruises* • *Dancing In A Golden Cage* – CD

YZ638CD

Extract From *Trois Chansons De Bilitis* • *The Days Of Pearly Spencer* • *Bruises* • *Dancing In A Golden Cage* – limited edition numbered holographic CD in card sleeve

YZ638CDX

Reached Number 4. *The Days Of Pearly Spencer* and Extract From *Trois Chansons De Bilitis* produced by Trvor Horn. *Bruises* and *Dancing In A Golden Cage* produced by John Coxon. *The Days Of Pearly Spencer* originally written and recorded by David MacWilliams, though Marc provided additional lyrics. *Chanson De Bilitis* written by Claude Debussy and sung by Sally Bradshaw. Elaine Vassell provides backing vocals on *Bruises* and *Dancing In A Golden Cage*. *Dancing In A Golden Cage* (Reflection In A Golden Eye) appeared on a one-sided 12" promo **SAM 956**. *The Days Of Pearly Spencer* • *Bruises* • *Dancing In A Golden Cage* was released on CD as a gold DJ-only promo on **YZ638CDDJ**. A 12" of *The Days Of Pearly Spencer* (With Extract From *Trois Chansons De Bilitis*) • *Dancing In A Golden Cage* • *Dancing In A Golden Cage* (Reflection In A Golden Eye) on **YZ638T** was withdrawn. A Japanese CD of *The Days Of Pearly Spencer* • Extract From *Trois Chansons De Bilitis* • *The Days Of Pearly Spencer* • *My Hand Over My Heart* (Grit And Glitter Mix) • *Bruises* • *Deadly Serenade* • *Night And No Morning* • *Deep Night* • *Money For Love* (Fiddle Mix) *Dancing In A Golden Cage* • *Dancing In A Golden Cage* (Reflection In A Golden Eye) was released on **WMC5-552**.

Mar 1993
What Makes A Man A Man (Live) • *Torch* (Live) – 7", p/s

WEA YZ720

Discography

What Makes A Man A Man (Live) • *Torch* (Live) – cassette

YZ720C

What Makes A Man A Man (Live) • *Torch* (Live) • *Stars We Are* (Live) – part one of a numbered two CD set

YZ720CD

What Makes A Man A Man (Live Studio Version) • *Tainted Love* (Live) • *Vision* (Live) • *Only The Moment* (Live) – part two of the above two CD set

YZ720CDX

Reached Number 60. *What Makes A Man A Man* originally written and recorded by Charles Aznavour – wrongly credited to Pizer on some releases. Produced by Gregg Jackman. All live versions were recorded during the **Twelve Years Of Tears** show at the Albert Hall on September 30th 1992.

ALBUMS

Jun 1990
Enchanted – LP
Madame De La Luna • *Waifs And Strays* • *The Desperate Hours* • *Toreador In The Rain* • *Widow Weeds* • *A Lover Spurned* • *Deaths Diary* • *The Sea Still Sings* • *Carnival Of Life* • *Orpheus In Red Velvet*

Parlophone CDP 79 4404 2

Reached Number 52. Produced by Bob Kraushaar and Gary Maughan except *Desperate Hours* produced by Bob Kraushaar and *A Lover Spurned* by Stephen Hague. Marie France provides solo voice on *Carnival Of Life*. The cover is by Pierre et Gilles. Also released on cassette **TCPCS 7344** and on CD **CDPCS 7344**. *Toreador In The Rain* is also included in the third Some Bizzare compilation **Some Bizzare Ish** available on CD **SBZCD 003**. Released in Japan with the extra track *City Of Nights* on **TOCP-6269**.

Oct 1991
Tenement Symphony – LP
Meet Me In My Dreams • *Beautiful Brutal Thing* • *I've Never Seen Your Face* • *Vaudeville And Burlesque* • *Champagne* • *Prelude* • *Jacky* • *What Is Love?* • *Trois Chansons De Bilitis* (Extract) • *The Days Of Pearly Spencer* • *My Hand Over My Heart*

WEA 9031-75518-2

Reached Number 39. Marc Almond is spelt Márc Almond. Subtitled *Kies Und Glanz* • *Grit And Glitter* • *Grés Et Paillettes*. The Tenement Symphony actually comprises the songs from *Prelude* to *My Hand Over My Heart* and was produced by Trevor Horn. *Meet Me In My Dreams* and *I've Never Seen Your Face* produced by The Grid. *Beautiful Brutal Thing, Vaudeville And Burlesque* and *Champagne* produced by Marc Almond/Billy McGee/Nigel Hine. *What Is Love?* was written by Trevor Horn and Bruce Woolley, *Prelude* was written by Dave Ball/Richard Norris, *Meet Me In My Dreams, I've Never Seen Your Face* and *My Hand Over My Heart* written by Marc Almond/Dave Ball/Richard Norris. Released on cassette and CD **9031-75518-2**.

Dec 1989
Jacques – LP
The Devil (Okay) • *If You Need* • *The Lockman* • *We Must Look* • *Alone* • *I'm Coming* • *Litany For A Return* • *If You Go Away* • *The Town Fell Asleep* • *The Bulls* • *Never To Be Next* • *My Death*

Some Bizzare BREL 1

Did not chart. Produced by Charles Gray and Marc Almond. All songs written and first recorded by Jacques Brel. *Alone, If You Go Away, The Bulls* and *My Death* were translated by Mort Shuman, all other translations by Paul Buck. Also released on CD **BREL 1 CD**.

Apr 1993
Twelve Years Of Tears – LP
Tears Run Rings • *Champagne* • *Bedsitter* • *Mr Sad* • *There Is A Bed* • *Youth* • *If You Go Away* • *Jacky* • *Desperate Hours* • *Waifs And Strays* • *Somethings's Gotten Hold Of My Heart* • *What Makes A Man A Man* • *Tainted Love* • *Say Hello Wave Goodbye*

WEA

Produced by Gregg Jackman. **Twelve Years Of Tears** was a two-and-a-half hour show involving a band, an orchestra and dancers at The Royal Albert Hall on September 30th 1992. This is a selection of edited highlights from that show. Also available on CD **4509-92033-2**. Also released as a video.

<u>Oct 1993</u>
Absinthe – *The French Album* – gatefold LP
Undress Me • *Abel And Cain* • *Lost Paradise* • *Secret Child* • *Rue Des Blancs-Manteaux* • *The Slave* • *Remorse Of The Dead* • *Incestuous Love* • *A Man* • *My Little Lovers* • *In Your Bed* • *Yesterday When I Was Young*
                            Some Bizzare sbz lp 021

Did not chart. *Abel And Cain, Secret Child, Rue Des Blancs-Manteaux, Remorse Of The Dead* and *Incestuous Love* produced by Marc Almond and Charles Gray, all other songs produced by Marc Almond and Martin Watkins. *Undress Me* written by Robert Nyel, *Secret Child* written by Juliette Greco, *Rue Des Blancs-Manteaux* written by Jean-Paul Sartre, and *In Your Bed*, all originally performed by Juliette Greco; *Abel And Cain* and *Remorse Of The Dead* are poems by Charles Baudelaire put to music and first performed by Leo Ferré; *Lost Paradise* and *A Man* were written and performed by Robert Nyel; *The Slave* written and performed by Serge Lamain; *Incestuous Love* written and performed by Barbara; *My Little Lovers* is a poem by Arthur Rimbaud put to music by Billy McGee; *Yesterday When I Was Young* was written and performed by Charles Aznavour. All translations are by Paul Buck except *Yesterday When I Was Young* by Marc Almond. Jim Thirlwell – credited as Kirt Rust – plays drums on *Undress Me* and *A Man*. Also released on CD **SBZ CD 021** initial copies of which came in a cardboard gatefold version. *Incestuous Love* had been included on a compilation CD entitled **Volume Seven** released in **Jul 1993** on **Volume 7VCD7**.

<u>1988–1993</u>
Treasure Box - double CD in slipcase
City Of Nights • *Waifs And Strays* (Grid Mix) • *King Of The Fools* • *The Libertines Dream* • *Only The Moment* (All The Time In The World Mix) • *Tears Run Rings* (La Magia Dance Mix) • *Everything I Wanted Love To Be* • *The Gambler* • *Something's Gotten Hold Of My Heart* • *Bitter Sweet*

(Big Beat Mix) • *The Frost Comes Tomorrow* • *She Took My Soul In Istanbul* (Blue Mosque Mix) • *The Stars We Are* (Full Length Mix) • *A Lover Spurned* (12" Version) • *Real Evil* • *Exotica Rose* • *The Desperate Hours* (Extended Flamenco Mix) • *Old Jack's Dream* • *These My Dreams Are Yours* (Through The Night Mix) • *The Sea Still Sings* (Demo Version) • *Madame De La Luna* (Demo Version) • *Death's Diary* (Demo Version) • *Toreador In The Rain* (Demo Version) • *Orpheus In Red Velvet* (Demo Version) • *The Sensualist* (Ultimate Ecstacy Mix)

A round-up of assorted B-sides, extended versions, demo versions and one unreleased track from Marc's period with EMI on Parlophone. A CD only release, finally released in 1995.

MISCELLANEOUS

Sep 1982
Discipline – 7", flexi

Flexipop 23 A

Recorded by Marc Almond And Friends. Originally written and recorded by Throbbing Gristle. A flexi disc given away free with issue 23 of *Flexipop* Magazine.

Nov 1982
Force The Hand Of Chance – limited edition LP with 12" and poster
Guiltless • Stolen Kisses

Some Bizzare PSY1

Recorded by Psychic TV. Marc takes lead vocals on *Guiltless* and backing vocals on *Stolen Kisses*. Both songs written by Psychic TV.

1983
The Whip – LP with insert
The Hungry Years

Kamera KAM 014

Taken from the musical soundtrack from **The Whip**, an imaginary film based on the writings of Isidore Ducasse. One track is written and recorded by Andi of the Sex Gang Children and Marc Almond.

Sept 1984
If You Can't Please Yourself You Can't Please Your Soul – LP with inner bag, insert and folder
Love Amongst The Ruined

EMI EJ 26 0663 1

The second Some Bizzare compilation album. Also includes tracks by sometime Marc collaborators Jim Foetus, Cabaret Voltaire, Psychic TV, The The and Coil. Also released on cassette **EMI EJ 26 0663 4**, and on CD.

Apr 1985
I Feel Love • Puit D'Amour – 7", p/s

Forbidden Fruit BITE 4

I Feel Love • Puit D'Amour – 7", diff picture disc

BITEPD 4

Love To Love You Baby/I Feel Love/Johnnie

Remember Me Vocal (Cake Mix) • *Love To Love You Baby/I Feel Love/Johnnie Remember Me* Inst (Fruit Mix)* – 10", diff red p/s

BITET 4

Love To Love You Baby/I Feel Love/Johnnie Remember Me Vocal (Cake Mix) • *Love To Love You Baby/I Feel Love/Johnnie Remember Me* Inst (Fruit Mix)* – 10", diff black p/s

BITET 4

I Feel Love • The Potatoe Fields • Puit D'Amour • Signs (And Wonders) – 12" p/s

BITEX 4

I Feel Love (Cake Mix) • *I Feel Love* (The Fruit Mix) • *Puit D'Amour* – 12", diff p/s

BITER 4

Reached Number 3. Recorded by Bronski Beat with Marc Almond. *Love To Love You Baby* and *I Feel Love* written by Giorgio Moroder and originally recorded by Donna Summer, *Love To Love You Baby* reaching Number 4 in Feb 1976 and *I Feel Love* reaching Number 1 in July 1977. *Johnnie Remember Me* written and originally recorded by John Leyton reaching Number 1 in Aug 1961. *I Feel Love* was also included on **Memorabilia – The Singles Collection** on CD **Mercury 848 512-2**.

Jul 1985
Skin – 12", p/s

Wide Blue Yonder WBY 121

Recorded by the Burmoe Brothers, music and lyrics by Guy Chambers. Marc provides the lead vocals.

1985
Annie Hogan Plays Kickabye – 12" EP, p/s
Burning Boats

Doublevision DVR9

Recorded by Annie Hogan. Marc provides lead vocals – credited as Raoul Revére – on one track for the **Kickabye** EP. The song was written by Annie Hogan.

1986
Horse Rotovator – LP

Force & Form/K.422 ROTA 1

Slur • Who By Fire

Recorded by Coil. Marc – credited as Raoul Revere – provides backing vocals on two tracks, *Slur* music by Coil and lyrics by John Balance, and *Who By Fire* originally written and recorded by Leonard Cohen. Also released on CD **FFKCD1**.

Sep 1986
Indigo Blue – LP

RM 5

Marc provides one track on a compilation album **Fruitcakes And Furry Collars** given away to readers of the *Record Mirror*.

Dec 1986
Violent Silence – import LP
Blood Tide • Healthy As Hate • Things You Loved Me For • Body Unknown • Unborn Stillborn

Virgin 208 050

Cycle of songs performed at **Violent Silence – The Celebration Of Georges Bataille** on 26th September 1984 at the Bloomsbury Theatre in London. The album was only ever available as a Belgian import. *Body Unknown* had been written for the Immaculate Consumptives, a musical revue cabaret featuring Lydia Lunch, Nick Cave, Jim Foetus and Marc Almond, who performed two shows in New York including a night at the Danceteria on New Year's Eve 1982.

June 1987
This House Is A House Of Trouble – 7", p/s
T.I.M. MOT 6
This House Is A House Of Trouble – 12", p/s
T.I.M. 12 MOT 6

Recorded by Sally Timms and the Drifting Cowgirls. Marc shares lead vocals with Sally Timms on a song he wrote. The 12" features an extended version.

1987
Slut • The Universal Cesspool • Bruisin Chain – 12", p/s
Some Bizzare SLUT 1

Recorded by The Flesh Volcano, who are Jim Thirlwell – credited as Clint Ruin – and Marc Almond.

1988
'Til Things Are Brighter – CD
Man In Black

Red Rhino REDLP 88

Sub-titled *A Tribute To Johnny Cash*, a compilation album featuring various artists covering Johnny Cash songs to raise money for the Terrence Higgins Fund. Also available on CD **REDCD 88**

1989
Scatology – CD

Force & Form FFKCD1

Recorded by Coil. The sleevenotes state that Marc plays guitar – credited as Raoul Revere – on *Restless Day*, an instumental track though it is hard to discern any obvious guitar playing on the track. This track is only included on the CD release. The track had also seen a very very limited release on Yang-Ki Records.

1991
Love's Secret Domain – CD
Titan Arch

Torso CD 181

Recorded by Coil. Marc provides lead vocals on one song on this album, with music by Coil and lyrics by John Balance.

Apr 1992
The Law Of The Dream – LP
Shivers In Red

Normal 133

Recorded by Melinda Miel. Marc provides vocals on one track. Also available on CD **133CD**

1992
Ruby Trax – *The NME's Roaring Forty* – triple CD
Like A Prayer

NME 40 CD

A triple CD featuring various artists covering No 1 records of the seventies to raise money for the Spastics Society. Marc chose the Madonna hit which had reached Number 1 in March 1989.

Dec 1992

Christmas In Vegas— 7" flexi

A flexi released for Christmas 1992, only available through the Vaudeville and Burlesque fanclub.

VAUDEVILLE & BURLESQUE

THE OFFICIAL MARC ALMOND FAN CLUB

Vaudeville and Burlesque has been established for
three and a half years and is currently going
from strength to strength.

On joining the club as a new member you'll receive
a presentation folder, numbered membership card,
special edition colour photo, colour postcard and
four newsletters throughout the year.
As well as keeping you up to date with the news
surrounding releases, concerts etc, the fan club newsletters
offer you the opportunity to put questions to Marc,
to buy and sell rare records and memorabilia,
to contact fellow fans and much much more.
In addition we also offer a selection of
Vaudeville and Burlesque merchandise.

New members are always welcome,
so if you're interested in joining,
why not drop us a line, with an S.A.E. or I.R.C,
to the address below and we'll send you an application form.

VAUDEVILLE & BURLESQUE,
THE OFFICIAL MARC ALMOND FAN CLUB
P.O. BOX 4RX,
LONDON W1A 4RX

JEREMY REED

Jeremy Reed was born in Jersey, Channel Islands. Acknowledged as one of Britain's foremost poets, he has been described by Kathleen Raine as "the most imaginatively gifted poet since Dylan Thomas".

Between 1984 and 1990 he published six books with Jonathan Cape. Four collections of poetry: **By The Fisheries, Nero, Engaging Form** and **Nineties**, and two novels: **Blue Rock** and **Red Eclipse**. Penguin published his **Selected Poems** in 1987, and he has been the recipient of major awards which include an Eric Gregory Award, the Somerset Maugham Award, and the Poetry Society European Translation prize for his version of Eugenio Montale's **The Coastguard's House**, published by Bloodaxe in 1991.

Among his recent novels are **Inhabiting Shadows, Isidore** – described by J.G. Ballard as "superb" – and **When The Whip Comes Down**, all published by Peter Owen. His autobiography **Lipstick Sex And Poetry** was published to acclaim in 1992, as were his books about the hallucinated imagination, **Delirium** and **Madness, The Price Of Poetry**. His collection of poems **Red Haired Android** was published by Harper Collins and in the US by City Lights, as was **Delirium**. **Chasing Black Rainbows**, a novel about Artaud, and the science fiction novel **Diamond Nebula** were published in 1994. The same year saw his first publication for Creation Books, **Kicks**. They have also published his novella of surreal erotica, **The Pleasure Château**.

Jeremy Reed lives in London, reads extensively on the subject of extra-terrestrials, avoids the literary scene, and is one of the most prolific of contemporary writers. His love of rock music is expressed in his Picador biography of Lou Reed, **Waiting For The Man**.

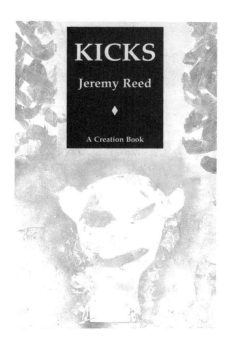

KICKS

Kicks is a brand new collection of poetry, prose-pieces, essays, translations and erotic film-scripts from award-winning writer Jeremy Reed, one of the most acclaimed poets and novelists of his generation. Reed's androgynous visions embrace a uniquely poetic universe, presided over by icons such as Jean Genet, Warhol, Hart Crane, David Bowie, John Ashbery, Proust, Baudelaire and Marc Almond – all of whom appear in this collection. *Kicks* reveals the most outrageous, sexually-outspoken side of Jeremy Reed, whilst demonstrating with consummate artistry how the spangled threads of his influences draw together to form a maverick blueprint for the future of literature and art.

Cover painting: William S Burroughs

"A brilliant and original talent."

– J G Ballard

Trade Paperback 1 871592 15 1
5½" X 8½" 192pp £8.95 • $13.95

THE PLEASURE CHATEAU

The story of Leanda, mistress of an opulent château where she tirelessly indulges her compulsion for sexual extremes, enter-taining retinues of deviants, transsexuals and freaks in pursuit of the ultimate erotic experience. When a dark stranger calls, schooling her in the ways of his bizarre cult, she is finally transported to a zone where sex transcends death itself, and existence becomes a never-ending orgy of the senses. In the decadent and erotic tradition of De Sade, Sacher-Masoch and Apollinaire, *The Pleasure Château* is a *tour-de-force* of perverse sexual delights; a careering midnight excursion through the labyrinths of a young girl's most secret desires. Jeremy Reed has turned his exquisite imagination to producing this masterpiece of gothic erotica.

Trade Paperback 1 871592 52 6
4½" X 7" 192pp £4.95 • $9.95

RAPID EYE 1   Simon Dwyer

KATHY ACKER • WILLIAM S BURROUGHS • BRION GYSIN • GENESIS P-ORRIDGE • COLIN WILSON • DEREK JARMAN • ALEISTER CROWLEY • CHARLES MANSON • HUBERT SELBY • AUSTIN SPARE • NEOISM

Rapid Eye is the much-acclaimed "Occulture" journal, probably the only British book which comprehensively explores the dark side of our popular culture, and examines the way society is really reacting to the coming end-of-millennium crises. Through its wide-ranging articles, which deal with subjects from Control and Conspiracy, Underground Art, Literature, Music and Film, to the Occult, Body Art, Psychopharmacology, Serial Killers, Virtual Reality, and everything between, RAPID EYE discloses a global society of inter-connected chaos, confronts this occult (hidden) network and both offers and encourages a real response to it. RAPID EYE is a truly post-postmodern phenomenon.

    While most of today's art and media describe appearance, *Rapid Eye* describes reality.

ARTS/CULTURE   Trade Paperback   1 871592 22 4   8½" X 11"   256pp   £11.95 • $17.95

RAPID EYE 2   Simon Dwyer

JORG BUTTGEREIT • RICHARD KERN • H P LOVECRAFT • MONDO MOVIES • PAUL MAYERSBERG • ALEX SANDERS • SAVOY BOOKS • AARON WILLIAMSON • MESCALIN • CUT-UPS • PLAGUE YARD: ALTERED STATES OF AMERICA

"This book is awesomely intoxicating...more ideas per square inch than in anything you'll read this year."
            – YOUR FLESH

"Book find of the year. Rapid Eye is great!"   – SHORT NEWS, NEW YORK

"Heavyweight periodical devoted to documenting apocalypse culture. Great pieces...recommended reading."
            – i-D MAGAZINE

"To read Rapid Eye is to descend into chaos...This is the first and final battle."   – MELODY MAKER

ARTS/CULTURE   Trade Paperback   1 871592 23 2   8½" X 11"   256pp   £11.95 • $17.95

RAPID EYE 3   Simon Dwyer

GILBERT & GEORGE • WILLIAM GIBSON • ROBERT HEINLEIN • ALAN MOORE • MAYA DEREN • KENNETH ANGER • PORNOGRAPHY • FREAK FILM • PROCESS CHURCH • K FOUNDATION • STEWART HOME

Painters, cyber punks, dog-boys, mad scientists, occultists, neoists, performance artists, film makers, writers, leopard girls and voodoo horsemen. In this age of transition and sensory overload, new ideas and organisations of perception form. To be marginalised, misunderstood, ignored, reviled. But melancholy can fuel creation. Imagination can replace fantasy. Hope can overcome fear. Different interpretations of the past and fresh approaches to art and technology can ensure the evolution of refinement of the perception of everyday life. In the virtual universe, there is no death.

ARTS/CULTURE   Trade Paperback   1 871592 24 0   8½" X 11"   256pp   £11.95 • $17.95

DIARY OF A GENIUS   Salvador Dalí

One of the seminal texts of Surrealism, revealing as it does the most astonishing and intimate details of the mind of Salvador Dalí, the eccentric polymath genius who became the living embodiment of that most subversive and disturbing of all modern art movements.

    Dalí's second volume of autobiography, *Diary Of A Genius* covers his life – and inner life – from 1952 to 1963, during which years we learn of his *mad love* for his wife Gala, and their relationship both at home in Cadaqués and during bizarre world travels; how Dalí draws inspiration from excrement, rotten fish and Vermeer's *Lacemaker* to enter his 'rhinocerontic' period, and preaches his post-holocaustal gospels of nuclear mysticism and cosmogenic atavism; and we follow his labyrinthine mental journeys to the creation of such paintings as the *Assumption*, and the development of his film script *The Flesh Wheelbarrow*. This new edition includes a brilliant and revelatory essay on Salvador Dalí, and the importance of his art to our century, by the author J G Ballard.

SURREALISM/AUTOBIOGRAPHY   Trade Paperback   1 871592 26 7   5½" X 8½"   208pp   £8.95

SATANSKIN
James Havoc

Visions of pure evil; a full-frontal assault on the senses, a surreal detonation of uttermost erotic horror.
"SATANSKIN is a remarkable collection of stories. The writing is black as hell, by turns violently obscene, repulsive, bizarre. No taboo goes unchallenged, no horror unexplored. It shouldn't be missed by anyone with an interest in the unusual." – OUTLOOK
"SATANSKIN is less a short story collection than an album of snapshots from Hell." – CRITICAL WAVE
"Havoc's prose is a kind of evil manitou crossover between Nick Cave, Mervyn Peake and Iain Sinclair...there isn't a paragraph which doesn't contain some batches of flaming phraseology or some livid welt of brilliance. As a literary bestiary of gratuitous horrors, SATANSKIN is up there with 120 Days Of Sodom." – DIVINITY
PULP FICTION   Trade Paperback   1 871592 10 0   5½" X 8½"   112pp   £5.95 • $13.95

INTERREGNUM
Geraldine Monk

In 1612, seven women from the Pendle area of East Lancashire were hanged as witches in the city of Lancaster. They had fallen victim to a patriarchal *language-magic* far more potent than their own. Present-day and historical abuse and misuse of language-magic, which determines degrees of freedom, is a recurring theme in the text of *Interregnum*, and culminates in the nemesis of the witches' monologues. The dualistic battleground of Pendle Hill forms the geographical and emotional nerve centre of the book. Using personal and historical coincidence, the writer integrates her own experience with inter-connected sources, ostensibly the writing of the Poet and Jesuit Gerard Manley Hopkins. *Interregnum* is a disturbing mating of private memory and public ghosts in the timeless dreamscape of Lancashire.
POETRY   Trade Paperback   1 871592 16 X   5½" X 8½"   128pp   £7.95 • $12.95

ANGELS FROM HELL
Mick Norman

England, turn of the millennium. Government repression has driven the Hell's Angels underground, yet they still exist – the final outlaws. From their hide-out in the mountains Gerry Vinson leads his chapter, The Last Heroes, into battle. Apart from police and government manipulation, the Angels must contend with The Ghouls – a satin-jacketed yet sadistic rival chapter – as well as unscrupulous rock promoters who want them as cannon fodder against the emerging breed of razor-wielding teen fans and, above all, the deadly new threat from gangs of strutting, scented, ultra-violent mod/skinhead hybrids: the Skulls. The result is a brutal, mythopoeic motorpsycho nitemare of sex, drugs, madness, betrayal and ultra-violent death; the outsider aesthetic taken to its logical extremes.   *Introduction by Stewart Home*
PULP FICTION   Trade paperback   1 871592 43 7   5½" X 8½"   368pp   £8.95 • $16.95

BRIDAL GOWN SHROUD
Adèle Olivia Gladwell

Bridal Gown Shroud is a collection of short stories and prose-poems, with an illuminating appendix of essays dealing with contemporary female issues. The book is centred about a 'taboo' cyclic motif of menstruation; steeped in bloody catamenial lore, we meet satyrs and vampire paramours, devils of death and rebirth, and other praetherhuman shadow figures cavorting to liberate the female imagination. The essays divulge a poetic undercurrent to the language of textual/post-feminist theory, and cover topics ranging from film, music, literature and performance to religious ecstasy, prostitution and pornography. The blood of women is ubiquitous in our cultural expression, yet never fully recognised – *until now*.
"Gladwell's debut evokes the cyclical nature of womanhood, throwing down a bloodied gauntlet." – THE FACE
FICTION/WOMENS STUDIES Trade paperback   1 871592 13 5   5½" X 8½"   208pp   £6.95 • $13.95

CATAMANIA
Adèle Olivia Gladwell

Catamania is a radical, compelling study of the female voice. Multi-contextual theorist Gladwell puts forward her analysis of the polemic of feminist rhetorical discourse as it presents a fresh and vital approach to an *anatomy* of female subjectivity through precise listening and the audacity to speak aloud.

Reconciling the body with the projected word or noise, CATAMANIA offers an extended reflection of female voices in mythology, the domestic nursery, the workplace and, specifically, in contemporary arts. In its uniquely poetic language, the book chronicles the work of many seminal female artistes and performers who are seizing hold of a new phonetics and sonic eloquence. Amongst subjects discussed are the lone siren wail, earliest recorded voices of blues, soul and attitude, through to the electric voice of the post-modern orator, and the assaults of frontline agitators such as Lydia Lunch and Diamanda Galas. *Catamania* also traces back to the *1st Voice* – brought to us through its only avenue of projection, semiotics – to the chattersome nymph Echo and the earliest story-tellers, to the screams of the 'madwoman' or hysteric, and to the rantings of the 'witch'; decoding the voice that speaks in many tongues, and invoking the engulfing, blanketing voice of the Mother.

The feminist voice of dissent is revealed as *the* subversive and enlightening agent of the new millennium, heralding a usurpation which is vital not only to women, but also to men in its ruthless condemnation and exposing of patriarchal oppression.
"A remarkable essayist and poet."   – THE SUNDAY TIMES
WOMENS STUDIES   Trade paperback   1 871592 25 9   5½" X 8½"   256pp   £7.95 • $13.95

DUST   Jack Hunter (Editor)

KATHY ACKER • ALAN MOORE • STEWART HOME • PIERRE GUYOTAT • GRANT MORRISON • JEREMY REED • JAMES HAVOC • AARON WILLIAMSON • GERALDINE MONK • ADELE OLIVIA GLADWELL and others.
"The crucifixion of modern literature, the resurrection of the imagination."
With this manifesto, Creation Books was inaugurated. Here is a selection from its pages past present and future, hallucinated or anatomical texts by writers estranged from the bind of linear narrative and 'literary' values, and the establishment which seeks to perpetuate it.
Dedicated to Dennis Hopper.
FICTION/POETRY   Trade Paperback   1 871592 44 5   5½" X 8½"   160pp   £6.99 • $10.99

EDEN, EDEN, EDEN   Pierre Guyotat

Eden, Eden, Eden – Pierre Guyotat's legendary novel of atrocity and multiple obscenity – finally appears in English. Set in a polluted and apocalyptic zone of the Algerian desert in a time of civil warfare, this delirious, exhausting novel brings scenes of brutal carnage into intimate collision with relentless acts of prostitutional sex and humiliation. The book's protagonist, a teenage Algerian boy, engages in a series of sexual acts which constantly escalate in intensity and number. Guyotat's language is welded into a headlong rush into the wild terrain of obscenity and murder; a courageous and unique exploration into the virulent matter of sex, language and the human anatomy; a continuous, malignant orgasm.
Pierre Guyotat is the most original writer alive, and this is his most livid, atrocious book. It will derange you and scar you.
FICTION   Trade Paperback   1 871592 47 X   5½" X 8½"   176pp   £7.95 • $13.95

THE GREAT GOD PAN   Arthur Machen

First published in 1894, *The Great God Pan* is Arthur Machen's first, and greatest, opus of Decadence and Horror. With his singular eye for the bizarre and macabre, Machen unfurls this tale of a young girl cursed by her supernatural parentage to become a creature of shape-shifting, polysexual, demi-human evil. Vilified upon publication, *The Great God Pan* can now be seen as a classic of *fin-de-siècle* erotic malevolence. This new, centenary edition, the first for many years, is illustrated by a set of complementary "automatic" drawings by Machen's contemporary and fellow mystic Austin Osman Spare, and also includes Machen's own illuminating introduction from the 1916 edition.
"Of creators of cosmic fear raised to its most artistic pitch, few can hope to equal Machen." —H P Lovecraft
PULP FICTION   Trade paperback   1 871592 11 9   6" X 9"   96pp   £7.95 • $15.95

BLOOD AND ROSES   Havoc & Gladwell (Editors)

BRAM STOKER • ARTHUR MACHEN • SHERIDAN LeFANU • POE • JOHN POLIDORI • TURGENEV LAUTRÈAMONT • BAUDELAIRE • MAUPASSANT • HUYSMANS • GAUTIER • WILDE • COUNT STENBOCK
A collection of 19th Century literature in which the vampire, or vampirism, both embodied and atmospheric, appears; seminal texts, covering the whole period from Gothic and Romantic, through Symbolism and proto-Surrealism to Decadence and beyond, in one single volume. With translators both old and modern including Lafcadio Hearn, Alexis Lykiard and Jeremy Reed. The book is a de-luxe edition, illustrated throughout by the Death/Erotic works of the 19th Century Belgian artist Felicien Rops, a disciple of Baudelaire obsessed with images of death, prostitution and Satanism.
DECADENT LITERATURE   Trade paperback   1 871592 14 3   6" X 9"   288pp   £7.95 • $15.95

CRAWLING CHAOS   H P Lovecraft

H P LOVECRAFT, one of the great obsessive writers of the 20th century, instinctively chose the field of "weird horror" in which to exorcise his acute anatomical alienation and existential torment; yet his best works easily transcend the limitations of this genre. Within the matrix of his grotesque yet complex mythology, Lovecraft was able to conjure a hideous universe lying just beyond our own; his relentless style and language forging a rich, convoluted literary form which ultimately achieves a veritable "pornography" of horror: the accumulation and repetition of his demonic visions climaxing in orgasms of cosmic revulsion. Revolving around such mythical texts as *The Necronomicon*, Lovecraft's labyrinthine demonology exerts a profound and enormous psychological attraction; articulating a kind of atavistic dread which, while archaic, yet has an increasingly modern application in its total effect.
   Writers such as Ramsey Campbell and Stephen King have acknowledged Lovecraft's influence, as have many film-makers. Others have applied the tenets of Chaos Magick to his work and found many hidden affinities – positing him as a Crowleyesque 'medium' for messages from what Kenneth Grant has termed the "Mauve Zone". The 23 stories in this volume comprise an essential, chronological collection of this unique writer's best work; from his early tales of the gruesome and bizarre, through his collaborative pieces and prose-poems, to the flowering of his personal cosmology, the *Cthulhu Mythos*. With a brand new introduction by Colin Wilson.
PULP FICTION   Trade Paperback   1 871592 18 6   7" X 10"   368pp   £9.95 • $19.95

PHILOSOPHY IN THE BOUDOIR   Marquis de Sade

In the boudoir of a sequestered country house, a young virgin is ruthlessly schooled in evil. Indoctrinated by her amoral tutors in the ways of sexual perversion, fornication, murder, incest, atheism and complete self-gratification, she takes part with growing abandon in a series of violent erotic orgies which culminates with the flagellation and torture of her own mother – her final act of liberation.

Philosophy In The Boudoir is the most concise, representative text out of all the Marquis de Sade's works, containing his notorious doctrine of *libertinage* expounded in full, coupled with liberal doses of savage, unbridled eroticism, cruelty and violent sexuality. The renegade philosophies put forward here would later rank amongst the main cornerstones of André Breton's Surrealist manifesto.

This seminal text is presented in a new, modern and authentic translation by Meredith X, herself a former dominatrix descended of Hungarian aristocracy.

EROTICA   Trade paperback   1 871592 09 7   4½" X 7"   192pp   £4.95 • $9.95

THE SHE-DEVILS   Pierre Louys

A mother and her three daughters...sharing their inexhaustible sexual favours between the same young man, each other, and anyone else who enters their web of depravity.

From a chance encounter on the stairway with a voluptuous young girl, the narrator is drawn to become the plaything of four rapacious females, experiencing them all in various combinations of increasingly wild debauchery, until they one day vanish as mysteriously as they had appeared.

Described by Susan Sontag as one of the few works of the erotic imagination to deserve true literary status, *The She Devils (Trois Filles De Leur Mère)* remains Pierre Louys' most intense, claustrophobic work; a study of sexual obsession and mono-mania unsurpassed in its depictions of carnal excess, unbridled lust and limitless perversity.

EROTICA   Trade paperback   1 871592 51 8   4½" X 7"   192pp   £4.95 • $9.95

FLESH UNLIMITED   Guillaume Apollinaire

The debauched aristocrat Mony Vibescu and a circle of fellow sybarites blaze a trail of uncontrollable lust, cruelty and depravity across the streets of Europe.

A young man reminisces his sexual awakening at the hands of his aunt, his sister and their friends as he is irremediably corrupted in a season of carnal excess.

Flesh Unlimited is a compendium edition of *Les Onze Mille Verges* and *Les Mémoires d'Un Jeune Don Juan*, two of the finest examples of wild literary erotica ever produced. Dadaist poet Guillaume Apollinaire fine-tuned his uniquely poetic and surreal vision to produce these two masterpieces of the explicit erotic imagination at the turn of the century, works which compare with the best of the Marquis de Sade.

Presented in brand new translations by Alexis Lykiard (translator of Lautréamont's *Maldoror*), these are the original, *complete and unexpurgated* versions, with full introduction and notes.

EROTICA   Trade Paperback   1 871592 56 9   4½" X 7"   192pp   £4.95 • $9.95

THE WHIP ANGELS   Anonymous

Victoria's journal reveals her darkest secrets, her induction into a bizarre yet addictive sexual underground at the hands of her immoral, incestuous guardians.

Behind the façade of everyday life seethes black leather mayhem, voluptuous eruptions of demonic angels from timeless torture zones, a midnight twist heralded by the bullwhip's crack and the bittersweet swipe of the cat.

Blazing with erotic excess and incandescent cruelty, *The Whip Angels* is a feast of dominance and submission, of corrupted innocence and tainted love. In the tradition of *The Story Of O* and *The Image*, this modern classic was written by an anonymous French authoress fully versed in the ways of whipcord and the dark delirium of those in both physical and spiritual bondage.

EROTICA   Trade Paperback   1 871592 53 4   4½" X 7"   192pp   £4.95 • $9.95

HOUSE OF PAIN   Pan Pantziarka

When a young streetwalker is picked up by an enigmatic older woman, she finds herself launched on an odyssey of pleasure and pain beyond measure.

Lost in a night world, thrown to the lusts of her anonymous captors, she must submit to their increasingly bizarre rituals of pain and degradation in order to embrace salvation.

House Of Pain is scorched earth erotica, an unprecedented glimpse of living Hell, the torments and raptures of a young woman abandoned to the throes of rage, violence and cruelty which feed the sexual impulse. Churches, hospitals, courtrooms, all become mere facets of the same unyielding edifice, a bedlam of desire and flesh in flame beneath the cold black sun of her own unlimited yearnings.

EROTICA   Trade Paperback   ISBN 1 871592 57 7   4½" X 7"   192pp   £4.95 • $9.95

HOUSE OF HORROR   Jack Hunter (Editor)

House Of Horror traces the complete history of Hammer Films, from its early origins through to its golden era of classic horror movies, and presents a comprehensive overview of Hammer's importance and influence in world horror cinema. The book features interviews with Hammer stars Christopher Lee and Peter Cushing, detailed analysis of all Hammer's horror and fantasy films and their key directors, and nearly 200 rare and exciting photographs including an 8-page full-colour poster section; plus a fully illustrated and updated appendix on the worldwide vampire cinema which followed in the wake of Hammer's *Dracula* – including the work of sex/horror kings Jean Rollin and Jess Franco – and a complete filmography.

CINEMA   Trade Paperback   1 871592 40 2   7" X 10"   176pp   £12.95 • $22.95

KILLING FOR CULTURE   David Kerekes & David Slater

Killing For Culture is a definitive investigation into images of death, both staged and real, which have been captured on film or videotape: the complete history of the so-called "snuff movie" aesthetic.
• FEATURE FILM. From *Peeping Tom* to *Videodrome* and beyond.
• MONDO FILM. From *Mondo Cane* to present day 'shockumentaries'.
• DEATH FILM. From *Faces Of Death* to real deaths captured on film such as live-TV suicides, executions, and news footage.
Illustrated by stunning photographs from cinema, documentary and real life, *Killing For Culture* is a necessary book which examines and questions the human obsession with images of violence, dismemberment and death, and the way our society is coping with an increased profusion of these disturbing yet compelling images from all quarters. Includes a comprehensive filmography and index.
"Well-researched and highly readable, Killing For Culture is a must-have."   —FILM THREAT
CINEMA/CULTURE   Trade Paperback   1 871592 20 8   7" X 10"   256pp   £11.95 • $16.95

DEATHTRIPPING   Jack Sargeant

Deathtripping is an illustrated history, account and critique of the "Cinema Of Transgression", providing a long-overdue and comprehensive documentation of this essential modern sub-cultural movement.
Including: • A brief history of underground/trash cinema: seminal influences including **Andy Warhol, Jack Smith, George and Mike Kuchar, John Waters.**
• Interviews with key film-makers, including **Richard Kern, Nick Zedd, Cassandra Stark, Beth B, Tommy Turner,** plus associates such as **Joe Coleman, Lydia Lunch, Lung Leg** and **David Wojnarowicz.**
• Notes and essays on transgressive cinema, philosophy of transgression; manifestos, screen-plays; film guide, with synopses and critiques, of key works of transgressive cinema; index.
Heavily illustrated with rare and occasionally disturbing photographs, *Deathtripping* is a unique document, the definitive guide to the roots, philosophy and development of a style of film-making which can no longer be ignored by the mainstream.
CINEMA/CULTURE   Trade Paperback   1 871592 29 1   7" X 10"   256pp   £11.95 • $16.95

INSIDE TERADOME   Jack Hunter

Freakshows – human anomalies presented for spectacle – have flourished throughout recorded history. The birth of the movies provided a further outlet for these displays, which in turn led to a peculiar strain of bizarre cinema: Freak Film. *Inside Teradome* is a comprehensive, fully illustrated guide to the roots and development of this fascinating, often disturbing cinematic genre. Including:
• *Teratology: freaks in myth and medicine.*
• *The history of freakshows, origins of cinema.*
• *Influence of sideshows on cinema.*
• *Use of human anomalies in cinema.*
• *Freaks and geeks.*
• *Bizarre cinema: mutilation and other fetishes.*
• *Illustrated filmography; index.*
From the real-life grotesqueries of Tod Browning's *Freaks*, to the modern nightmare vision of *Santa Sangre, Inside Teradome* reveals a twisted thread of voyeuristic sickness running not only through cinema, but through the society of which it has always been the most telling mirror.
CINEMA/CULTURE   Trade Paperback   1 871592 41 0   7" X 10"   256pp   £11.95 • $16.95

THE STARRY WISDOM   D M Mitchell (Editor)

J G BALLARD • WILLIAM S BURROUGHS • RAMSEY CAMPBELL • JOHN COULTHART •
MICHAEL GIRA • RICK GRIMES • JAMES HAVOC • ALAN MOORE • BRIAN LUMLEY •
GRANT MORRISON • DON WEBB • SIMON WHITECHAPEL *and many others*

Contemporary visions of cosmic transformation, mutation and madness – many inspired directly by the thoughts and writings of H P Lovecraft, others reflecting his strangely presentient themes, perhaps unwittingly, in their own bizarre sub-texts. Here the primal beings of Lovecraft's *Cthulhu Mythos* stalk a post-modern landscape of social collapse, ethnic cleansing, genetic engineering and nuclear devastation – nightmare prophecies from his pulp pages which have now come chillingly true. The undercurrents of sexual and ecological displacement which powered Lovecraft's work have finally been laid bare, providing this maligned genius with a long-overdue retrospective and revealing him to be a true prophet of the 20th century.

   The Starry Wisdom includes a host of brand new, previously unpublished prose and graphic works, plus select reprints which are now shown in a brand new light, forming a fascinating document which will appeal not only to readers of H P Lovecraft, but to all lovers of innovative art and literature in the science fiction, horror and fantasy genres. *Over 50 pages of original graphics*

PULP FICTION   Trade Paperback   1 871592 32 1   7" X 10"   368pp   £9.95 • $15.95

A HOLYTHROAT SYMPOSIUM   Aaron Williamson

Exploratory penman, explosive performer, Williamson is profoundly deaf and has evolved a physical approach to demonstrating a text in live settings, creating a combination of voice, anatomy and rhythm which produces contorted, volatile displays aspiring to a bodily evocation of deafness itself. At the heart of this book is an unspeakable surdity, a silent flickering language ravenous for release, possessing any and every faculty. A primal world of violence and estrangement is explored from within the frustrations and verbal rages of one who is 'anatomically exiled' from the language he uses; liberating, re-instating the real life of words by alchemising their traces through juxtapositions, rhythms, repulsions and secret affinities; vertiginously layered, accumulating a trip-hammer impact.

POETRY   Trade Paperback   1 871592 17 8   5½" X 8½"   112pp   £7.95 • $14.95

you have just read
the last star
a creation book
published by:
creation books
83, clerkenwell road, london ec1, uk
tel: 0171-430-9878 fax: 0171-242-5527
creation books is an independent publishing organisation producing fiction and non-fiction genre books of interest to a young, literate and informed readership.
creation products should be available in all proper bookstores; please ask your uk bookseller to order from:
bookpoint, 39 milton park, abingdon, oxon ox14 4td
tel: 01235-400400 fax: 01235-832068
non-book trade and mail order:
ak distribution, 22 lutton place, edinburgh eh8 9pe
tel: 0131-667-1507 fax: 0131-662-9594
readers in europe please order from:
turnaround distribution, 27 horsell road, london n5 1xl
tel: 0171-609-7836 fax: 0171-700-1205
readers in the usa please order from:
subterranean company, box 160, 265 south 5th street, monroe, or 97456
tel: 503-847-5274 fax: 503-847-6018
non-book trade and mail order:
ak press, po box 40682, san francisco, ca 94140-0682
tel: 415-923-1429 fax: 415-923-0607
readers in canada please order from:
marginal distribution, unit 102, 277 george street, n. peterborough, ontario k9j 3g9
tel/fax: 705-745-2326
readers in australia and new zealand please order from:
peribo pty ltd, 58 beaumont road, mount kuring-gai, nsw 2080
tel: 02-447-0011 fax: 02-457-0022
readers in the rest of the world, or any readers having difficulty in obtaining creation products, please order direct (+ 20% postage outside uk) from our head office
our full mail order catalogue is available on request (please enclose sae/2 ircs)
booksellers may order the full creation books trade catalogue free of charge from any of the above addresses.